The City in Europe and the World

Edited by

Stephen Barber

European
Research
Forum at

LONDON
metropolitan
university

European Research Forum at London Metropolitan University
Department of Governance and International Relations
London Metropolitan University
Old Castle Street
London, E17NT

www.europeanresearchforum.com

First published 2005

ISBN: 0 9547448 1 0 (paperback)

Printed by Print Solutions Partnership

Contents

Foreword

Rt. Hon Peter Mandelson, European Commissioner for Trade

The City sits at the centre of the British economy and in turn is at the centre of the European financial system. It generates some 3% of the UK's GDP and some 13% of London's. The City's prospects are interlinked with European economic development, both affected by it and able to drive it. Some 72,000 jobs in the square mile depend in some way or other on decisions made by the European institutions.

This truth is reflected in the wider economy. The prosperity of the British economy is directly connected to the rest of Europe. After all, 50% of UK trade is with the rest of Europe. We share a market, certainly the largest and potentially one of the most vibrant in the world. And the reason that the European Union matters to Britain generally, and the City more specifically, is that the continent's economic success or failure contributes directly to Britain's economic success or failure.

The openness to trade and investment across European borders accounts for a quarter of productivity gains in Britain and is a major instigator of growth. This single market is important to the City, but it is impossible to maintain without the supranational institutions that make it work. These include the Commission, of which I am a member, to ensure fair competition; and the Court of Justice that can hold member states to account. So it is a contradiction for the City to want free trade in Europe but reject Brussels. The institutions of Brussels created the Single Market and without Brussels, the Single Market would quickly disintegrate.

Not everyone agrees with this view of course, and importantly this book encompasses wide and thoughtful opinion across a variety of issues facing the City. London faces rivals to its primacy, an ongoing need to adapt and innovate as well as global economic challenges. The same is true of Europe as a whole as it faces up to the economic challenges of the rise of Asia. A great debate is opening up about Europe's economic and social future, in which the City should play a leading part.

What these issues demonstrate, however, is that while we may argue in terms of raw economics, the real debate is political. The City is important to politicians of all parties and the decisions politicians make can affect growth in the square mile. But it is worth remembering that collectivity can make those decisions more palatable. The combined negotiating authority of the member states means that, in my own responsibilities as commissioner for trade, for instance, I speak for a developed market of 450 million people. This can only be positive for City institutions.

The City remains one of the dominant financial centres of the world but it has never been and cannot now be complacent. It is crucial for City interests that Europe presses on with economic reforms. Reforms will safeguard economic success allowing markets to flourish and easing trade. But let me be clear, this is not to Americanise Europe, economically or socially, as some suggest, but rather ensuring the sustainability of the European model of society that we now enjoy. I would argue that to prioritise growth and jobs is not to be neo-liberal. Opening up European markets creates not only wealth but also opportunities. It means that issues such as financial exclusion can be tackled or worker rights protected. But it is a fiction to think that these things can be achieved through tariffs and protectionism. The City in Europe will only prosper if it has access to free and ever open markets. And it can only benefit from Europe's bargaining power to open markets if it embraces the European political model.

A critical decision for coming years is whether the UK should join the Euro. This has not gone away as an issue for all time. The British economy has prospered outside of the single currency but with increasing harmonisation in other areas of financial services, the long term case for staying outside is becoming weaker. The City itself will reap major cost and efficiency benefits from sharing a currency with its trading partners, as the British Government acknowledged in its assessment of the "five tests". But first there needs to be a debate in Britain and that debate will be political as much as economic. This debate, which is already developed in the investment services industry, needs to be advanced further. The City will be one of the most influential players when it comes to deciding if Britain joins the single currency and, once joined, will be a crucial factor in its success or failure.

The City of London is the economic powerhouse of Europe: internationalist, innovative and open. It has been the hub of cross-border trade for centuries, adapting to economic, political and societal change. Europe not only provides the greatest opportunities for growth in this still young twenty-first century, but also the best protection to its primacy. If the City is to continue to prosper as we all wish, it must recognise the momentousness of the political decisions ahead on Europe, and Britain's place in it.

Contributors

Stephen Barber is Research Director of the European Research Forum at London Metropolitan University. A frequent contributor to the financial press, he has spent a decade working in the City of London's investment industry. He is author of *Political Strategy: Modern Politics in Contemporary Britain*.

stephen.barber@europeanresearchforum.com.

Graham Bishop is an independent analyst of European financial affairs and is principal of GrahamBishop.com founded in 2000. In June 2003 he was appointed as Specialist Adviser to the House of Lords Select Committee on the European Union in its inquiry into The Barriers to Competition in the Internal Market for Financial Services and in September 2002, was nominated by the European Parliament to be one of its two members of the Inter-Institutional Monitoring Group, as foreseen by the Lamfalussy Report. In December 2002, Mr. Bishop was appointed as a Special Advisor to the Treasury Committee of the House of Commons in its examination of the implications for United Kingdom membership of the Single Currency. He is a member of the European Commission's Consultative Group on the Impact of the Introduction of the Euro on Capital Markets (the Giovaninni Group). He was a Member European Commission's Strategy Group on Financial Services (1998 – creating the Financial Services Action Plan) and Committee of Independent Experts on the preparation of the changeover to the single currency (the 'Maas' Committee 1994/5). He is also a Council Member of both Britain in Europe and The City in Europe and was a Specialist Adviser to the Treasury Committee of the House of Commons on recent EMU Enquiries; Chairman, the London Investment Banking Association (LIBA) Committee on converting London's capital markets to the single currency.

Alex Brassey is Managing Partner of SFI (financial engineering consultancy), and a North London School Teacher. He is formerly an Assistant Vice-President of Citibank and Director of Lehman Brothers. He holds an MA in Philosophy from Kings College London and is currently completing a Doctorate in Psychology at the Institute of Education. He is also a Dad of three lovely girls.

Mario Cerrato is a Senior Lecturer in Finance at the Department of Economics, Finance and International Business, London Metropolitan University. His current research interests include option pricing, risk management and econometric theory. He has published several articles in major finance and economic journals.

Patrick Diamond is a Senior Visiting Fellow at the Centre for Global Governance at the London School of Economics, and a Transatlantic Fellow at the German Marshall Fund. He is a former Special Adviser to the Prime Minister, and member of the No.10 Policy Unit. He edited *New Labour's Old Roots: Revisionist Thinkers in Labour's History 1931-1997* and co-edited *Rethinking Social Democracy*, with Matt Browne and *The New Egalitarianism*, with Anthony Giddens.

Brendan Donnelly has been Director of the Federal Trust since January 2003. He is a former Member of the European Parliament (1994 to 1999). He was educated at Oxford, where he obtained a double first in classics, and later worked in the Foreign Office, the European Parliament and the European Commission.

Howard Flight is a senior City figure. Until 2005, he was Member of Parliament for Arundel & South Downs He was appointed Shadow Economic Secretary to the Treasury in 1999, having served on the Environment and Social Security Select Committees. In September 2001, he was appointed Shadow Paymaster General and in July 2002 was made Shadow Chief Secretary to the Treasury. In September 2004, he was appointed by Michael Howard as Special Envoy to the City of London and Deputy Chairman of the Conservative Party. He has 30 years experience in the investment management industry and has built up a successful investment management company. He regularly contributes to political and economic articles and his book, *All You Need to Know about Exchange Rates*, was published in 1988.

Alexandra Forter is a Project Worker at SAFE (Services Against Financial Exclusion) at Toynbee Hall where she works to increase access to banking for benefit recipients. Prior to her work in the United Kingdom, Alexandra worked for non-profit organisations, research institutions, and think tanks in the United States and Latin America on economic development projects and asset building policy development. The think tanks included ShoreBank Advisory Services in Chicago, IL and Instituto Interamericano de Derechos Humanos in San Jose, Costa Rica and the community based organisations of Association House of Chicago, Chicago, IL and ASAPROSAR, Santa Ana, El Salvador. She graduated with dual masters in International Relations and Public Policy at the University of Chicago.

Chris Huhne was elected to the House of Commons for the Liberal Democrats in the 2005 general election, and was shortly appointed treasury spokesman. Before that he was MEP for South East England and the European Liberal Democrat and Reformist Group's economics spokesman. He has sat on the parliament's Economic and Monetary Affairs Committee and chaired the expert group on Britain's adoption of the euro. An award winning former economic journalist on the *Guardian*, *Independent*, *Economist* and *Evening Standard*, he is author of four books including two on European monetary union. He founded and headed of one of the largest teams of economists in the City as group managing director at Fitch IBCA.

Mario Jung is an economist specialising in Monetary Macroeconomics and European Economic Policy. He studied at the universities of Trier, Germany, and Maastricht, Netherlands. Until February 2005 he worked at the Ernst-Moritz-Arndt-University of Greifswald, Germany, at the Chair of Monetary Economics. In March 2005 he took a senior industry position.

Angela Knight is Chief Executive of the Association of Private Clients Investment Managers and Stockbrokers (APCIMS). A former Member of Parliament for Erwish, she was Economic Secretary to the Treasury between 1995 and 1997 and Parliamentary Private Secretary to the Chancellor of the Exchequer between 1994 and 1995.

Agnes Oestreich is an economist specialising in Monetary Macroeconomics and European Economic Policy. She studied business administration at the University of Greifswald, Germany. Until June 2002 she worked as research assistant at the Ernst-Moritz-Arndt-University of Greifswald, Germany, at the Chair of Monetary Economics. She is completing a doctoral thesis in the monetary policies of different countries, especially in the field of monetary policy and asset prices.

Giancarlo Perasso is Head of Emerging Markets Research at West LB AG. Before joining West LB, he was responsible for economic research and strategy for Central and Eastern Europe at Chase Manhattan and then JP Morgan-Chase. Previously, he worked at the OECD in the Centre for Co-Operation with Non-Member Countries and in the Economic Directorate. He holds degrees in economics from Bocconi University in Milan and The Johns Hopkins University in Baltimore.

Alice Rogers joined Services Against Financial Exclusion (SAFE) in March 2003 and has worked to expand the areas of financial inclusion work SAFE has been involved in. In June 2004 she helped launch the Financial Inclusion Forum supported by The Royal Bank of Scotland. This national forum brings together financial inclusion projects, providing an arena to share good practice and network. SAFE recently created the Access Project an off-shoot of SAFE supporting clients and organisations across London and the South East in the move to Direct Payment of benefits. As Coordinator, Alice oversees SAFE's research into banking, as well as maintaining an interest in asset building and affordable credit. Alice can be contacted on alice.safe@toynbeehall.org.uk or 020 7392 2954.

Sanjiv Sachdev is Principal Lecturer at Kingston University Business School which he joined in 1999 after working as a Research Fellow at Cambridge University. Previously a full-time trade union Research Officer at UNISON for eight years, he has also worked in Brussels for an international trade union confederation. His research interests are threefold: (i) the employment relations implications of Public Private Partnerships and the Private Finance Initiative, which has led to publications in journals, by Unison, the think tank 'Catalyst' and some news media. (ii) the HR implications of Corporate Social

Responsibility, for which he has written a chapter of a forthcoming book, (iii) low pay issues including the minimum wage, for which he has published work in journals, books and think tanks. He has also co-written an HR textbook *Managing in a Business Context* (with Huw Morris and Brian Willey).

Professor Lucio Valerio Spagnolo holds the Jean Monnet Chair and teaches Macroeconomics and European Integration Economics at the University of Salerno in Italy. He was a promoter of the EU students exchange programmes, pioneering this activity from the very beginning. In the framework of it he has been lecturer at The Liverpool John Moores University, UK, and at the Escuela Universitaria de Estudios Empresariales of the University of Barcelona, Spain. He gave the course The Theory of Union at the University of Oklahoma, USA, and has been Relator at the European Week: a learning resource organised by the Institute of Higher Education at The Hague, NL. He is author of a number of books including: *Teoria delle decisioni e analisi economica*, Napoli, *La convergenza di Maastricht: una misura della divergenza*, Torino and *L'equilibrio in un'economia aperta*, Napoli and articles as *The Role of the European System of Central Banks in the European Integration Process* in Building the New Europe, Vol. I: The Single Market and Monetary Unification, edited by Baldassarri M. and Mundell R. The Macmillan Press, London and New York, 1993; and *European Economic Convergence and The International Monetary System* in De Pecunia, (Number dedicated to the memory of Robert Triffin) Bruxelles, 1993.

Richard Woodward is a lecturer in political economy at the University of Hull. He is currently writing up his PhD thesis on multilevel governance of global financial markets and recently co-edited *Governing Financial Globalisation: The political economy of multi-level governance* (Routledge, 2005). His research interests include the City of London, the globalisation and governance of financial markets, and the role of the OECD. His first book *The OECD* will be published by Routledge in 2006.

Acknowledgments

Many people have been supportive in the process of producing this book of essays, not least the authors themselves who have helped to produce a diverse and stimulating collection of papers. I would also like to thank Peter Mandelson for writing the foreword and Roger Liddle and Karen Ramsey of his office for facilitating, Rhydian Peters of GreenEgg.net who designed the cover, Maria Farrell for her editorial assistance and Stephen Haseler Director of the Forum.

About the European Research Forum

The European Research Forum at London Metropolitan University promotes analysis and debate of the politics and economics of the European Union, its member countries, Britain's relationship to them and its place in the world.

For more information about the Forum's activities, seminars, papers and publications, visit the website at

www.europeanresearchforum.com.

Chapter One

The Political Economy of the City

Stephen Barber

This book is a collection of essays on political economy. It is about an industry, economic and political policies, ethics, internationalism, globalisation and an urban environment. The City sits as the pre-eminent financial centre in Europe, part of but often strangely detached from its home economy in the United Kingdom. It is affected by, or affects, the economic policies of governments, not only in Britain, but also in the United States and the European Union. It is an international economic powerhouse rivalled only by New York. But its position is not unassailable and at times seems unusually vulnerable.

London is home to two powerful cities. The financial centre, the City, and the political city of Westminster sit at either end of the Thames, interconnected yet oddly separated. Neither city fully understands the other. A notion of both suspicion and admiration characterises this long and indispensable relationship. But indispensable is right. Although perhaps the balance of power is now with the powerful international financial markets whose home from home is London. London and New York remain the two most important financial centres in the world. While Wall Street might be the senior partner, as Richard Woodward demonstrates in his analysis of the regulatory environment, the City is by far the most internationalist. Consider that London is home to more foreign banks, instigates more off-shore business, the stock exchange lists more foreign companies and handles a greater turnover of foreign equities. Most Eurobond trades, most over the counter (OTC) derivatives business, almost all of the world's metal trading, happen in London. London is the main centre for fund management. The Baltic exchange dominates marine services, Lloyds dominates international insurance. The list goes on[1]. In terms of international financial services, London leads. The scale of this and the importance to both the British and wider European economies is reflected to some degree in various chapters in this book, including Angela Knight's, *Future of the City in Europe*, Giancarlo Perasso's discussion of the City and central and Eastern Europe, and Mario Jung and Agnes Oestreich's paper on foreign exchange. Howard Flight, a seasoned City figure and former Conservative City spokesman when a member of parliament and Patrick Diamond, former adviser to Tony Blair, respectively show the importance of the City to our political leaders. And the City is important. On a very basic level, according to the Centre for Economics and Business Research, the Square Mile contributes something like £10 billion a year in taxation, some 4% of total tax revenue. London's gross domestic product as a whole was said to be 21% of UK national income, with finance and business services accounting for 31% of London's GDP and an 11% contribution from financial intermediaries[2]. Also notable is that in the predominantly service economy that Britain has become, since the de-industrialisation which occurred under the premiership of Margaret Thatcher, the UK imports more goods than it exports. Without the overseas earnings generated by the City, Britain's balance of payments would look decidedly less healthy. According to the Office for National Statistics, business and financial services constitute the largest single sector of the UK economy, in 2003 accounting for some 32% of total UK gross value added (GVA)[3].

The institutions that the City represents also develop and administer the many domestic financial products and schemes devised by the Treasury. These range from Personal Equity Plans (PEPs) Tax Exempt Special Savings Accounts (TESSAs) and Individual Savings Accounts (ISAs) to Self-Invested Personal Pensions (SIPPs), Stakeholder Pensions and the Child Trust Fund (CTF). In each case the rough political drafts of government policy are shaped into workable form by the City. That government can draw on City expertise in these matters is clearly beneficial to policy implementation and can fulfil economic aims of, for instance, encouraging share ownership in the case of the PEP, a savings culture for the TESSA, social policy, capital based head start for all children in the case of the CTF or, as Alexandra Forter and Alice Rogers discuss, tackling financial exclusion with a savings gateway scheme.

But there is more than that as New Labour recognised in the build up to the 1997 general election and indeed Shadow Chancellor John Smith had understood before 1992[4]. No British government can hope to implement a successful economic policy without the buy-in from the financial markets and they happen to live, conveniently, just a few miles away from Whitehall in the City. If a government has the co-operation of the financial markets, it can be more powerful. If the markets turn on a government, economic policy can be left in tatters as Norman Lamont discovered in September 1992, when Sterling was unceremoniously ejected from the Exchange Rate Mechanism (ERM) at the behest of the powerful markets[5]. And powerful they are. For instance, in January 2005, the UK had net foreign currency reserves worth a not inconsiderable $18685 million.[6] By comparison, as Jung and Oestreich report, *daily* foreign exchange turnover reached $1.9 trillion in April 2004. What this shows is that individual countries' reserves are dwarfed by the foreign exchange market and consequently that market can decide the cost of any country's borrowing and disrupt any country's economic policy.

It is not difficult to assert that the City is small 'c' conservative: uncertainty, unwelcome change, is the bane of the market. Yet, the rapidity of support New Labour affected from the square mile before and in the aftermath of the 1997 general election, suggests it is not wedded to the Conservative party. The City, it could be said, is ideologically non-partisan. Nevertheless, it is partly inhabited by the self same public school educated elite or the self-made 'Essex man', who sustained the Tories in government past their sell by date in the 1980s and 1990s. What it wishes to maintain is free, market-based economics and low tax, low inflation economic management. An aspiration that appeared to be assured when the new Labour government granted independence to the Bank of England's Monetary Policy Committee to set interest rates, shortly after the election in 1997.

The City welcomed the arrival of Margaret Thatcher in 1979 at the end of a decade which had seen economic crisis and stockmarket returns eroded by runaway inflation. Throughout the 1980s individuals in the City saw themselves as having benefited from Conservative party policy. What was to become characterised as the 'greed is good' generation saw little attraction in the policies of a Labour party which still harboured the image of class war and punitive taxation. The 1983 Labour manifesto was a disjointed and left wing document, a threat to those who made a good living in the market. The privatisation programme of the Tories, by contrast, offered the opportunity for money to be made – even if to begin with the City displayed little enthusiasm for the policy which had been conceived not only to reduce the public sector and stimulate market forces but it also generated a further source of income after the failure of the Howe / Thatcher medium term financial strategy (MTFS)[7] . While the Thatcher government's economic policies decimated large chunks of British industry, the markets prospered, not least as a result of the artificial benefits of North Sea oil. Unemployment continued to rise in the north, but taxes began to fall and for the parochial, short-termists based in the City, good times seemed to have arrived once again. A degree of self-interest, therefore, underpins the City's relationship with party politics at least. Even if its vision is infuriatingly short, the market can have a long memory. For those engaged in investing massive sums of capital, the economic record of Labour governments in the 1960s and 1970s was enough to persuade most of the City that it wanted a Conservative government. This changed with the arrival of New Labour with its market friendly policies and the loss of trust in the Tories after the ERM debacle.

It is little wonder then that political parties and governments seek City approval of their economic plans. But what this means is that, at election time, voters have little real choice when it comes to economic policy. This is particularly true of an economy the size of Britain's but one should not pretend that even one the size of the United States is immune. Given this, it is reasonable to challenge the oft made argument that European integration means surrendering great swathes of powers to EU institutions (in return for the 'clout' that offers) when those powers can only really be exercised where they meet the approval of the financial market. Some 'market popularists', as set out by Thomas Frank[8], believe that the market is more democratic than the electoral process since it forces competition and promotes consumer preferences day-by-day, minute-by-minute, not once every four or five years at the ballot box. While this view might be astounding to many, it is just this type of political thinking that has led to, City sponsored, market forces being introduced into the running of many British public services, as Sanjiv Sachdev highlights in his chapter on Public Private Partnerships. The ability of the market to exert its influence over increasingly greater aspects of our lives can be empowering to some and de-emancipating to others. And yet it often goes without questioning. Its great power can only be tempered to support the type of society an electorate wants by a revival in society's belief in democratic politics and co-operation with other countries, especially within Europe, accepting the sort of structural harmonisation of markets discussed by Graham Bishop in chapter two. Government and inter-governmental co-operation have a great role to play, balancing the competition and open markets which generate wealth and innovation with the dangerous consequences of 'free-for-all' market hegemony. Without this role, democracy becomes increasingly a privilege of the wealthy, exercised by the market.

And while this market might 'live' in London, it is not British. The City is perhaps no longer the 'market place' even if it is, or represents, 'the market', to use Slater and Tonkiss' terms[9]. The City has seen a move towards impersonal relations between its principal actors as the 'club' of old is replaced by a vast global market. The City is the hub of financial globalisation. Financial markets are international with modern communication facilitating huge capital transfers across the globe at the click of a mouse to wherever the greatest returns can be achieved. Such a market, herd-like in its instincts, will pull away great sums of cash from economies wherever it detects government policy to which it takes exception. It is for this reason that international financial markets, not international trade, determine economic policy and lead the world economy. After all, trade is connected to national economies (or trading blocs); the markets interweave those national economies. Critics such as Beck characterise this globalisation as inherently anti-political, the trans-national forces which have little regard for nation states[10]. While the City is a great asset to the British economy, it is not contained or controlled by it.

The City is not even led by British firms or with British assets as Chris Huhne points out in his chapter. The square mile is a massive source of employment in London, but most people in the City are employed by overseas firms. The 1980s and 90s saw British owned finance businesses swallowed up by large international institutions. The conditions which created the environment in which this was possible were politically driven. A combination of 'big bang', the de-regulation of the City in 1986, and closer European integration can be seen as being responsible. As Roberts and Kynaston demonstrate in their excellent book *City State*, when the Thatcher government decided to abolish exchange controls after its election in 1979, British stock broking firms were shown to be relatively uncompetitive and insular failing to capitalise on the new demand for overseas equities. Foreign firms took the business and politicians hastily agreed to abolish fixed commissions, end the separation of broking and market making and loosen the rules on the ownership of stock exchange firms, allowing, for the first time, brokerages to be owned by banks[11].

Secondly, as the process European integration became a reality, the Single European Act being signed in 1986, US firms took the decision to enhance significantly their European presence and the natural base was London. However, the pressure this put on domestic firms also meant that many fell into the hands of overseas institutions.

The downside of this is diminished domestic power in the square mile but with the upside that these developments secured greater and greater shares of international financial business. British firms might not control London's financial centre, but it is difficult to argue that the City is or has been in any way in decline. In any case, is there now an alternative? Despite the coming European debate of protectionism versus free markets, it is not realistic for the British government to intervene, offer 'protection' to an industry which in its own day-to-day behaviour acts in a short-term profit seeking manner and which is prepared to undermine the stability of almost any other company, industry, currency, commodity or even, as we have seen, government. An industry that lives by the sword (or market) must be prepared to die by it.

And the financial markets have been prepared to undermine other British companies and industries for short-term profits. A further effect of the abolition of exchange controls by the Thatcher government was to expose British firms, quoted on the stock exchange, to international competition; British shares had to compete with the best returns in world stockmarkets. As a result both aggressive asset stripping and demands for short-term returns, often by means of corporate actions or merger and acquisition activity, became increasingly prevalent. When the Trade and Industry Select Committee investigated the issue in 2003, it found that institutional shareholders had markedly increased the percentage of UK equity they hold from 30.3% in 1963 to 51.9% in 1999[12]. Since liquidity is too poor in smaller companies for such institutional investors, this figure is significantly higher among the larger companies of the FTSE 100 and 250 in which they hold shares and control. Companies have found themselves under pressure from the markets to concentrate on producing better returns from their shares, with the sanction being a fall in share price and vulnerability to being taken over, often to be dismantled. And it is a fact of life that a successful hostile bid is likely to provide better shareholder returns than one which has management support. The short-term activities of fund managers or other institutional shareholders, highlighted in the Myners Review, does not necessarily mean rapid turnover, but it does mean constant pressure on the company to increase shareholder value as a primary objective. The Myners Review, set up by Chancellor Gordon Brown and headed by former investment banker Paul Myners, noted the "extreme vagueness about the timescales over which fund managers' performance is to be judged. This is a real – but wholly unnecessary – cause of short-termism in fund managers' approach to investment". [13] And short-term means a financial quarter or a year, not three, five or ten. Quoted industry in Britain or the USA struggles to take on substantial projects with long-term paybacks. According to a study by academics from Duke University, of 401 senior financial executives surveyed, a staggering 78% said they "would sacrifice an initiative they expected would create economic value if it would negatively impact on their ability to smooth earnings"[14].

But perhaps this is being too fair to many company directors. Theory suggests a company will float to raise funds for long-term growth and investment. In practise, City fund managers have limited interest in the activities of the company beyond its short-term profits. But there is also a breed of CEO who, sympathetic to this concept of 'shareholder returns', acts accordingly in their own relationship with the company. Alex Brassey picks up some of these arguments in his chapter on the ethics of the City. They deliver the short-term returns demanded by their institutional shareholders. As their reward, shareholders are complicit when the same directors award themselves large pay, bonuses and share options. In the 10 years between 1994 and 2004, median pay, before bonuses and share options, among FTSE 100 CEOs grew by 92% to £579,000. This compares to UK male average of £21,000, having largely kept up with inflation[15]. It is unsurprising that Total Shareholder Returns (TSR), that is share price growth plus dividend, is a predominant method of calculating directors' bonuses in FTSE 100 companies[16]. Similarly, directors' collusion in the venture capital and mergers and acquisitions processes can see, even very mediocre, company directors amassing personal fortunes created with little personal risk or ability and at the expense of other 'stakeholders', to use Will Hutton's term, the employees and customers. Some non-institutional shareholder activism in recent years has put pressure on directors' pay, especially 'golden goodbye', pay-offs for failure. But these are few and far between. Indeed, the first time that shareholders in a British company voted down a director's pay package came in 2002 when proposals to pay Jean-Pierre Garnier, CEO of drugs giant Glaxosmithkline, a massive $35m (£22m) if he left the job early, were rejected. Significantly, however, this rare opposition came at the end of a two year slump in the company's share price during Garnier's tenure at the top. Glaxosmithkline's share price had slumped by more than 30% in the 12 months before the shareholder meeting, while profits fell by 25% in the previous financial year. There were a handful of other examples of shareholder activism to follow including supermarket Tesco whose board came under criticism from for its two-year rolling contracts for directors, which "maximise 'rewards for failure' because they oblige firms which dismiss underperforming executives to pay them larger than usual severance packages"[17].

It is not only shareholders who have been critical of board-room pay. According to a survey by Robert Half Finance in 2002, 70% of UK accountants agreed that "some senior executives are paid far too much"[18]. Indeed, in 2003, the government went so far as to publish proposals aimed at curbing such pay-offs for directors who leave failing companies. The paper, *Rewards for Failure*[19], which recommended connecting pay to performance, came under attack from the Confederation of British Industry with its Director General, Digby Jones, claimed that it is "transparency and shareholder activism are the ways to police directors' pay, not legislation"[20] Perhaps it is only fitting that after a period of bearish stockmarket returns, and perhaps correspondingly reduced pay awards, PA Consulting reported in its 2004 annual survey of shareholder value, the first reduction in the number of top executives world-wide who agreed with the statement: "we believe that the overarching objective of our business is to maximize long-term shareholder value"[21].

Board-rooms are still closed off to an elite, wealthy, few who award themselves and each other the pay they believe they can justify. According to the *Financial Times*, drawing on research conducted by consultants BoardEx, a typical FTSE director is "white, male, aged 58 and likely to have had a finance background"[22]. Even at the beginning of the twenty-first century, 'chairman' means just that. There are more people called David amongst the chairs of FTSE 100 companies than there are women. As at August 2005, Sarah Hogg (3i) alone was the only women chair of a FTSE 100 Company. And there was only Marjorie Scardino as CEO (Pearson). There is scant representation of ethnic minorities. According to a report commissioned by the DTI, in December 2004, almost a third of FTSE 100 companies had male-only boardrooms and that only 17% (albeit improving) of new board room appointments during the survey year had been to women[23]. The Higgs review, set up by Chancellor Brown to investigate non-executive directorships and which reported in 2003, found similarly that such directors were white, males approaching retirement age and that just 6% of non-executive directors were women. The thrust of Higgs' conclusions was that such a 'narrow pool' of talent is detrimental to the potential effectiveness of a company and that recruitment practices should change[24]. The City itself may have opened its doors to a degree since deregulation, but it and the companies quoted on its exchange have some way to go.

Even if boardrooms come under pressure, the City's financial institutions seem politically secure; continuing to prosper in the way they have come to enjoy. Certainly no British government dares to do anything which might undermine its competitiveness. It seems willing also to fight European originated proposals, such as Currency Transaction Tax (or 'Tobin tax') on foreign exchange transactions or withholding tax on savings and investments seen as likely to hit the bond market. Chancellor Gordon Brown even made City interests one of his famous 'five tests' to determine whether the UK would join the European single currency.

If its appearance in the various chapters of this book is a guide, the question of the euro, and Britain's potential participation, remains one of crucial importance to the City. Professor Spagnolo and Mario Cerrato, and Brendan Donnelly, respectively set out the economic and political issues surrounding the British debate. But looked at from purely City interests, might entry ever be advisable? Given that with Britain outside, foreign exchange business increased since the euro's introduction, with trading in the single currency centring firmly in London, the great fear that Frankfurt, the home of the European Central Bank, would steal the FX market has proved unfounded. It is also difficult to see quite how the City, a truly internationalist financial centre, fits into an economic system which primarily serves its own 'domestic' markets. For the City to prosper, it must continue to operate almost symbiotically with New York because London facilitates global financial trade which the US leads. Inevitably, this means that the economic cycle of the City will be torn between the American economy to which it is closer and the major European ones that are its political abode.

Britain of course needs to decide which system it wishes to be part and the type of capitalism it wishes to promote. As ultimately does Europe. The type of capitalism which has prospered in post-war

France and Germany, but which has come under pressure in the 1990s and early part of the twentieth century particularly in the wake of German re-unification and sustained levels of unemployment, sees promotion of shareholder value as just one the many missions of a successful company. As a result, as Hutton points out, directors (though very well paid) receive much lower remuneration than their British or US counterparts, the dividend pay-out to earnings ratio is lower, proportionally more funds are devoted to research and development, there are far fewer hostile takeovers which, indeed, are legislated against, workers benefit from higher levels of protection, work fewer hours and enjoy greater levels of consultation, and investment is greater with capital stock in France and Germany growing 150% and 175% respectively between 1965 and 1991, compared to a mere 65% in the US[25]. This is one of the reasons why European financial institutions are the world leaders. According to Jeremy Rifkin, fourteen of the largest twenty commercial banks in the world are European (including three of the top four: Deutsche Bank, Credit Suisse and BNP); eight of the top ten re-insurance companies, all top five life and health insurance are European and the story is repeated in other areas of industry such as engineering, consumer products and telecommunications[26]. Some of these companies are indeed British. But it is striking that although the City dominates financial services, it is not dominated by British companies and many of the successful, European, businesses which occupy the glass-fronted offices of the square mile and inhabit the global financial markets play by different capitalist rules in the management of their own affairs. Undoubtedly, continental Europe will move a little closer to the US capitalist model embraced only partly by Britain; a move which will please the City. But political decisions in the UK may see Britain gradually accepting some of the lessons of European capitalism as it moves closer to European economic union.

The City will adapt to the political environment with which it is faced. But for it to achieve optimal benefit for Britain and for Europe, it should examine some of its practices. The criticisms of the City highlighted in this chapter are not those of the radical left, who would rather the financial market not exist, but can be found in the professions which service those markets, the City's 'village newspaper' The FT, and many of the City's senior figures whose advice to government on the reform of market practices have so often been kicked into the long grass. Judging by reports and proclamations, government is often concerned about short-termism, board room pay, elitism, exclusion, but is little prepared to act.

The contributions and contributors to this book vary greatly. They represent a number of different viewpoints which do not always agree and at times diametrically oppose. The book itself does not argue in a single tradition or ideological position; indeed quite the contrary. But each of these diverse essays demonstrate the need for continued debate about the role of the City in modern Britain and Britain in Europe. They may even stimulate that debate. They show that the City highlights the great strengths of the British economy but also harbours many of its great weaknesses. As an introduction to the book, this chapter demonstrates the indispensable connection between politics and the financial markets of the City. The City epitomises political economy in the UK and indeed in Europe. Perhaps that alone is a message which runs through each of the distinct chapters in this book.

Notes

[1] See www.london-first.co.uk

[2] See *London's Contribution to the UK Economy*, CEBR, July 2001; Roberts, Richard and Kynaston, David, 2002, *City State,* Profile. p 79; "London — the country's wealth generator - London's contribution to the UK economy - Centre for Economics and Business Research - Statistical Data Included", *New Statesman*, July 9 2001.

[3] *Business and financial services economic impact is double manufacturing UK Input-Output Analyses*, Office for National Statistics, 19 August 2005.

[4] See Barber, Stephen, "City Policy: A Matter of Trust", *Securities and Investment Review*, June 1998.

[5] For an interview with Norman Lamont on the subject, see Barber, Stephen , 2005, *Political Strategy: modern politics in contemporary Britain*, Liverpool Academic Press. pp 114-117

[6] *UK official holdings of international reserves, HM Treasury*, 3 March 2005.

[7] Marsh, David and Rhodes, R.A.W. 1992, op cit. p.178.

[8] Frank, Thomas, 2001, *One Market under God: extreme capitalism, market popularism and the end of economic democracy*, Seker and Warberg.

[9] Slater D. and Tonkiss F, 2001, *Market Society: markets and modern social theory*, Polity.

[10] Beck, Ulrich, 2000, *What is Globalisation?,* Polity, London.

[11] Roberts and Kynaston, op cit. p.93.

[12] Trade and Industry Sixth Report, April 2003.

[1313] *Myners Review of Institutional Investment: Final Report*, HM Treasury (March 2001) p.2.

[14] Paper for National Bureau of Economic Research, cited in Themotheram, Raj, "The Enhanced Analytics Initiative: Investing as if the Long-term Really did Matter", *Gresham Lecture*, 2 June 2005.
[15] "Time to thin down fat cat pay", *Personnel Today,* 17 February 2004.
[16] Roberts and Kynaston, op cit. p.153.
[17] Pension Investment Research Consultants, Press Release 20 May 2002.
[18] "UK accountants condemn 'Fat cat' pay", *Robert Half Finance & Accounting*, Press Release, January 21, 2004.
[19] *Rewards for Failure*, DTI, June 2003.
[20] Reported, BBC, 3 June 2003.
[21] *Managing for Shareholder Value – International survey 2003/04,* PA Consulting, 2004. The survey had been run for 5 consecutive years.
[22] "Boardrooms fail to pick up on diversity", *Financial Times*, 5/9/05.
[23] *The Female FTSE Report 2004*, sponsored by the DTI and Shell. Undertaken by Cranfield School of Management
[24] *Review of the Role and Effectiveness of Non-Executive Directors*, Derek Higgs Review, 2003, DTI.
[25] Hutton, Will, 2002, *The World We're In*, Little Brown. pp. 242-246.
[26] Rifkin, Jeremy, 2004, *The European Dream: How Europe's vision of the future is quietly eclipsing the American dream*, Polity. P. 68.

Chapter Two

Economic and Structural Developments of Financial Markets: the Lisbon Strategy and Beyond

Graham Bishop

In March 2000, the EU Heads of States and Governments agreed, at their summit in Lisbon, to make the EU "the most competitive and dynamic knowledge-driven economy by 2010". But they were also more specific in areas that are vital to the financial sector in general and the City in particular. They set themselves tests where success or failure could be measured on a reasonable horizon, and agreed that: "To accelerate completion of the internal market for financial services, steps should be taken: to set a tight timetable so that the Financial Services Action Plan is implemented by 2005."[1] The goal was simple: to create a genuine single market in money and financial services throughout the EU.

The benefits of a liberalised market in financial services throughout the EU have been championed actively by the UK for the last two decades. The changes in that time are nothing short of revolutionary – and yet there is still a strong feeling that much remains to be done. But that feeling is tempered by creeping doubts about whether something is in the process of 'going wrong'.

A single financial market should be defined broadly for all users across the EU – savers, users of equity and fixed income funds, retail, wholesale, intermediaries –but the specific challenge of 'securities' was taken up at the 2001 Stockholm Summit: "The regulation of securities markets needs to be sufficiently flexible to be able to respond to market developments, while recognising the need for transparency and legal certainty." The process of developing new regulations for this single securities market has become known as the Lamfalussy Process (LP). It was judged to be sufficiently successful that it has now been extended to cover banking and insurance, with mutual funds and financial conglomerates also rolled in. It is this process that is now being questioned. But what are the driving forces for structural change?

Technological Advance

The staggering technological advances in the last couple of decades have provided an opportunity to re-assess the way in which financial services are delivered to citizens. Naturally that extends to their financial intermediaries in the capital markets. That progress, fortuitously, opened the door to radical change just at the time when political leaders were recognising that some more general economic reforms were necessary. The advent of the euro also called into question the nationally-organised financial silos of the past.

So structural change in the financial markets came to be seen as a necessary development – epitomised by the Lisbon Summit commitments. But it was always going to be a lengthy process for the euro zone to extract the full benefits of its monetary union.

The EU's need for Economic Benefits

A single financial market is taken as a necessary condition for boosting economic growth and the November 2000 *Initial Report by the Committee of Wise Men on the Regulation of European Securities Markets* (The Lamfalussy Report) devoted its first chapter to confirming this analysis. Their Final Report made the strong point that "the European Union has no divine right to the benefits of an integrated financial market. It has to capture those benefits by building an integrated European market… If it does not succeed, economic growth, employment and prosperity will be lower, and competitive advantage will be lost to those outside the European Union."[2] The entire EU stands to gain from success, whether it uses the single currency or not. So the UK supported the creation of the Lisbon Strategy in 2000, including financial services as a key element.

The original Lamfalussy Report cited evidence about the overall welfare gains, and other studies have quantified specific aspects. This author calculated that the gains highlighted by these studies might add up to nearly €200 billion annually after 10 years. To out-weigh these public benefits, the private costs of each of the 40 FSAP (that

Chris Huhne considers in this book) measures would have to average €5 billion. However, the Commission analyses of the day made no attempt to estimate the costs involved in securing the assumed benefits, underlining the weaknesses of such impact assessments as the costs usually fall on private sector players who legitimately require costs to be minimised. These costs are now crystallising for the financial sector – and causing questions to be raised about the purpose of it all. This is the moment to keep the desirable goal of enhanced economic activity firmly in mind.

Creating Appropriate Financial Assets for Aging Citizens' Savings

The economic benefits are widely discussed but there is another powerful driver for structural change in Europe's capital markets: the need for citizens to build up financial assets to provide some of their own income during retirement. It is worth analysing these requirements in more depth as they are already having a specific influence on financial market re-structuring.

The influence can only be expected to increase in the years ahead and it is not an optional extra: the aging of society is already set in stone and a "pension crisis" is at hand in the EU. By 2050, life expectancy will soar to 85 for a 65 year–old man; the old age dependency ratio is set to rocket (pensioners rising from 40% of the working age population today to 70% by that time); and the population of several major states will have declined by more than 10%. Such statistics can be seen every day in many newspaper articles and they raise disconcerting questions about the long-term sustainability of economic growth.

Many interpret the ageing society as being the driver of this crisis and increasing longevity will certainly create problems for the age structure. But that is not the whole of the story. In the long run, the decline in fertility rates is a clear threat to economic growth, but that is a social question that cannot be influenced by financial markets. Their role is merely to try to intermediate savings flows and investment opportunities in the next few decades for the benefit of the retired citizens.

Forty years ago, Europeans retired at age 65 but the effective age has been falling ever since and is now fluctuating around 60. The Heads of Government may have set a target of reversing that decline but it will be some years before it happens. In the meantime, the improvement in health care has lengthened the life span of the elderly, and continues to do so at a rate that is rising and may now be about 1.5 extra years per decade.

The combination of earlier retirement and increasing longevity is having a dramatic effect on the length of retirement — the 'term' to be funded by savings. That term has risen from 12.8 years in 1960 to more than 20 years today. However, this does not yet reflect the (perhaps alarming) improvements in longevity that are now the reality.

Using data from the UK — which has slightly lower longevity than the Eurozone — the 60- to 64-year-old age group is now experiencing a rapid improvement in longevity. In the 1960s, the improvement seemed to have stalled but nowadays it is accelerating — to a 2.5% annual improvement, and life expectancy for this group may rise by two years in the next decade, versus the 1.5-year improvement in the last decade.

Whatever the future may hold, the present already exists and is quite different from the past. Social *mores* shape legal structures and even in the mid 1980s German government bonds did not have a maturity longer than 10 years — originally stemming from legal concepts about the prevention of usury. But these laws permitted assets that would comfortably last most retired people for their life span during the 1950s and 1960s.

Today, retirees would be seriously exposed to "roll-over risk" when a 10-year bond is redeemed about halfway through their retirement when they may be less able to cope with difficult economic problems. Roll-over risk is the possibility that they may find that interest rates at the time of the redemption of their bond are significantly lower, thus cutting their actual income. In the past, they may have welcomed such a mismatch as it offered the possibility of recovering from "surprise inflation." Today, the inflation risk seems much reduced and more attention is likely to be paid to the possibility of a cut in income. This is the problem that has faced European savers, and their intermediaries, for the past decade.

The Institutionalisation of Financial Markets

In practice, most citizens will not hold financial assets themselves but will use a financial intermediary such as a pension fund or life insurance company. The new retiree is likely to look for some form of guarantee from the intermediary that they will continue to pay the income throughout their remaining life. After a string of shocks about the stability of life companies, the EU has embarked on a major re-assessment of capital adequacy and a directive called Solvency II, is the likely result.

It is not only Europe where there is a drive to encourage citizens to provide their own retirement income; there is a global trend towards saving via financial institutions such as life and pension funds. These institutions' behaviour is especially important for developments in financial markets because they may issue guarantees – explicit or more informal – about investment returns, and thus retirement income.

The world's accountancy profession is looking at the appropriate accounting treatment for both insurance and pensions. A key element is that any mismatch between the term of the liabilities – the length of the promises to pensioners or insured lives – and the assets should be backed by adequate capital. For a capital-constrained industry, this proposal will create a major incentive to match the term structure of promises/liabilities with assets more closely.

That turns out to be a difficult task. Analysing the Citigroup index of "tradable" bonds, the average time for redemption of all bonds in the Eurozone is only seven years – about a third of the life span of the average retiree. Importantly, the non-central government sector is only five years – and constitutes only a third of outstanding bonds. Thus, the important sector is that of bonds issued by central governments – where the average life is nearly eight years.

It turns out that decisions by central governments are crucial to the ability of financial intermediaries to give real certainty to the promises to retirees. Will governments recognise their responsibility to issue bonds that will provide that type of certainty, even if it costs more? Or will they continue to insist that their debt managers minimise the interest cost – which inexorably leads to shorter maturity bonds? The recent decision by several governments to issue 50-year maturities is a welcome step in dealing with the unfolding pension crisis.

The International Monetary Fund's *Global Financial Stability Report* (September, 2005) provides some useful statistics to illustrate the global trends in the development of these financial institutions. City financial firms compete to supply services to all these

Institutional Investors – not just the European ones - so the global trends are vital to the City's future.

Assets Under Management by Institutional Investors

	1990	1995	2000	2001	2002	2003	2004
			(In trillions of U.S. dollars)				
Institutional investors	13.8	23.5	39.0	39.4	36.2	46.8	. . .
Insurance companies	4.9	9.1	10.1	11.5	10.2	13.5	14.5
Pension funds	3.8	6.7	13.5	12.7	11.4	15.0	15.3
Investment companies	2.6	5.5	11.9	11.7	11.3	14.0	16.2
Hedge funds	0.03	0.10	0.41	0.56	0.59	0.80	0.93
Other instl investors	2.4	2.2	3.1	3.0	2.7	3.4	. . .
				(In percent of GDP)			
Institutional investors	77.6	97.8	152.1	155.3	136.4	157.2	. . .
Insurance companies	27.8	37.8	39.4	45.3	38.4	45.4	44.0
Pension funds	21.2	27.8	52.6	50.1	42.9	50.4	46.4
Investment companies	14.8	22.7	46.3	45.9	42.7	47.2	49.0
Hedge funds	0.1	0.4	1.6	2.2	2.2	2.7	2.8
Other insl investors	13.6	9.1	12.3	11.7	10.1	11.5	. . .

Source: *IMF Global Financial Stability Report September 2005*. Sources: International Financial Services, London; OECD; and IMF staff estimates.

It can be seen that, in the past decade and a half, the growth in global assets has been explosive: up 340% in nominal terms and more than 200% relative to GDP. Within these broad categories, the major sector of yesteryear – life insurance – has slipped into third place. Investment funds have just overtaken pension funds as the largest group – probably aided by the strong showing of equity markets. Hedge funds have risen dramatically in recent years but are still under 3% of GDP. Nonetheless, that scale illustrates why there is growing pressure to bring them within some sort of formal regulation – even if it is only a reporting requirement so that the implications of tier growth can be understood better.

However, the salient feature of this table is that assets that have to be matched against some form of calculated liability – pension and life insurance – have increased from around 50% of GDP in 1990 to almost exactly 100% of GDP. The principal liability is to provide some retirement income for long-lived pensioners in a world of stable prices. That suggests that the fixed income content of portfolios is likely to be on a rising trend relative to other assets, with a probable bias towards longer maturities.

Outstanding Domestic Debt Securities, Stock Market Capitalisation, and Bank Credit, 2004

	Total Outstan -ding	Govt Securities	Financial Instit-utions	Corpo-rate Issuers	Stock Market Cap	Bank Credit
			(In billions of U.S. dollars)			
Euro area	9,570.2	5,495.0	3,051.6	1,023.4	5,595.2	10,652.3
Japan	8,866.7	6,836.7	1,240.6	789.4	3,805.8	4,577.9
United States	19,186.6	5,526.4	11,078.8	2,581.3	15,132.2	5,370.3
			(In percent of GDP)			
Mature markets	140.2	66.5	57.3	16.4	91.4	76.8
Euro area	93.3	53.6	29.8	10.0	54.6	103.9
Japan	182.9	141.0	25.6	16.3	78.5	94.4
United States	163.5	47.1	94.4	22.0	129.0	45.8

Source: *IMF, Global Financial Stability Report, September 2005*. Sources: Bank for International Settlements (BIS); Bloomberg; Standard and Poor's; and IMF staff estimates.

The trend towards the institutionalisation of savings is vital for the City as it is the financial centre for the issuance of securities, whereas bank intermediation of savings can take place locally. In the search for the higher returns they are promising investors, institutions overwhelmingly hold securities rather than bank deposits. This is inevitable otherwise, there would be little incentive for the saver to do anything other than invest in capital-certain bank deposits.

But Europe is still strikingly dominated by bank credit rather than the US equity-dominated model. However, that is changing and led by the governments in search of cheaper funding. The ECB reports bank credit to governments of about $1 trillion, versus government securities outstanding of more than $5 trillion. One of the strategic aspirations of monetary union was to open the possibility to companies of funding themselves more cheaply in the capital markets, rather than from bank credit. In other words, the cost of capital should fall and thus the incentive to invest to raise productivity should increase – a clear economic benefit. The issue for savers trying to match their life expectancy is both the safety and the term structure of these assets.

IMF shows that monetary union certainly stimulated a surge in corporate bond issuance. Initially, some of this was to fund major take-overs but the equity crash slowed that business. The recent revival in take-overs may lead to another upsurge in debt issuance.

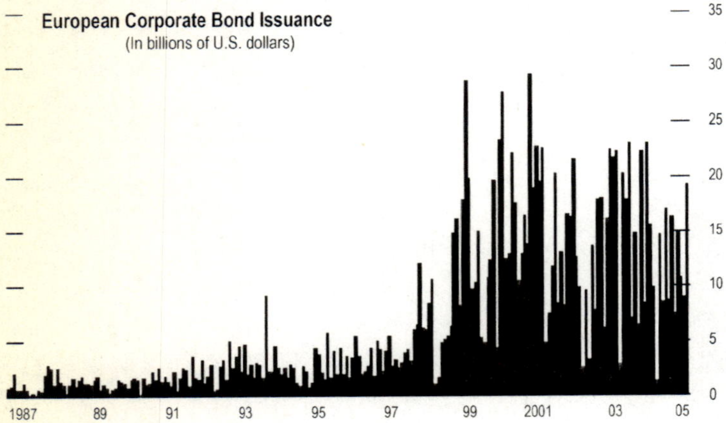

Source: *IMF Global Financial Stability Report 2004.* Sourced from Bondware, Datastream. Details non-financial corporate bonds, spread between yields on a Merrill Lynch High Yield European Issuers Index bond and a 10-year German government benchmark bond.

Regulatory Changes

This brings the analysis full circle: Have the regulatory steps taken so far been enough to permit a wave of mergers – especially cross-border? The answer seems to be "No" – except for the fierce struggles in Italy about banking mergers. That could herald a wave of activity as the top 30-50 banks seek to establish themselves as genuinely pan-European groups.

As Chris Huhne points out in this volume, in 2005, the FSAP measures were moving into the implementation phase so it will be vital to monitor how well they are succeeding in opening up capital markets. First, securities firms themselves have to bear the costs of the changes needed to bring the massive public benefits that are expected. So this is the moment when it seems likely that there would be the maximum complaints about the burden of costs. That is exactly what is happening – amidst complaints that the whole process has gone wrong in some way. But, why could things be seen as 'going wrong'?

Delays in Transposing Measures agreed at the European Level

The "Kok Report" produced an assessment of progress on the Lisbon Strategy and, as one of its key recommendations, highlighted the need to complete all the transposition of the FSAP measures by the end of 2005. There is an absolute need for Member States to honour the transposition deadlines - underlining that the deadlines should be realistic – otherwise this may turn out to be a significant bottleneck to the whole Lamfalussy Process that was agreed at the Stockholm Summit.

The political commitment of all the European institutions to enact the Level 1 measures has been impressive but the Kok Report also points out that "one of the most persistent obstacles is the failure of too many Member States to act on the commitments they make in the Council within the agreed time limit"[3]. The Commission recently published a new 'Lamfalussy league table' on Member States' success in meeting deadlines for writing into national law a series of securities Directives that were adopted as part of the FSAP.

The league table is astonishing given the professed high-level commitment to the process. No less than 20 Member States failed to implement the Prospectus Directive before the deadline of 1 July 2005. And 16 Member States had not yet fully implemented the Market Abuse Directive (MAD), and it's implementing measures when the deadline had been 12 October 2004. Correctly, the UK made implementation one of its Presidency priorities, when it took over in July 2005, and it was clear that it should start with transposing the EU framework directives into national legislation before even considering the lower levels of technical detail. The Commission has started to fulfil its commitment to launch infringement procedures, and took action in August 2005 against the 16 States that had not implemented MAD fully – ironically, including the UK

Excessive Detail in Primary Legislation

The entire philosophy of the Lamfalussy Process is to avoid excessive detail in the primary legislation (Level 1) as any subsequent changes are difficult and time consuming. Instead, Level 1 should be about principles. Yet there are continuing pressures from stakeholders to put much detail into the primary legislation. This tendency may decline as confidence in the flexibility of the process builds up, but all stakeholders should constantly be aware that secondary (Level 2) legislation is the place where detail should be.

So there is a fundamental tension between the political desire to meet deadlines – to avoid the charge of failing to reform - and the proper need to get the details right. But the real dilemma for many stakeholders is the risk of forgoing the opportunity to get complete legal certainty for their business needs at an early stage –in Level 1 legislation. Or should they be prepared to wait, and play the new game at Level 2 where they may have more flexibility in the longer term?

The evidence so far is that market practitioners have chosen to play the old game, with the inevitable result of large and unwieldy legislation that is extremely complex. The Inter-Institutional Monitoring Group (this author was the Rapporteur) examined this problematic tendency in some detail but correcting it may take some time – and growing trust between all the stakeholders.

Better Regulation

The European Commission's Green Paper on Financial Services Policy 2005- 2010 is right to stress the political orientation of acting in ways that ensure societal legitimacy. The new *Impact Assessment Guidelines* – only published in June 2005 - offer a sound approach to achieving the necessary rigour, but there are inherent limitations in the process. In part, these are logical and stem from the nature of the legislative process. If any Member States have solved these problems decisively within their own political framework, then the EU could learn from them.

The UK Presidency made *Better Regulation* a priority because there is a strong political will to capture these aggregate benefits and that means change – often as a result of legislation. Making the necessary changes requires the formal political system to act but there must be *societal legitimacy* so that all the players feel that it is fair and right. They must be consulted, together with their customers, to make sure they have *bought-in*, to use the usual terminology, to this legislation. A crucial part of that process of generating legitimacy involves the preparation of an *impact assessment* so that the necessary consultation can be focussed on the areas of private cost as well as public gain.

Two examples during the UK Presidency illustrate the Better Regulation approach. The first shows the system working to quantify the public gain balanced with private costs that may be unevenly borne by the commercial winners and losers. But the second example seems to show what happens when the EU's politicians decide on action for political reasons:

1. The Commission's Green Paper on Mortgage Credit was accompanied by a weighty assessment from a UK economics consultancy, highlighting the cost/benefit analysis. They calculated the possible costs of the changes to be around €2.5 billion annually – though some private associations have questioned this calculation. EU mortgages amount to €5 trillion, equivalent to 45% of GDP, so any improvement in financing could have significant economic effects. Annual costs to the mortgage bankers may seem substantial but the study estimates the economic gain to be very large (a net present value around €95 billion). So the benefits from a major legislative programme seem well worthwhile.

In this case, statistics are available to support these calculations. But a weakness of the Green Paper is that it does not address the inadequacies of EU financial data – a prerequisite for convincing and thorough impact assessments. The current moves to harmonise reporting requirements for some financial institutions offer a *golden opportunity* to correct this and, more importantly, lay the necessary foundations for the eventual possibility of a lead regulator for cross-border financial activities. This is an insistent demand from many large financial institutions.

Some of these institutions may even find it hard to have an internal position on subjects like this. A key part of the benefits flow from enhancing the mortgage-backed bond market – where the City of London-based trading desks should gain. But the costs are likely to fall on a wide swathe of banks across the EU that specialise in mortgage origination.

2. However, another example shows how policy-making can still be subject to political desires – even if they are for the common good. The tragic bombings in London in July 2005 underline the seriousness of the fight against terrorism. Co-incidentally, the Financial Action Task Force (FATF) has made a seventh recommendation: to require further details on wire transfers of money. This proposal was launched on 26 July 2005 with only 6 weeks for comment – half the norm. The UK accorded this proposal priority so that it could be enacted within six months. The Commission has not provided an impact assessment at all and the UK Treasury published only a Partial Regulatory Impact Assessment that specifically states "Estimates of the costs of the following would be very welcome"[4] and then lists all the components of the activity to be regulated. The effectiveness of the proposal is not particularly considered as there must be a clear risk that it can be circumvented by putting some high-value euro notes in the post.

Conclusion

Grand slogans have an immediate appeal but the reality of the task facing the EU must be different because, in Lamfalussy's wise words again, "the European Union has no divine right to the benefits of an integrated financial market"[5]. The benefits will only come by pushing forward – step by step – the creation of soundly-based policies of liberalisation. But that means change, and change cannot be free.

For the City, the potential benefits are enormous as the European financial system moves to create the required assets for savers to fund their lengthy retirement. Crucially, these savings seem likely to be channelled via financial institutions that are virtually certain to hold securities. That gives the City the opportunity to issue and trade securities for the entire EU financial system. Moreover, a successful EU system is likely to be a magnet for foreign savings, whilst it also gives a better chance for EU firms to compete on the world stage.

Notes

[1] Lisbon European Council communiqué 2000

[2] *Lamfalussy Report on the Regulation of European Securities Markets*, 2001, p.8.

[3] *Facing the Challenge*, Kok Report on Lisbon Strategy, November 2004.

[4] *EU Regulation on Wire Transfers Consultation Document*, HM Treasury, July 2005, p.7.

[5] Lamfalussy op cit. p.8.

Chapter Three

European Rhetoric and European Reality: the Financial Services Action Plan[1]

Chris Huhne

Ambrose Bierce once defined the future as that period of time in which our affairs prosper, our friends are true and our happiness is assured. I imagine that there are enough readers with grey hair to have seen such futures come and go, and to have found the reality fall a little short of the expectations. By contrast, the expectations of those us involved with the Financial Services Action Plan were as I remember relatively low when it was launched. Yet here we are, only a few years later, 39 out of 42 measures completed. We have been through controversies that looked as if they would sink the whole ship. We have surmounted obstacles that looked enormous and even insuperable at the time. Many of the routes around those obstacles are curious and do not go in a straight line. But overall, the body of legislation is an achievement of which I think all of us can be proud. As the period of primary legislation nears its end, it is worth remembering just how far we have travelled.

What is more, it has been over particularly hazardous terrain. Adam Smith, in a gloomy passage in The Wealth of Nations, said that free trade would never be completely attained even in Great Britain, for which he had higher hopes than most. 'Not only the prejudices of the public' he said 'but what is much more unconquerable, the private interests of many individuals, irresistibly oppose it'.

And in financial services, free trade is even more difficult because of the political sensitivity of the field. It was not an accident that financial services was the great left over of the single market programme. This is the allocative heart of the market economy that switches savings into investments. Not only do savers have a legitimate expectation of receiving their cash back when they want it, but the system itself crucially determines the efficiency of the whole economy. Finance has to say yes or no, and those choices are crucial.

My main criterion in approaching all the proposals from the Commission has been the liberal one. Will it make competition easier? Will it open up the market? Will it extend choice? And I have asked these questions for the simple reason that, whenever I am trying to buy something, I prefer to have two people trying to sell me something than one. And three is even better. The best means of consumer protection is choice and free markets. But I am not naïve enough to believe that open markets are enough: financial services products are often so complex that their intricacies are way over the head of many customers, and those customers need help. So competition is crucial for consumers. But so is information. And so is understanding. And so often is regulation where we cannot rely on informed consumers.

The key is balance, and the appropriate balance shifts. Professional investors need little if any regulation. It is no disrespect to my aunt Agatha to say that she needs a lot of help with financial matters. But that regulation must be non-discriminatory between member states and their businesses. It must allow as much competition as possible.

Indeed, a single market programme that merely replicates excessive levels of regulation in some member states across the whole union would be actively counter-productive. Basic welfare economics tells us that protection moves prices away from a market-clearing price. If that protection is extended, more prices will move further away from market-clearing prices, and overall economic welfare would be reduced. So a single market programme only makes sense to the extent that it introduces more competition and choice, and moves prices towards the free market.

Enough of the generalities, I intend to provoke. To call a spade and spade, and say when the Emperor has no clothes. So let me turn to unfinished business, and particularly to failures of understanding and logic in some of the member states. As a representative of Britain's most pro-European political party, I find my own fellow citizens' inability to follow the logic of the single market deeply curious.

It seems obvious to me that there can be no really effective single market without a single currency. Could the single US market be a reality without the US dollar? Of course not. It is also obvious that participation in the euro should be a logical step onwards from the thinking of so many British people who championed the single market, not least the Conservatives. Given our own track record of sterling crises, I cannot see that we would be giving up much. But I can see real benefits from tearing down the tariff barrier of having a separate currency.

I am also astonished at the lack of UK debate on the subject: the fact that our Chancellor of the Exchequer can still congratulate himself on Britain's relative economic performance when he is paying more to borrow ten year money than every other of the 15 old member states, including countries like Greece and Italy with public debt ratios three times as high. And the plummeting share of the UK's foreign direct investment into the EU - down from 27 per cent in 1998 to 7 per cent in 2002 - would worry me if I were in his shoes. Britain is performing worse than many of the euro-area's members such as Spain, Ireland and Greece.

But one of the difficulties of selling the euro in Britain is the sluggish performance of France and Germany, the two countries with which we most naturally compare ourselves, and the political economy of which deeply concerns me. Start with Germany, which was responsible for perhaps the biggest defeat of the single market legislation during the last parliament when the hard-negotiated Takeover directive was defeated in July 2001 on a tied vote in the parliament. After a massive national campaign, every single German MEP except one - honourable mention should go here to Christoph Conrad - voted against the directive. Why? In theory, because it did not go far enough to open up a cross border market in corporate control. In reality, because German public opinion thought it went too far.

The warning signs were there when Vodafone took over Mannesmann in a contested takeover bid. Reading the German press, you would have thought that it was the rape of the Sabine women. There is a marvellous doctrine in economics called revealed preference, which says that you should judge people by what they do, not what they say. And Germany just does not like foreign investors: equity capital owned by foreigners is worth just 12.1 % of GDP. France, by the way, is 11.9% of GDP. That compares with twice as much - 24 % of GDP - in Britain. Or 33 % in the Netherlands. Or 21 % in Spain. Or 104 % in Ireland.

By the way, the comparisons are even worse when you look at a sensitive sector like financial services. The proportion of bank assets that are foreign controlled in Britain is 51% - more than half. The proportion in Luxembourg is 94 %. In Belgium, it is 25%. But the proportion in Germany is just 4.7 %. Looking at these numbers, you have to ask yourself whether Germany really wants to integrate with its neighbours. And so we have the delicious irony that the most reluctant European when it comes to political integration - Britain - is wholly relaxed about foreign ownership. Siemens is one of the biggest manufacturing employers in Britain. But Germany, the champion of political integration, hates the idea of working for foreign bosses. Germany is all in favour of European politics, just so long as Germany does not have to integrate with other European economies.

Germany is going to have to face these nationalist demons, and for a simple reason. Monetary union without free capital flows is not going to work. The single currency deprives member states of the adjustment mechanisms of a separate interest rate and a separate foreign exchange rate. It keeps the adjustment mechanisms of separate price levels and wage levels. And it adds a powerful new adjustment mechanism - crucial to the working of the US monetary union when for example Texas went into recession following the 1986 oil price dip - of free capital flows. These capital flows can be much larger within a monetary union precisely because of the lack of exchange rate risk, but if countries block one of the most important avenues, this mechanism cannot work. So I very much hope - for the sake of the euro area - that the Commission brings forward a new takeover proposal. And that the Commission holds the German government's feet to the fire.

I have criticised my own country, Britain. I have criticised Germany. Let me now turn my attention to France. I was a student in France. I speak French. I am an enormous admirer of France and the French. But I am astonished by the extraordinary hypocrisy of the French Government. According to President Chirac, we need to abolish more vetoes in the new constitution so that we can build Europe more quickly. There are even hints of moving forward with a select group in enhanced cooperation. And he is highly critical of Britain for putting a brake on European progress. Well, all I can say is that people should learn to walk before they try to run. Pehr Gyllenhammar pointed out that some of the most sceptical countries are the ones that best apply the EU's rules. He did not say that the Government that likes to employ the most high-flown European rhetoric and deliver the most stern lectures to others is the worst of all when it comes to European reality.

If you look at the latest single market scoreboard, France is the worst EU member state for directives that are overdue by more than two years. As at June 2004, it has 9 overdue, more than twice the number of Germany or Britain. France also has the longest delay of any EU member state in implementing directives after their deadline, with an average of 14 months, more than double the time of the UK, Sweden, Finland or Denmark. And France has the worst record of any member state when it comes to open infringement cases for breach of EU law: 220 cases at the last count compared with 200 in Italy, 136 in Germany and 121 in Britain. If I came from a country with a track record for failing to apply European agreements like France's, I would not feel it appropriate to be lecturing anyone else about being good Europeans. I would want to put my own house in order first.

That track record is now particularly relevant to the next stage of financial services legislation, where implementation will be all. Just to ensure that I can maintain my reputation for biting the hand that feeds me, let me say that I very much hope that the Commission puts the resources into making this area work. Generally, the Commission has been far too slow to allocate staff to areas that have become 'hot', like merger control in competition, or financial services in the internal market. The Commission employs 22,453 people, about the same number as an average sized county council in my own country, and fewer people than Gordon Brown managed to add to the British civil service payroll in just one year to April 2003. But I would not argue for more Commission officials, just for a much more responsive allocation to important areas. And to a much more ruthless pruning of areas that are frankly unnecessary. The Commission tries to do too much, and that is one of the reasons why it does not always do what it does at all well. It needs to prioritise its tasks and do less, better.

Now that I have laid about me with fair abandon, you are entitled to ask 'what about the European parliament?' And my response is that the list of needed improvements in my own institution would be far too long, but elections show that the parliament needs to improve its game if it is to perform the essential function of any parliament, which is to create consent among the electorate for the decisions that it takes. Overall, though, the parliament has I believe been on the side of the angels when it comes to the financial services programme, and indeed the single market more widely. The big exception is the Takeover directive. But generally, we have toughened up those provisions that open up markets and ensure more choice. And that it is a real achievement both for us and for Europe. Freeing up markets is difficult politics. It is never easy to introduce changes that benefit many millions of people a little, while disadvantaging a few people a lot. The many millions of winners do not get very enthusiastic, while the few losers tend to get very angry. But we - the Commission, Parliament, Council - have done it, and it's a real achievement.

Notes

[1] Based on a speech delivered to European Commission conference on the Financial Services Action Plan, Brussels, Speech at the dinner for speakers, Palais d'Egmont on Tue 22nd Jun 2004.

Chapter Four

No Euro Please, We're British!

Lucio Valerio Spagnolo and Mario Cerrato[1]

When comparing the economic performances between UK and Euroland, the appropriate and obvious question should be why does not Euroland replace its euro with the British pound? However, the economy does not represent all the interests of the human beings. They believe in values beyond the economy. Right! It may well be that Euroland citizens, once with the euro, feel much more confidence in themselves, as part of a larger world, as they trust the monetary and political decision makers of the EU institutions. If that was the truth, the European integration process should proceed just like a ball thrown against standing skittle-pins. Unfortunately, that is not the case. The authors try to point out some reasons to understand those British people who love to look at the euro experience, sitting in their armchairs and, above all, without loosing their national pound.

From January 1st, 1973, the UK became, in every respect, a member country of the European Union (EU) and consequently is one of the addressees of its huge legislation and effects deriving from it. On February 27th, 1992 the *Treaty on European Union* (thereafter Treaty) is signed in Maastricht and represents the beginning of the European Economic and Monetary Union (EMU) creation to be achieved through three stages. On October 1997, the British government, by means of the Chancellor of the Exchequer Mr Gordon Brown, using the Treaty *opting-out* clause, announced the intention of non-participation to the third stage, the one that would have led the twelve member states of the EU to adopt one European currency, the euro. Hence, the UK maintains its own autonomy in the fields of *monetary policy* and *exchange rate policy*. The UK maintains its British pound as national currency unless a popular referendum indicates the will of replacing the British pound with the euro. The UK, however, participates in the European System of Central Banks (ESBC) where the EU monetary policy is decided through the Governor Council and the Executive Committee. In other words the presence of the UK in the EMU is testimony to the fact that monetary union and one single currency are not mutually exclusive[2].

Nevertheless, the passage towards a monetary union with a single currency makes complete and mature an incomplete union[3]. The British choice comes from a number of criticisms either of EU economic policies, the monetary policy and the rate of exchange policy to be accepted by accepting the euro, or on the negative result of a number of economic tests, which will be explained in the next sections. In this chapter we point out that the British opting-out choice might be explained not only by economic concerns, but more importantly, by political concerns. We shall start however with the former.

Exchange Rate Policy

Building a single currency implies the disappearance of the exchange rate policy for a country within a union. A country will be keen to accept a new currency if it is convinced that the advantages of having it will prevail over the disadvantages. Therefore, is the UK convinced that the loss of exchange rate policy implies more advantages than disadvantages? Though this point should not be the most important one, it still it helps us to understand the British view on the euro.

As Mundell (1961) showed[4], the evaluation of costs and benefits of building up a monetary union with a single currency takes place through the *theory of the optimal currency area (Oca)*[5]. An Oca will be justified if advantages exceed disadvantages.

According to this theory, in the presence of fixed rates of exchange, an eventual negative asymmetric shock that hits the economy of country A will cause, at the same time, a worsening in its balance of payments and an improvement in that of country B. Because of the presence of a fixed rate of exchange, the re-equilibrium of the balance of payments between the two countries will take place if, and only if, at least two conditions are met: a perfect flexibility of wages and a high mobility in the labour market. In fact, country A, because of a lack of demand will experience lower prices, higher unemployment, a weakening of trade unions, and consequently lower wages. Country B will experience exactly the opposite effect: an excess of demand, higher prices, higher employment, a strengthening of trade unions, and consequently, higher wages. Thus, country A, because of the lower wages, will increase the demand of labour, employment and output. Country B, because of the higher wages, will decrease employment and output. Prices and wages will increase in country A and decrease in country B, re-establishing the external equilibrium in both the countries.

In the presence of flexible rates of exchange, an eventual negative asymmetric shock on country A will cause a worsening of its balance of payments, deriving from a worsening either in its current account balance, due to a decrease in the exports, or in the short run capital flows, due to an increase in the short run capital outflows. The domestic currency will depreciate and, at the same time, the currency of a country B will appreciate. Such depreciation and appreciation will increase exports and capital inflows in country A and decrease exports and increase capital outflows in country B. The balance of payments of country A will improve, while the one of country B will worsen, re-establishing the external equilibrium in both the countries.

On one side, flexible rates of exchange reflect the ups and downs of the markets, and the only danger with them might be due to high exchange rates volatility and inflation without the possibility for it to be exported to the rest of the world. On the other side, fixed rates of exchange need the fulfilment of the two above conditions (i.e. perfect flexibility of prices and wages and high mobility in the labour market), conditions that the UK believes do not exist, or, at least, do not *yet* exist within Euroland. Evidently, apart from the above mentioned advantages of having flexible rates of exchange, the UK believes that the danger linked to the flexible rates of exchange is preferable to the non existence of the flexibility of wages and labour mobility within the EU member countries.

Thus, the EU area might not be an Oca and consequently the disadvantages of abandoning the exchange rate policy is not at all balanced by the advantages of replacing the British pound with the euro.

In fact the exchange rate policy, if successful, may only temporary help an economy to draw a sigh of relief, but cannot be thought of as the right one for pursuing stability and growth.

On one hand it is true that for an exchange rate policy to be successful we need i) the fulfilment of the Bickerdicke-Robinson condition, according to which the balance of the current account improves, when the national currency depreciates, if, and only if, it will result $(p_X X/p_M M)\ \Sigma_X+\Sigma_M>1$, where X and M are the quantities of exports and imports, p_X and p_M their prices, and Σ_X and Σ_M their elasticises, to a devaluations of the rate of exchange[6], and ii) that the other countries with which the country devaluating has more exchanges will not also devaluate their own currencies. On the other hand it is also true that, in the absence of prices and wages perfect flexibility and high labour mobility, there will not be a convincing reason to participate in a union.

However, examples of success, in using appropriate exchange rate policy to help the national economy, come from the government decisions in France during the years 1982-83, when the devaluations of the franc helped the domestic economy to recover from years of stagnation. Denmark during 1982, and above all Belgium, whose devaluation of 8.5% improved the current account from -3.5% in 1981 to +2.0% in 1986, and of employment, in the same period, from -2.0% to +1.0% when the average within the Union was +0.8%.

If, as we mentioned above, under certain conditions fixed exchange rates might be appropriate, why should the UK believe that those conditions (i.e. perfect flexibility of wages and high mobility in the labour market) are not met in Euroland? The answer passes through two basic points: the institutional differences in the labour market of the countries participating to the union *and* the political attitude of the governments of those countries towards unemployment and inflation.

About the first point, countries may be different according to the degree of concentration of their trade unions: the higher that degree, the higher the proportion of workers represented by the same institution, the stronger the pressures put on employers to obtain higher wages[7]. Within the Union, the UK is characterised by a low degree of concentration of the trade unions, compared with that of other countries[8], and it might be difficult to achieve one homogeneous degree within the Union.

About the second point, countries assign different weights to the *trade off* between the rate of increase of wages and the level of unemployment. Some of them are more prone than others to accept a lower employment rate, due to higher wages; others will advocate the idea that the rate of unemployment must not go beyond a maximum level, which, if exceeded, will imply the use of expansionary fiscal and monetary policies. That is to say each country has its own utility function satisfied at the point where the government utility function (the demand of labour of the whole community) meets the trade union's utility function (the level of real wages claimed by trade unions)[9].

Traditionally, on one hand the UK has always considered economic liberalism as an unquestionable priority to help growth and development and, on the other one[10], has never forgotten to support families, schools, researchers, and social services in the light of the Beveridge philosophy[11]. Any complete union entails agreement about the two points above, and the UK might be convinced that the compromise for accepting the euro would weaken and worsen its freedom of decisions.

As mentioned above, the second point for building an Oca is the existence of a high labour mobility[12]. From this point of view the lack of such mobility is evident in the EU area. Lack due to a number of important reasons such as, differences in the language[13], culture, law, uses, traditions etc. Therefore, it might be possible that one currency, the euro, will not fill all the gaps involved by such differences or, at least, will not be a substitute for them, unless a higher degree of social feeling and cultural harmonization between EU countries is achieved. Until then, the abandonment of the pound, and exchange rate policy, might be an unreasonable cost to pay.

On The Diversity of Monetary Policy in the UK and Euroland

Once it has accepted the euro as the national currency, the UK will cease to decide its own monetary policy. However, while exchange rate policies will become a nonsense within Euroland, the UK, once belonging to Euroland, has to share decisions, and management, on Euroland monetary policy. Such a policy can only be one, and precisely the one representing the expression of the emerging will of all the countries belonging to Euroland.

In principle, national monetary authorities may have, and generally have, their own view about objectives to pursue and the means to achieve them. The diversity derives from different economic realities, perspectives and evaluations of such objectives and means. However, in the end, those authorities have to reach only one decision. Inevitable adjustments will be accepted, in the end, in the name of belonging to a union and, inevitably, part of the power of deciding their own monetary policy will be given to the new authority. As often happens in many fields of economics, social and political environment, and also in our case, there could be an interval of much (infinite) diversity, varying from the most insignificant to the deepest of them. No matter about the former, but what will happen in case the latter prevails?

Firstly, there is an urgent need to find out an acceptable way of making the smallest countries count when important decisions are taken. Secondly, should the (new) monetary policy institution have only one objective, for example, assuring price stability, or more objectives, say, price stability, growth, external equilibrium, etc? Furthermore, should the monetary institution be absolutely independent of political power, transparent in its decisions, and accountant towards other institutional powers? What kind of intermediate targets should it firstly achieve, before achieving the final goal? The above are only some of the disquieting, or at least uneasy questions, which may arise when trying to tackle the delicate problem for a country to cease control of part of its monetary sovereignty to a new institution in the name of belonging to a union.

On the Differences in the Objectives

In principle, price stability (that is controlling the rate of inflation) is the ultimate goal of any monetary policy. In order to achieve that goal, monetary authorities, generally, use three means, that is, fixing the rate of interest, using open market operations and fixing the rate of the bank reserve-ratio. In the absence of diversities in the objectives to be achieved and considering the three means mentioned above, why should not the UK accept the euro? An acceptance of the euro would lead to more price stability in the advantage of both, the UK and the Euroland. The reason might be that any monetary policy spreads its effects over the financial market, only if monetary policy actions are synchronised with financial markets. That happens if, and only if, the latter trusts the former. Financial markets are in synchrony with monetary policies only when, traditionally, monetary policy announcements have been proved to be true for a long time, which implies monetary policy credibility. It might well be that the UK is concerned about maintaining such a credibility once monetary policy decisions are to be shared with other culturally different oriented decision makers.

The reason lies in the definition of the different task of the British monetary authority, in comparison with that of the ECB (European central bank), when dealing with inflation. The main goal of the ECB, in terms of controlling inflation, is achieved when the rate of increase in the *Harmonised Index of Consumer Prices (HICP)* is, within the euro area, somewhere between 0% and 2%, however less than 2.0%[14]. To On the other hand the Bank of England fulfils that goal at a *Retail Prices Index excluding mortgage interest payments (RPIX)* increasing at a maximum of 2.5%. However, due to a different method of calculating the rate of inflation in the UK and Euroland, *it may happen*, in the long term, that the two values might be coincidence. What if they will not? What if the value measured by the ECB were lower than the other one? Will an EU deflationary process involve, in the UK too, a fall in employment and output?

This is the reason why the ECB, at the beginning of its activity, stated precisely that the above rate of 2.0% has to be referred to as a *medium term rate.* However, the definition of medium term itself, given by the ECB, is still rather unclear.

Further, how can one accept a 2.0% rate of increase in the HICP, as referring to the whole euro area when it is clear that the euro area is not yet a homogeneous area? In fact, prices for the same good vary not only between countries belonging to the euro area, but also between adjacent areas belonging to the same country or even to adjacent areas of the same town. It would be very unlikely that we will ever achieve price homogeneity across the different countries participating to the EU.

In other words, one monetary policy for one (euro) area needs one common market, a market that, as already stated by the Treaty of Rome (1957), assures perfect mobility of persons, goods and capitals. Though undeniable progress in this respect has been made during the past half a century, there is a lack of flexibility in the adjustment of real and monetary variables that prevents the euro area from being a perfectly competitive one.

The uncertainties over a number of points involved by too many unanswered questions represent a threat to the above mentioned crucial requirement of any respectable monetary authority, that is the credibility of the latter with financial markets. In this respect, one may well believe that the UK, being aware of the long time the British authority took to build up that credibility, might be concerned about maintaining the euro once accepted.

However, neither the Bank of England nor the ECB have the single task of assuring price stability. In fact, for example, the Bank of England has to help government make effective its economic policy. The stability of prices appears to have the same importance as other government objectives. The ECB has also a number of objectives belonging to the real economy such as employment, output, and so on. Therefore, there is no difference between the two. But, in fact, the meaning is not the same; the former, through the monetary policy, is asked to co-operate with the government in implementing its economic policy[15]; the latter has, first of all, the task of assuring price stability, and only after having achieved that, it looks at the real economy. The difference will appear clear in the next section.

On the Diversities of the Means

In the previous section we pointed out that the main objective of a monetary authority is price stability. However, is the path any monetary policy has to follow to achieve price stability unique? That is, is there any choice between a number of intermediate targets to be achieved before achieving the final goal, or rather there is only one path. If there are different paths and therefore different intermediate targets, how should one choose between them?

With respect to the first and secondary tasks, the ECB monetary policy is based upon two pillars, a monetary pillar and a second one made up of a set of variables of the real economy. The first one, the so-called *money targeting*, that allows achieving price stability, is the ECB's main choice. It comes from the ECB conviction that inflation is essentially a monetary phenomenon, and consequently it depends on the quantity of money in the economy. Thus, once fixed, let us say, at a maximum of 2.0%, the increase of the rate of inflation, supposing an increase of GDP by 1% and an increase of the money circulation velocity by 0.2%, the amount of money supply has to increase by 2.8%[16]. The second pillar sweetens the strong and true first one, as it shows an ECB keeping also into account the real economy. Final decisions however are taken essentially on the basis of the first pillar, although not automatically as in such cases, expectations would lead to speculative activity.

The *direct inflation targeting* is the British authority's choice according to which the rate of inflation represents both the intermediate target *and* the final goal. In other words, the British monetary policy deals with the elimination of the gap between the *expected* and *planned* rate of inflation. That is pursued by monitoring and using any variables able to reduce that gap, not only the quantity of money supplied. At the same time, the whole of its action is extremely *transparent* towards public and, broadly speaking, the financial markets. Therefore, it is implicit in our example that, by accepting the euro the UK has to replace its direct inflation targeting with the money targeting. That might carry on a high cost indeed for the UK for a number of reasons.

The first reason is linked to the concept of the *neutrality of the money*[17], which appears to belong to the ECB, and does not belong to Bank of England. Consequently, the Bank of England has to help government in implementing its policy, while pursuing its duty of price stability; the ECB only addresses a yearly report on its activity to the European Parliament, the Commission and the Council of Europe. On the other hand, since in the British view the money is *non neutral* then the Bank of England is *accountant* towards the government.

The second reason is a consequence of the first. In fact, the multi-purpose Bank of England task (to assure the stability of prices *and* help government in realising its economic policy) implies a co-operative action with government. Monetary policy and fiscal policy are to co-operate to achieve price stability and growth. There are two objectives and two means. Co-operation does not mean the presence of a leader and follower. On the contrary, since there are two objectives and two independent means to be used to achieve them, it is respected the well known *Tinbergen Principle*, according to which a model with predetermined objectives (i.e. with n independent objectives) must have n independent means and all of them have to co-operate to the achievement of the objectives[18]. The ECB philosophy of the two pillars yields to the inevitable consequence of giving priority to monetary variables when compared with the real ones: the Tinbergen Principle is not satisfied[19]. For example suppose that, in the absence of coordination, the rate of interest is increased in order to reduce inflation and that, at the same time, government decides an expansionary fiscal policy to reduce the rate of unemployment. Monetary policy will fade away fiscal policy expectations, contributing to lead the economy towards undesired effects. It would not appear hazardous to imagine the British not willing to weaken their co-ordination philosophy and respect of the Tinbergen principle.

The Independence of the ECB

The creation of the ECB proved to be a revival of the ancient debate about whether a central bank should, or should not, be independent of the political power[20]. As to the ECB, the principle of independence from the political power is stated by article 107 of the Treaty: *"When exercising the powers and carrying out the tasks and duties conferred upon them by this Treaty and the Statute of the ESCB, neither the ECB, nor a national central bank, nor any member of their decision-making bodies shall seek or take instructions from Community institutions or bodies, from any government of a Member State or from any other body...."* The passive defence of such a principle is *institutional*, being exerted from external interferences when ECB is pursuing statutory objectives, *personal*[21], through the process of nomination and the length of the charges[22] and *functional*, since the ECB is given a number of financial and accountant tools and the responsibility of drawing up the ESCB (European System of Central Bank) consolidated balance sheet[23]. The active defence of that principle takes the form of the prohibition, stated by the article 104 of the Treaty *"Overdraft facilities or any other type of credit facility with the ECB or with the central banks of the Member States (hereinafter referred to as "national central banks") in favour of Community institutions or bodies governed by public law, or public undertakings of Member States shall be prohibited, as shall the purchase directly from them by the ECB or national central banks of debt instruments."* and the art. 104 A *"Any measure, not based on prudential considerations, establishing privileged access by Community institutions or bodies, central governments, regional, local or other public authorities, other bodies governed by public law, or public undertakings of Member States to financial institutions shall be prohibited."* In fact, the independence of the ECB from the political power is a *condition sine qua non* of the existence of the ECB herself. Moreover, a number of economic models, as the *representative agent* model by Rogoff[24], have been developed to advocate the thesis according to which the ECB should minimise the function of the loss

$$L=(p-p^*)^2 + b(u-u^*)^2$$

where L is the loss, p-p* is the difference between *current* and *planned* rate of inflation, u-u* is the difference between *current* and *planned* rate of unemployment and b is the value the minimizer assigns to the relative importance between inflation and unemployment[25]. According to the model, the lower the value assigned by the central banker (the agent) to b, the more conservative she is. Her credibility is higher, the lower the value assigned to b since a low value means more control on the rate of inflation. Consequently, at the beginning of the ECB activity, it was essential for the ECB to show that it was conservative, above all, that it was even more conservative than most conservative existing central banks. However, is the priority given to the rate of inflation over unemployment justified?[26] Is it true that the degree of credibility of a central banker increases with the degree of conservativeness? Is it true that more conservativeness means more credibility? Is it true that more independence means more credibility and, hence, more conservativeness? Most important, who should the minimiser be: the representative agent (the central banker) or, rather, the society, that is to say, the government chosen by the society? Further, once accepted the idea of a rate of inflation mainly linked to the quantity supplied of money, would not the ECB, with its monetary policy, make dependent the fiscal policies of the governments of the member countries? These are only some of the questions needing a satisfactory answer.

The British model of central bank, though is left independent in the accomplishment of the main task, on the other hand, it is essentially considered, as explained above, an institution helping government in achieving the goals set by the government itself. That comes from the fundamental UK conception of the *non-neutrality* of the money.

However, the principle of independence might be also seen in a slightly different way. In fact, is the ECB really an institution independent, *super-partes*, above the will of the member States expressed by their Governors? And how many activities are, still now, maintained by the national central banks and how many delegated to the ECB[27]? Finally, is monetary policy really conceived by the ECB or, rather, influenced by the view of national bankers?[28] If monetary is influenced by the view of national bankers then it would be a difficult for the UK to see its view accepted! In all cases, the ECB independence can only be *relative*: it cannot be *absolute*, since it depends on the international rate of exchange systems[29]. Keeping into account the international rate of exchange context, there could be different views on what policy is advisable. At the same time all of them could probably be justifiable on the basis of different arguments. However, they will imply different consequences in different member countries.

A Pragmatic View

British Prime Minister Tony Blair described the decision on whether or not joining the euro as the most important decision of the Labour government and promised to call a referendum on the issue. As a consequence of the Labour pro-Euro policy, in 1997 the Treasury announced five economic tests on UK entry to the Euro. The tests are essentially based on assessing the convergence of the UK business cycle with the European business cycle; assessing the degree of flexibility of the UK economy to adapt and adjust to changes; considering the effect on investment in the UK; considering the advantages for the financial services sector once joined the euro; finally, considering employment and growth prospects.

Despite the five economic tests, for quite few people the decision to join the euro will not be an easy one, and it will be based more on the "emotional facts" of having to scrap the pound than economic concerns.

The Treasury considers the test on convergence an important step towards a successful single currency. It says that, in order for the UK economy to fully be able to benefit from a single currency, it has to converge with Europe and show that the convergence is sustainable. With regard convergence, in the past the UK's economic cycle has been, most of the times, divergent and more volatile than others in Europe and more linked to the USA cycle. The early twenty first century saw Britain experience a period of good economic growth and stability while most of the European countries (see for example France, Germany, and Italy amongst the others), suffered low growth with relatively high levels of unemployment. The British cycle therefore seems to be still invariably out of phase with respect to most of the major European countries. Furthermore, the UK mortgage market historically depends on variable interest rates while the European market is mainly characterised by fixed interest rate. The boom in the housing markets with the consequent increase in the value of properties across the country has increased the borrowing power of the UK residents. The consequent increase in disposable income has increased consumption. On the other hand as a consequence of the boom in housing market, house prices have seen a two-digit increase in various areas of the country. The different rate of borrowing between Euroland and UK, and the house price inflation might be more than a simple concern for Tony Blair in order to schedule a reasonable time for joining the Euro. In fact, this concern has been recently expressed clearly by Gordon Brown when he announced that the UK was not ready yet for the euro and the Prime Minister accepted the Chancellor's view.

Another important test is about the flexibility or ability of the economy to adjust to changes. In fact as we stressed in the previous sections a single currency leads to a loss of domestic control over monetary policy. Given the risk of future shocks, firms would need to be flexible in terms of pricing and margins in order to respond to asymmetric shocks, and employees would need to increase their skills in order to adapt to changes in the labour market.

With regard investment the Treasury believes that a single currency, by creating an area of low inflation and high stability, and by removing currency changeover costs, would attract investment in Britain. However, perhaps the impact of the euro on the thousands of small business across the country might have been miss-calculated. In fact, the adoption of the euro will imply additional costs deriving from new accounting systems, price labels etc. Therefore, small business will not benefit from it and will pass on to customers the increase in costs by rounding up prices.

The City of London has always been one of the major financial centres in the world. According to the Treasury the euro will affect financial services immediately, therefore it is important to see if the City is prepared for it and if the introduction of the euro is advantageous for the sector. It is not difficult for anyone involved in the financial sector to see that the level of euro transactions on the UK stock exchange and secondary markets has been growing fast. Therefore, apart from operational costs and operational risk involved with the system, the City should be able to fully adapt in short time to the new currency.

The final test concerns employment and growth. The introduction of the euro should lead to low inflation and high stability for the whole Euro area (Britain included) and therefore a high growth and employment. However, as mentioned above, convergence and flexibility are two important factors in order to achieve these goals. Therefore a decision on whether or not this test has been satisfied is to be taken by the Treasury by looking at the fundamental structure of the UK economy and considering flexibility and convergence. However, it is unclear what convergence may imply in this context given that the UK GDP has been growing much faster than the GDP in most of the largest economies in Europe.

On the Political Reasons[30]

According to Disraeli[31] *Great Britain is governed by its Parliament, not by its logic* [32]. That was to lay stress on the British undeniable and unquestionable principle of national sovereignty, which is the legal capability of the national decision-makers to make their choices without being subject to any external restrictions. Coherently, from the very beginning of European integration process[33], the UK has been the advocate of the inter-government confederal model rather than the supranational federalist one[34]. The main difference between those two models is that only in the former is national sovereignty assured. On the other hand, the latter keeps into account either the interests and needs of the members, regions or States, that it is part of, or those of the new entity, the federal State. The tasks of the members and of the new entity should have to be exactly defined. EU, though represents none of the two models, having elements of both, it is moving towards the direction of the latter. Disraeli's sentiments perhaps no longer ring true.

EU laws are based upon the *self-executing*, *supremacy* and *pre-emption* principles. The UK, with the European Act of 1972, accepted the self-executing, or direct applicability principle[35] and consequently its logical consequence, that is the supremacy principle, according to which community law prevails over national law. Principle that is the same for all the member countries.[36] The supremacy principle revolutionises the law system of the member countries, by transferring part of the national sovereignty to the Union in the name of the principle that there cannot be a case of clashing interest between any of the member countries and the Union. However, since such a principle is more an aspiration than a reality, it is understandable that all the member countries have difficulties in accepting it, as it is. However, once accepted, in the case of a clashing law, the UK would be judged by the European Court of Justice. Therefore, in order to accept that principle, the UK should be convinced that the democratic power is stronger and better represented in the community law system than at home, and that a democratic deficit no longer exists at the heart of EU law making process. It is also because of this, once the euro is accepted, since the ECB will be the EU monetary policy decision maker, the UK will have to accept the principles of neutrality of the money and independence of the ECB, which contrasts its traditional view.

Regarding the *pre-emption* principle[37], it is known that, under the pressures of a number of member States, including UK and Germany, it became, with *The Treaty*, the *subsidiarity principle*. Such principle is based upon the presumption that, within the EU, the state has competence in making law unless explicitly assigned to the Union[38]. Generally, federalism needs this principle and, as in the case of the legislative Scottish Assembly (i.e. so-called *devolved matters*), clearly defined.

The subsidiarity principle in the EU seems to work in the opposite direction. That is, it assigns more and more competence to the Union and the less and less to the member states, in the view of building up a super state with a dangerous hierarchy that might appropriate the law competence of the member states.[39]

Participating in a union, in itself, needs one identity. A European Union needs its own identity, which means one feeling and one will to belong to the same Union well beyond belonging to the member country. Furthermore, a Federal Union needs the right interpretation of the subsidiarity principle, that is leaving the law making process to the member states in the respect of their diversities in any subject but those for which the "common feeling" delegates the Union.

At present, it is hard to recognise the existence of one feeling of belonging to the same economic, social, cultural and political reality. In other words it does not seem possible to believe in the existence of one voice for the European Union towards the rest of the world, before having built one identity for one European people.

Moreover, while the EU institutional democratic deficit needs to be tackled, the increasing community law making process is steadily increasing. At the same time, such process is not at all balanced by an increasing accountability of the institutions representing it.

The UK might not be encouraged to replace the pound with the euro until a true EU identity has emerged.

In our view, the UK's reasons for not joining the euro should not be seen as sterile, vanishing or disrespectful of the EU integration process. Rather, all the possible reasons mentioned above, ought to be seen as to contribute to the creation of a better Europe.

Notes

[1] The authors wish to thank Alizabeth Parvin for constructive comment. Financial support from the University of Salerno for economic research ex 60%, 2000-2002 is gratefully acknowledged.

[2] AAVV, 1991, *Dal Piano Delors All'unione Economica e Monetaria* Cedam, Padova, p.85.

[3] Delors Report.

[4] Mundell, R. "A Theory of Optimal Currency Areas" in *American Economic Review*, 1961, pp.657-665. Mundell's analysis is the first exposition of the subject and is preceded by the works of Meade (Nobel 1977) such as Meade, J. "The Balance of Payment Problems of a European Free Trade Area" in *Economic Journal*, 1957, pp.379-396. and Scitovsky, T. 1961 *L'Integrazione Economica dell'Europa Occidentale dal Puntodi Vista della Teoria,* Feltrinelli, Milano.

[5] The concept of Oca, the traditional one, is linked to the debate on the choice of a fixed or flexible rates of exchange regime to achieve a re-equilibrium of the balance of payment, debate developed in consequence of the crisis of the fixed rates of exchange international monetary system built up in 1944 at Bretton Woods and of the establishment, of a flexible rates of exchange regime. (Spagnolo, L.V. 2002, "L'Equilibrio in un'Economia Aperta" in *Editoriale Scientifica*, Napoli, p.160). More exactly, once cleared the inability of both the regimes to assure an international stability, the Oca was an alternative model represented by a monetary union within which there had to be one currency. In the Mundell view, as not all countries take advantage from a flexible rates of exchange regime, it was better that i) a number n of countries be grouped in a number m of monetary areas, ii) inside each monetary area it was appropriate a fixed rate of exchange, iii) between the m monetary areas there ought to be flexible rates of exchanges iv) the flexible rates of exchanges between monetary areas would be optimal if internal mobility and external immobility of factors, labour and capital, (ricardian) hypotheses were respected (Spagnolo, L.V. 2002, op. cit. p.161).

[6] See, among others, Spagnolo, L.V. 2002, op. cit.

[6] De Grauwe, P. 2000, *The Economics of Monetary Union,* Oxford University Press, Oxford.

[8] Sachs, J. D. and Bruno, M. 1995, *Economics and Worldwide Stagflation,* Harvard University.

[9] Solow, R. *La moderna teoria macroeconomica* Laterza, 1998; Solow, R. 1998, *Inflazione, Disoccupazione e Politica Monetaria,* Etas, §4.1.

[10] Apart from the Thatcher government.

[11] Beveridge, J. 1943, *Il Piano Beveridge. La Relazione di Sir W. Beveridge al Governo Britannico sulla Protezione Sociale.* Rapporto Ufficiale.

[12] See, in particular, Johnson, C. 1996, *In with The Euro, Out with The Pound. The Single Currency for Britain,* Penguin, London.

[13] See, among many others, Bini Smaghi, L. 1998, *L'euro* Il Mulino.

[14] To be precise: *"Although it clearly establishes the maintenance of price stability as the primary objective of the ECB, the Treaty does not give a precise definition of what is meant by price stability. In order to specify this objective more precisely, the Governing Council of the ECB announced the following quantitative definition on October 13th, 1998: "Price stability shall be defined as a year-on-year increase in the HICP for the euro area of below 2%"* in ECB *The monetary policy of ECB* ECB, Frankfurt am Main, 2001, p.38. Further, p.39, *"First, neither prolonged inflation nor prolonged deflation is consistent with the definition. The phrase "below 2%" clearly delineates the upper boundary for the rate of measured HICP inflation that is consistent with price stability. At the same time, the use of the word "increase" in the definition shows that deflation, i.e., declines in the level of the HICP covers a wide range of consumer expenditure"*.

[15] Other objectives of the Bank of England are the maintaining of the stability of the financial system both at home and assure the efficiency of UK financial services.

[16] According to the *quantitative theory of money*, $\Sigma m=\Sigma p+\Sigma y-\Sigma v$, where m is the quantity of money, y is the real GDP, v is the circulation velocity of money. Thus 2,8%=2%+1%-0,2%.

[17] Money is considered neutral if her variations do not affect variations in the real variables, but only in the level of prices.

[18] Tinbergen, J. 1956, *Economic Policy: Principles and Design,* North Holland Publishing Co., Amsterdam.

[19] It might be argued that the Tinbergen principle is not only respected by the ECB, but even stated by the Treaty (of the European Union): the ECB has to act in harmony with the Ecofin Council and the Economic and Financial Committee. However, the ECB co-operative activity cannot be interpreted and put in practice as the Tinbergen principle would suggest, because of the simple reason that, once again by statute, the ECB takes, primarily, responsibility for the stability of prices. That comes from the conviction according to which, without assuring the stability of prices, any economic policy is destined to fail.

[20] See, among many others, Habib, M. M. "Saggio Sull'indipendenza della Banca Centrale" in *Studi Economici,* n.70, 2000/1; Spagnolo L.V. "The Role of the European System of Central Banks in the European Integration Process" in *Building the New Europe, Vol. I: The Single Market and Monetary Unification,* 1993, Baldassarri M. and Mundell R. (Eds) The Macmillan Press, London and New York.

[21] The same art. 107 "*The Community institutions and bodies and the government of the Member States undertake to respect this principle and not to seek to influence the members of the decision-making bodies of the ECB or of the national central banks in the performance of their tasks.*"

[22] The art.11 of the Protocol (of the Treaty) statues the length of the charge of the members of the Executive Board in eight years.

---

[23] See Protocol, Chapter V, art. 25-27.

[24] Barro, R. and Gordon, D. 1983, "Rules, Discretion and Reputation in a Model of Monetary Policy" in *Journal of Monetary Economics,* 12, pp.101-120; Kydland, F.E. and Prescott, E.E. 1977, "Rules Rather Than Discretion, The Time Inconsistency of Optimal Plans" in *Journal of Political Economy.*

[25]In the Rogoff model, the *agent* (the conservative central banker), optimizes the *trade off* between inflation and unemployment minimizing the Loss function. In fact, she cannot reach such objective because of the simple reason that she has no autonomy in deciding both the rate of inflation and unemployment. She can only fix the former as objective, and not the latter. In any case a central banker is said to be conservative if she assigns more importance to the rate of inflation than to unemployment.

[26] Spagnolo, L.V. 1997, *La convergenza di Maastricht: una misura della divergenza* Giappichelli, Torino.

[27] Graziani A. thinks of the ESCB chosen as a hybrid one. Apparently, it looks like a highly centralized system in which every decision is made by the ECB, which finances directly national banks of the member countries. That can be seen by the ECB balance sheet, where the assets include financements in favour of national banks of the member countries and do not those in favour of the national central banks. However, the system is deeply modified being the implementation of the monetary policy assigned to the single national central banks, to which has been left a set of large powers. Graziana, A. "La politica monetaria della Banca Centrale Europea" in *Rivista Italiana degli Economisti* 2004, No. 1, Supplement dedicated to the works of the 44° yearly scientific meeting, Salerno, October, 24th-25th, 2003, Il Mulino, Bologna, Italy.

[28]The art.10 of the Protocol of the Treaty statues *"In accordance with Article 109a(1) of this Treaty, the Governing Council shall comprise the members of the Executive Board of the ECB and the Governors of the central banks."* At present, the Executive Committee consists of six members (art. 11), consequently the Governor Council includes the six members of the Executive Committee and twelve national central banks Governors. Though the Executive Committee decisions are independent, those of the national central bank Governors might be not. In the case when Euroland were hit by symmetric shock, the Governing Council decisions might coincide with the Executive Committee ones. But what will happen in case of an asymmetric shock? See the interesting discussion of De Grauwe, P., Dewachter, P. and Aksoy, Y. "The European Central Bank Decisions, Rules and Macroeconomic Performance" in *CEPR*, Discussion Paper No. 2067.

[29] Spagnolo, L.V. *L'equilibrio,* ,op.cit. pp.174-175; Spagnolo L.V. 1993, "European Economic Convergence and The International Monetary System" in *De Pecunia*, (number dedicated to the memory of Robert Triffin), Bruxelles.

[30]The subject of this § needs, obviously, a width and depth well beyond the objective of this paper, which only represents an attempt to give an understandable and condensed synthesis of the reasons why the UK might not been keen to joint the euro.
[31]Disraeli, Benjamin (1804-81), 1st Earl of Beaconsfield, British Conservative Prime Minister (1868, 1874-80).
[32]Bogdanor, V. "The United Kingdom and the European Union: Light on the Relationship" in *Britain in Europe*, The London School of Economics and Political Science, p.28.
[33] Duff, A. 1998, "Britain and Europe. The Different Relationship", in Westlake M. (ed) *The European Union beyond Amsterdam. New concepts of European integration*, Routledge. Zurcher, A.J. 1963 "La lotta per l'Europa unita 1940-1958", in *Cultura e Società* n. 29, Opere nuove.
[34] As we know, the debate on federalism against confederalism comes out at from the *functionalism,* a doctrine according to which *the form of a thing should be determined by its use.* For a definition of the term *functionalism*, see Collins English Dictionary, Glasgow, 1990, p.614. In the European integration process, the functionalist pragmatic view was applied to economic sectors of the economy through common policies to be managed by common supranational agencies, and leaded to the throwing down of the custom barriers to build a common way to political sectors. The functionalism adaptability to the member states needs was, at the same time, its strength and its weakness. The development of common economic policies was not followed by net abandon of the political sovereignty. On the contrary, the crude reality represented by the endless and still unsolved debate between federalism and confederalism re-emerged. Pinder J. 1998, *The building of the European Union,* 3rd edition, Oxford University Press. Wallace W. 1990 "Less than a Federation, More than a Regime: the Community as a Political System" in *Policy in the European Community*, John Wiley & Sons.
[35] Kent P. 2001, *Law of the European Union* 3d Ed., Pearson Education, p.58. See also *eurotreaties.com.*
[36] Constantinescu, L.J. 1965 , "La specificité du Droit Communautaire" in *Revue Trimestrielle de Droit Européen.*
[37] The *pre-emption* principle is *the purchase of or the right to purchase property in advance of or in preference to others* . See Collins, op. cit., u.v. *pre-emption*, p. 1208.
[38] Centre for Economic Policy Research *La distribuzione dei poteri nell'Unione Europea. Il principio di sussidiarietà nel processo d'integrazione europea* Il Mulino, 1995; Beck C. H. *European Union law: cases.* Frank Emmert, 1999; Vandamme J. *European Federalism. Opportunity or Utopia*? In Westlake M. (editor) *The European Union beyond Amsterdam. New concepts of European Integration* Routledge, 1998.
[39] Ferrari Bravo L., Moavero Milanesi E. 2000, *Lezioni di Diritto Comunitario* 3rd Edition, Edizione Scientifica. Delors expects an 80%

legislation coming from the EU against a 20% of member States competence. De Leonardis, M. 1997, "L'Integrazione Europea e la Gran Bretagna" in Rainero R.H. (editor) *Storia dell'integrazione europea* Vol.II *L'Europa dai Trattati di Roma alla Caduta del Muro di Berlino* Marzorati Editore.; Gozi S. 2000, *Il governo dell'Europa* Il Mulino, Bologna.

Further Reading

AAVV 1991, *Dal Piano Delors All'Unione Economica e Monetaria* Cedam, Padova.

Barro, R. and Gordon, D. 1983, "Rules, Discretion and Reputation in a Model of Monetary Policy" in *Journal of Monetary Economics*, 12.

Beck, C.H. 1999, *European Union Law: cases.* Frank Emmert.

Beveridge,W. 1943, *Il piano Beveridge. La Relazione di Sir W. Beveridge al Governo Britannico sulla Protezione Sociale.* Rapporto ufficiale.

Bini Smaghi, L. 1998, *L'euro* Il Mulino.

Bogdanor, V. "The United Kingdom and the European Union: Light on the Relationship" in *Britain in Europe*, The London School of Economics and Political Science.

Centre for Economic Policy Research, 1995, *La Distribuzione dei Poteri nell'Unione Europea. Il Principio di Sussidiarietà nel Processo D'Integrazione Europea* Il Mulino.

Craig, P. 2002, "Costitutzioni, Costituzionalismo e Unione Europea" in *Rivista Italiana di Diritto Pubblico Comunitario.*

Cukierman, A. 1995, *Central Bank Strategy, Credibility and Independence: Theory and Evidence* The MIT Press.

De Grauwe, P. 2000, *The Economics of Monetary Union*, Oxford University Press, Oxford.

De Grauwe, P., Dewachter, P., and Aksoy, Y. "The European Central Bank Decisions, Rules and Macroeconomic Performance" in *CEPR,* Discussion Paper n. 2067.

De Leonardis, M. *L'Integrazione Europea e La Gran Bretagna* in Rainero R.H. (ed) *Storia dell'integrazione europea* vol.II *L'Europa dai Trattati di Roma alla caduta del muro di Berlino* Marzorati Editore, 1997.

Duff, A. 1998, *Britain and Europe. The different relationship*, in WESTLAKE M. (ed) *The European Union beyond Amsterdam. New concepts of European integration*, Routledge.

ECB, 2001, *The Monetary Policy of ECB,* ECB, Frankfurt am Main.

Farnararo, P. 1999, *Dalla Comunità all'Unione Europea* Centro Jean Monnet Editor, Salerno.

Ferrari Bravo, L. and Moavero Milanesi, E. 2000, *Lezioni di Diritto Comunitario* 3rd Edition, Edizione Scientifica.

Forster, A. 1999, *Britain and the Maastricht Negotiations,* St. Anthony's Series College, Oxford.

Graziani, A. "La politica monetaria della Banca Centrale Europea" in *Rivista Italiana degli Economisti* n. 2004/1.
Gelber, H.G. 1997, *Sovereignty through Interdependence* Kluwer Law.
Gozi, S. 2000, *Il governo dell'Europa* Il Mulino, Bologna.
Habib. M.M. "Saggio sull'Indipendenza della Banca Centrale" in *Studi Economici*, n.70, 2000/1.
Hurd, D. "Making Europe Safer: Foreign Policy & Defence" in *Britain in Europe* The London School of Economics and Political Science, Fraser Maurice Editor, 1998.
Johnson, C. 1996, *In With The Euro, Out With The Pound. The Single Currency for Britain* Penguin Books.
Kydland, F.E. and Prescott, E.E. "Rules Rather than Discretion, the Time Inconsistency of Optimal Plans" in *Journal of Political Economy,* 1977.
Lamont, N. 1995, *Sovereign Britain* Duckworth.
Masson, P. and Turtelboom, B. *Characteristics of the Euro: the Demand for Reserves and Policy Coordination under EMU* presented at the Foundation Camille Gutt, IMF Seminar on EMU and the International Monetary System, Washington, 1997, March 17-18.
Muet, P.A. 1997, *Deficit de Croissance et Chomage: le Cout de la Non-Cooperation* Etude n.1, Paris, Centre d'Etude Notre Europe.
Mayhew, J. "London: Financial Centre of Europe" in *Britain in Europe,* The London School of Economics and Political Science, Fraser Maurice Editor, 1998.
Meade, J. "The Balance of Payment Problems of a European Free Trade Area" in *Economic Journal,* 1957, pp.379-396.
Mundell, R. "A Theory of Optimal Currency Areas" in *American Economic Review*, 1961, pp.657-665.
Panizza, R. "Il Declino del Ruolo Degli Stati Nazionali nella Definizione della Politica Economica" in Teoria Politica XVIII, n.1, 2002.
Paesani, P. *Will the Monetary Pillar Stay? A Few Lessons from Britain* ciclostilato, Università di Roma La Sapienza, 2003, february.
Sachs, J.D. and Bruno, M. 1995, *Economics and Worldwide Stagflation* Harvard University.
Scitovsky T. 1961, *L' Integrazione Economica dell'Europa Occidentale dal Puntodi Vista della Teoria* Feltrinelli, Milano.
Solow, R. 1998, *La Moderna Teoria Macroeconomica* Laterza.
Solow, R. 1998, *Inflazione, Disoccupazione e Politica Monetaria* Etas.
Spagnolo, L.V. 2002, *L'Equilibrio in un'Economia Aperta* Editoriale Scientifica, Napoli, p. 160
Spagnolo, L.V. 1997, *La Convergenza di Maastricht: Una Misura della Divergenza* Giappichelli, Torino.
Thygesen, N. *Relations among the IMF, the ECB and Fund/EMU members* paper presented at Foundation Camille Gut, IMF Seminar on EMU and the International Monetary System, Washington, 1997, March 17-18.

Tinbergen, J. 1956, *Economic Policy: Principles and Design* North Holland Publishing Co., Amsterdam.
Vandamme, J 1998, *European Federalism. Opportunity or Utopia*? in Westlake M. (ed) *The European Union beyond Amsterdam. New Concepts of European Integration* Routledge.
Williamson, J. *Estimating Equilibrium Exchange Rates* Washington D.C., Institute for International Economics, 1994, September.
Woodard, S. "Britain in Europe. History of a Relationship." In *Britain in Europe,* The London School of Economics and Political Science, Fraser Maurice Editor, 1998.
Zurcher, A.J. "La Lotta Per L'Europa Unita 1940-1958", in *Cultura e Società* n. 29, Opere nuove, 1963.
www.treasury.org

Chapter Five

The Euro in British Politics

Brendan Donnelly

In recent years, most of those British journalists or academics who have written about British policy towards the European single currency have been influenced in their writings by their own partisan standpoint, either as advocates or opponents of British participation in the euro. Frequently, this has led both camps to overstate the extent of the genuine enthusiasm felt by Mr. Blair and his government for the project of joining the European single currency. Opponents of British membership have been eager to mobilise funds and campaigning resources by presenting the New Labour government as working relentlessly towards British integration within the Eurozone. Proponents of membership have understandably concealed any doubts they may have had about the government's commitment to the single currency in the hope of generating a political and campaigning momentum towards the referendum which Mr. Blair had promised as a precondition of any governmental decision to take Britain into the euro.

Now that it is clear that any serious attempt to secure British membership of the European single currency has been indefinitely postponed by Mr. Blair and his likely successor, Mr. Brown, it may be possible to review more objectively the role the European single currency has played in the political life and discourse of the United Kingdom over the past ten years. In particular, it may be possible to come to more considered view of the New Labour government's approach to this issue since 1997. Other contributors to this collection have described the economic background to the debate, and many who favour in principle British membership of the euro would argue that the economic landscape of the past five years has in any case made impossible or inadvisable any moves in that period by the British government to join the European single currency. This may be so, but quite apart from the evolving economic background, it is equally clear that powerful political factors (mostly domestic political factors) have coloured and shaped the approach towards the European single currency adopted by the British government elected in 1997 and still in power. This essay seeks to describe and analyse these political factors.

Historical Background

In the 1990s, the British political system was profoundly changed by the election to the Labour leadership of Tony Blair and his espousal of the revisionist politics known as "New Labour." Central to the political philosophy of New Labour was the belief that the traditional Labour Party was fatally harming its electoral prospects by its continuing association in the public mind with a number of unpopular policies and attitudes, such as punitive tax rates, poor management of the economy, commitment to wide public ownership in crucial areas of the economy and excessive tolerance of law-breaking. The consequence of this wilfully and self-indulgently unattractive image was, in the New Labour analysis, the series of four electoral defeats since 1979, culminating in the General Election of 1992, when an unpopular Conservative government was unexpectedly re-elected. To some extent, Mr. Blair's predecessor as Labour leader, John Smith, had shared this analysis and worked to "modernise" the policies of the Party until his sudden death in 1994. But the decade since Mr. Blair became leader of the Labour Party has seen an acceleration and generalisation of this process, which it is difficult to imagine his predecessor could have executed or indeed would have wished to execute.

As a result of Mr. Blair's wholesale and ruthless remodelling of Labour policies and presentation, the British electorate's perception of the Labour Party is today qualitatively different from that of fifteen years ago. Its management of the economy has been at least respectable, its rhetoric and policies on domestic security are deliberately robust and it carefully avoids the rhetoric of egalitarianism. To his critics within the Labour Party, arguing that traditional principles have been abandoned for short-term electoral interests, Mr. Blair can plausibly point to the unprecedented reversal of electoral fortunes which he has bestowed on the Labour Party since his election to government since 1997. The continuing difficulty which the Conservative Party finds in its attempts to develop a coherent critique of the Prime Minister's policies acceptable to its own potential voters is eloquent witness to Mr. Blair's success in this regard. Today, it is not the Labour Party, but rather the Conservative Party which is seen as the defender of outdated and unpopular attitudes having only marginal resonance with the wider electorate outside the diminishing ranks of its traditional supporters. If Labour's traditional principles have been sacrificed to electability, the sacrifice has certainly been successful in attaining its goal. It shows every sign of continuing to be successful. If there is in modern Britain a "mainstream" political party, it is New Labour.

In this radical remodelling of the Labour Party, European policy has played some role, particularly in the early years of the Labour government elected in 1997. But New Labour's European policy should not be viewed as something distinct from the general political and electoral matrix from which New Labour springs. As we shall see, for New Labour is simply one of a number of instruments subserving its fundamental political objective of the greatest possible electability for the Labour Party. The independent traction of the European Union within the Labour Party is relatively small. New Labour has been described by opponents, critics and itself as a "pro-European" party. A more accurate description might be that it has found it electorally advantageous to act as an "anti-anti-European" party. This distinction will emerge more fully in the course of this article.

New Labour and Europe

Since the 1960s, Europe has been a deeply controversial question within the Labour Party, and for much of that period the Party saw itself as distinctly politically hostile to the European Community. When Britain signed the Treaty of Rome in 1972, only a minority of Labour Members of Parliament supported that step. The Labour government elected in 1974 came to power deeply divided on the question of continuing British membership of the Community. After a limited renegotiation of the terms of British membership, the Labour Prime Minister Harold Wilson put the results of that renegotiation to a referendum in 1975, a referendum in which some serving members of the Labour government were allowed to campaign (in the event unsuccessfully) against Britain's continued membership of the European Community. When Labour lost power in 1979, the increasing hostility of its membership and leaders towards the European Community was an important factor leading to the fracture of the party and the founding of the Social Democratic Party, many of whose leaders such as Shirley Williams and Roy Jenkins, had been among the minority of Labour MPs supporting Britain's signature of the Treaty of Rome in 1972.

As the Labour Party moved to the left in the early 1980's, so its institutional hostility to the European Community increased. The most common criticism of the Community from Labour spokesmen was to claim that its core values of free trade and political integration would prevent the implementation of genuinely socialist policies in the United Kingdom by any future Labour government. In the General Election of 1983, the Labour Party manifesto called for withdrawal from the Community. In the General Election of 1987, the Party stopped short of calling for withdrawal, but could not hide its distrust of and distaste for the Community. Many current leading figures in New Labour fought in the elections of 1983 and 1987 without disavowing their Party's manifesto at the time.

It was only in the late 1980s that the traditional hostility of the Labour Party towards the European Community began to soften, not least in response to an influential speech given by Jacques Delors to the British Trades Union Congress in 1988. In this speech, the President of the European Commission argued that the Community had much to offer the British Labour movement in the way of new social legislation, a claim that greatly pleased his audience, while simultaneously fuelling the growing hostility to the European Community of the then British Prime Minister, Margaret Thatcher. In 1992, John Smith (one of those Labour MPs who in 1972 had voted for British membership of the European Community) became leader of the Labour Party. His leadership saw a narrowing of the gulf between the Labour Party and other left-wing parties in continental Europe, almost all of whom, with the exception of some national Communist parties, were enthusiastic supporters of deeper European integration. Even so, when the Conservative Party found itself divided in the early 1990s on the question of the ratification of the Maastricht Treaty, the Prime Minister John Major received little help from John Smith's Parliamentary Labour Party. In contrast to his decision of twenty years before, John Smith decided to exacerbate growing Conservative divisions on Europe by opposing the Treaty's passage through Parliament. The adversarial and tribal nature of British politics provides a standing temptation for political parties to exploit the divisions of their opponents, almost irrespective of any wider political context. John Smith's tactical approach to the ratification of the Maastricht Treaty was an illuminating example of that phenomenon.

When Tony Blair became leader of the Labour Party in 1994, he concluded that one of the elements which needed to be jettisoned in the remodelled Labour Party was its still well-entrenched anti-Europeanism. A number of considerations seem to have weighed with him in this decision. His own personal and intellectual background led him to regard with some disdain the cruder manifestations of left-wing and trades union hostility to all things European. Such unreflective hostility was in Mr. Blair's view part of the package of "Old Labour" attitudes, so unacceptable to the middle class voters whom New Labour was now attempting to woo. A significant tranche of these latter voters was also coming to be repelled by the growing shrillness with which the European question was debated within the Conservative Party. It was good party politics to remind such electors that New Labour now rejected old-fashioned nationalism, whether of the Old Labour or modern Conservative variety. But the new-found Europeanism of Mr. Blair's Labour Party was not one unreflectively or unconditionally embraced. Electoral calculation was at the heart of New Labour's approach to the single European currency in particular.

In the months leading up to the General Election of 1997, Labour strategists were consciously pursuing a double track in their pronouncements on British membership of the euro. While remaining generally convinced that the Labour Party's abandonment of reflexive anti-Europeanism was electorally advantageous, these strategists were equally mindful of the need to protect themselves from accusations of uncritical acceptance of every proposal emanating from the European Union. The British electorate might reject the virulent and obsessive tone with which the Conservative Party discussed European issues, but most British voters believed in 1997 (and no doubt still believe) that a determined defence of British interests within the European Union is a primary responsibility of the British government. It was in order to allay such concerns that Mr. Blair echoed before the General Election of 1997 the Conservative government's pledge to hold a referendum before taking Britain into the euro, and shortly before the election itself published an article in the notoriously Eurosceptic newspaper the "Sun" telling its readers about how much he "loved" the pound. New Labour was determined not to jeopardise its favourable electoral prospects by opening itself to the criticism of excessive European enthusiasm. New Labour's "love affair" with the European Union and specifically with the euro was from the beginning a relationship of calculated self-advantage rather than one of passionate conviction.

New Labour in Office

New Labour's rationalistic and politically measured view of the single European currency came to prominence early in the new government's term in office. That minority of New Labour ministers genuinely eager for Britain rapidly to join the euro hoped that the newly-elected government would use some of its immense political capital to hold and win shortly after the General Election a referendum on the principle of joining the euro, the precise date of Britain's accession to the single currency to be decided by the government later. Instead, after a confused and confusing set of discussions between the Prime Minister and his Chancellor, Gordon Brown, the new government adopted a set of five criteria (economic convergence, employment, outside investment, impact on the City, economic flexibility) which it would apply in the coming years to judge whether it was to Britain's economic advantage to join the euro, and only recommend British membership of the single currency if and when these criteria were met. It was stressed at the time and since that the decision whether to join the euro was at least primarily and perhaps exclusively an economic one. In this the government was undoubtedly responding to well-entrenched preconceptions among the British electorate which stress the economic component of European integration and disregard, or even reject, its manifest political aspect.

Formally, the five criteria remain the basis even today of the government's approach to British membership of the single currency. An interim assessment of them was made in 2003, which concluded that the criteria had not yet been met. Apparently the tone and terms of this assessment were matters of long and acrimonious discussion between the Prime Minister and his Chancellor. Immediately after the assessment was completed, a minority of commentators claimed that its contents opened the way for a relatively speedy entry into the single currency by the United Kingdom. Later remarks by the Chancellor and, more recently, the Prime Minister, have shown how little substance there was in these hopes. It is now very clear that British membership of the euro is at the earliest a number of years away, perhaps as many as the ten years mentioned recently by Kenneth Clarke, a former advocate of early membership. But since their formulation in 1997, the five criteria for British membership of the euro have proved strikingly helpful to the political positioning of the New Labour government. They are sufficiently elastic and general to be interpreted either as barriers or gateways to the single currency. Above all, they have been admirably adapted for use as an argumentative weapon in the government's domestic political controversy with the opposition parties.

Until recently, the Prime Minister in particular regularly presented the position of his government as equidistant between two misconceived and extremist attitudes, represented respectively by the Conservative Party and the Liberal Democrats. For Mr Blair, the former Party sinned by refusing ever to join the single currency, even if it was economically advantageous to do so; the latter by advocating membership of the euro even if contrary to Britain's economic interests. For his government, the Prime Minister insisted, the matter was not one of doctrine or ideology, but rather a pragmatic decision to be taken in the light of evolving economic circumstances. This was a view well attuned to British public sentiment in the late 1990s, when the euro was first set up. The British electorate was clearly uneasy at the prospect of ruling out for ever membership of the single currency but equally deeply hesitant before taking the decisive step of engaging further in European monetary and political integration through membership of the Eurozone. New Labour's Janus-like commitment to the five "criteria" for euro membership was a successful "triangulation" between the contrasting views of its political opponents, which faithfully mirrored the uncertain attitude of the British electorate.

It has often been claimed that the Prime Minister is emotionally more committed to Britain's eventual membership of the euro than is his Chancellor, and that the Chancellor in his turn has used the issue of the single currency as a weapon in his joust with Mr. Blair to ensure his early succession to the premiership. There is good reason to believe both these claims. New Labour's approach to the European single currency has been a matter not merely of political positioning by the Labour Party, but also of political positioning within the Labour Party. As the custodian of the five "criteria," Mr. Brown has been able to stress his own independence of the Prime Minister by thwarting any desire of the latter to declare the "criteria" met. Indeed, he has gone further, making more difficult the winning of any eventual referendum on the euro by his frequent and well-advertised diatribes against the European Commission, the supposed economic inflexibility of Britain's neighbours and the iniquities of the European budget. The Prime Minister has been unable to mobilise the determination or perhaps even the political capacity to overrule his Chancellor. No doubt many of his advisers were counselling him that a rupture with the Chancellor over European issues was politically dangerous ground on which to provoke a conflict. The need to preserve the internal and external political equilibrium of New Labour has clearly taken precedence in his calculations over any personal inclination he may have, or have had, to move to quick resolution of the single currency issue.

Conclusion

One frequently-voiced criticism of New Labour as a political philosophy is its supposedly reactive nature, its over-emphasis on following existing public opinion as determined by polling or focus groups. The government's friends would point to at least one major policy of recent years contradicting this criticism, namely Iraq. They would not, however, be able to cite European policy as an argument to establish their case for a New Labour party defying and moulding public opinion. On many occasions since 1997, press reports have claimed that the government, and the Prime Minister in particular, was resolved upon a systematic campaign to change increasingly hostile British attitudes towards the single currency. No such campaign has ever been mounted or even seriously attempted. New Labour has not tried to win the argument in favour of British membership of the euro and failed. It has not made any serious attempt to promote this argument. Given the purely instrumental role allocated to European questions by New Labour's political philosophy, this outcome is perhaps less surprising than it has appeared to many observers over the past decade.

In that decade, the political debate concerning British membership of the euro has revolved essentially around two poles, the pole of those hostile to British membership of the euro and the governmental position which could envisage, but would not seek to promote Britain's joining the European single currency. The former pole of debate was well-financed, favoured by important elements of the media, and supported by the official opposition. The latter pole was only intermittently promoted by a divided government, which was at least as interested in exploiting the divisions of its Conservative opponents and scoring Parliamentary points against all its political opponents as in securing British membership of the single currency. From the beginning, the New Labour government's commitment to the euro has been tentative, conditional and instrumental. It is unsurprising that in the contest of ideas with those who propagated a clear message against British membership of the Eurozone, the latter have marked a clear victory.

With the demise of the European Constitution, which on occasion the Prime Minster seemed to regard as an opportunity to combat the Euroscepticism which has flourished so vigorously under his Premiership, the interest of New Labour in the European Union seems at an unprecedentedly low ebb. This disengagement has been reinforced by the realisation of many in the current government that winning a referendum on the Constitution in 2006 might well have been an impossible challenge. There is little appetite in their ranks to run the gauntlet of another referendum on Europe in the foreseeable future. When, in order to deprive the Conservative Party of a tactical advantage in the European Elections of 2004, Jack Straw persuaded the Prime Minister to reverse tack and promise a referendum on the European Constitution, he was taking a definite risk. The success of that gamble, arising from the rejection of the Constitution in the French and Dutch referendums, could not be guaranteed to repeat itself in two or three years time.

The disappearance of the European Constitution in its present form is not the end of the evolving process of European integration. In the single market, in matters of internal security, in monetary policy and even in foreign policy, an institutional and political momentum exists which is far from having run its course. Mechanisms already exist whereby Britain can if it wishes participate only partly or not at all in these developments. But the price of this semi-detachment is that for the foreseeable future this New Labour government will be unable to secure for the United Kingdom (except perhaps in the field of foreign policy and probably in the field of defence policy) any leading or determinant role in the scope and pace of further European integration. The development of the euro's structures of governance in particular will take place without any significant British contribution to this process.

This ambiguous position may well be an outcome with which the great majority of the British electorate are content to live indefinitely. But two unfavourable possibilities for the long term should not be entirely discounted, namely that the continuing integration of the European Union without Britain develops in a way inimical to British interests; or that European integration without Britain is so economically and politically successful that Britain will wish in ten years time to "reconnect" with the European mainstream on terms less favourable than it might have achieved but for its hesitation. If the government confronting this latter circumstance were a Conservative one, and the Prime Minister seeking to join the European single currency a Conservative, the irony of the situation would be palpable. Until Mrs. Thatcher it was the Conservative Party which in British politics was the primary advocate and initiator of Britain's whole-hearted membership in the European Community. The move towards radical Euroscepticism in that party, stopping only just short of calls for withdrawal from the Union, has created a new equilibrium (from the author's point of view a disequilibrium) in British political discourse on the European Union. This new equilibrium (disequilibrium) may now seem a permanent element of the British political scene. Nothing, however, is permanent in democratic politics. Europe may well still have surprises in store for the British political parties and their leaders.

Chapter Six

The Political Power of Economic Ideas: Understanding Relations between 'New' Labour and the City in the Post-War Era

Patrick Diamond

On reflection, it is astonishing what little interest relations between the Labour Party and the City - 'Britain's London-based financial institutions and markets'[1] - have received in recent decades, given the powerful hold of the City over the British economy. The City has been pivotal in reconstructing British politics and the British state in the post-war era, and in determining the economic basis on which parties hope to govern.

The last thirty years have also witnessed great changes within the Labour Party and the City itself. 'New' Labour has abandoned apparently irreconcilable conflicts with financial capital and its institutions, and is now working co-operatively with the City. This shift in outlook is set to become permanent, reflecting Labour's enlightened acceptance both of the limits imposed by the liberalisation of global markets on the British state, and the new realities of the international economy.

This paper focuses on the period between 1989 and 1997 as the 'New' Labour project was evolving under Neil Kinnock and John Smith, and achieving its apotheosis under Tony Blair and Gordon Brown. But it also examines the history of both the Labour Party and the City of London over a long process of development. It seeks to understand why Labour replaced conflict with co-operation in its relationship to the City during those years, as 'New' Labour thoroughly reconstructed the party's economic strategy. To those such as Colin Hay in *Labour's Thatcherite Revisionism* who doubt its legitimacy - citing naked electoral ambition as the sole motivating factor in the policy transformation inaugurated by 'New' Labour - it presents a more nuanced interpretation.[2]

The argument is that this change in Labour's attitude to the City is the result of a fundamental shift in the climate of ideas within the traditions of British and European political economy since the late 1970s, forcing Labour to re-appraise its governing strategy, but with the complex interplay of the financial markets on electoral opinion still a decisive factor.

It rejects the claim that Labour simply embraced the City because it was prepared to sacrifice its principles for electoral gain - an exercise in 'triangulation' known as 'market research socialism'. There is scant evidence that polling pushed Labour into particular positions on economic policy. Nor was Labour compelled to accept the basic tenets of the Thatcher settlement - Hay's 'Thatcherite revisionism' thesis. It is also misleading - as will be shown - to argue that Labour was forced to shift policy to accommodate business, given the dependence of governing parties on owners in industrial capitalist economies - 'structural dependence' theory.[3]

It is certainly true that Labour made a conscious effort to woo the City from 1989 onwards. This initiative was dubbed 'the prawn-cocktail offensive' by economic commentators[4]. But it reflected the importance attached to the financial markets and their willingness to accept Labour as a credible manager of the economy. The overriding imperative was neutralising negative City comment on Labour's macro-economic and fiscal policy, projecting its reputation for economic competence to the wider electorate at a time of new upheavals in the global economy.

Its leaders came to understand that a coherent governing strategy was required so that it would not be 'blown off course', plunged into crisis by panic on the financial markets as afflicted every previous Labour Government. In the late 1970s, the Callaghan administration had been crippled by 'gilt strikes' in which a crisis of City confidence led the financial markets to refuse to fund Britain's public sector deficit.

The renegotiation of Labour's relationship with the City was about 'statecraft' as much as an election-winning strategy, of which gathering votes is but one element in the art of achieving the necessary degree of governing competence in office[5]. 'New' Labour could be seen as a political project aimed at restoring the conditions - electoral, ideological, economic, and political - for the Labour Party to assume a leading role in British politics. This requires a conception of economic policy and political action that is unified, coherent and bounded by realistic assumptions about the relationship between the state and the economy, re-drawing the contours of domestic political argument both within the party and outside it.

Labour's embrace of the City also reflected the relative weakness of Japan and Germany in the early 1990s, as alternative institutional models were severely compromised. Under such conditions, Labour was inevitably constrained in its room for manoeuvre, compelled to accept the limits imposed by the prevailing economic orthodoxy. There was no serious alternative intellectual framework for economic management that could inform 'New' Labour's domestic statecraft. Indeed, efforts to provide one in the mid-1990s - such as Will Hutton's 'stakeholder' model elaborated in *The State We're In* - did not prove viable.

There is an important general point here. As J.M. Keynes famously argued, in the long-run, the quality of argument does matter[6]. Accounts of the recent period that stress the importance of political marketing, and claim that the Labour Party's policy-making process was driven by opinion polls, focus groups, and the desire for electoral popularity, are wrong both empirically, and because they under-estimate the importance of economic strategy to a political party[7]. This paper is an attempt to redress the balance, giving adequate weight to debates about economic strategy in conditioning Labour's attitude to the institutions of financial capital.

By the late 1990s, the party shifted its attention to how it might harness the energies of the City to fit its broader social and economic goals - of creating a fairer, more inclusive society - a process that Richard Hill describes as 'preference-shaping', where it seeks to win the underlying arguments while reshaping the climate of opinion.[8] The intention is to work effectively in co-operation with, rather than in thrall to, City institutions, for example in devising 'Public-Private Partnerships' (PPP) to finance the revitalisation of Britain's public infrastructure.

The Strength of the City: Britain as a 'World Island'

The City is a unique feature of the British economy that has persisted for more than 400 years. Britain's financial services sector continues to lead the world. Andrew Gamble has observed that Britain was the pre-eminent world power by 1750, but of a very odd kind and that, "this historical relationship has had a lasting impact on the development of the City of London".[9]

Britain was the 'world island': the centre of an informal network of trading relationships and capital movements, of which her formal

Empire was merely a part. This has made Britain by tradition a market economy and a supporter of free trade. "One distinctive feature of the British economy was always its extensive and deep-rooted overseas commitments", Gamble argues - ensuring Britain's dominant position in world trade throughout the 19th century - and enabling the City to become one of the world's leading financial centres.[10]

The City developed as the pre-industrial expansion of the world economy proceeded apace, financing both Britain's trading activities, and the extension of Britain's overseas commitments into new colonies and markets. The City was strongly orientated towards the international economy from the outset, reinforced in the early 19th century by its interest in buying and selling money in all its forms.[11]

City institutions were concerned with 'commercial' activities - financing trade, insuring commodities and transport, and undertaking foreign exchange transactions. This not only affected Britain's relationship with other states, but also had ramifications for capitalistic enterprise on a global scale. The City manages the domestic currency as 'world money', an international means of exchange. It makes its profits by selling intermediary services to those who are directly engaged in the productive use of capital.

This had major consequences for British industry, and it was argued, created a disjuncture of practices and interests. While the City was orientated towards short-term gains from high-volume, fast-turnover commercial transactions, industry was working for long-term profitability, since investments took time to implement and mature. British economic policy fought to maintain the City as an open, unrestricted marketplace with a currency strong enough to facilitate international transactions.

From the mid-1950s to the mid-1970s, Labour and Conservative Governments were caught in a vicious cycle struggling to satisfy the demands of both industry and the City. "No industrialised society found it easy to adjust to the upheavals in the world economy, but Britain found it uniquely difficult"[12]. The UK appeared to be caught in a 'pincer movement' between low-wage competition from the developing world, and high-wage sophisticated competition from the US, Japan and the EEC.

The period since 1970 had also been a time of great change in the City, as macro-economic policy has adjusted to a more interdependent global economy - symbolised, for example, by the abolition of credit controls in 1979. The demise of the Bretton Woods system in 1971 based on fixed exchange rates for the development of trading nations had imposed a degree of restraint on the world economy. Its collapse - followed by the oil price shock of 1973 - set in train a series of events leading to greater liberalisation and globalisation of world markets.

It was against this backdrop that during the 1980s, the financial institutions and markets of the City came to represent the 'powerhouse' of the British economy, enabling successive Conservative administrations to argue that relative decline was being steadily reversed[13]. The collapse of the historic compromise between capital and labour in the British economy during the mid-1970s appeared to highlight the limitations of traditional social democracy, engineering a new mood of 'anti-collectivism'. The discrediting of so many of the assumptions on which post-war policy had been based allowed the New Right to argue that a quite new approach to the problems of British decline and modernisation had to be developed. Labour gradually assumed a more realistic view of the limits imposed on national governments by global economic forces. It was against this background that the Labour Party came to revise its historical relationship with the City.

The City occupies a peculiar position, being both part of Britain and yet separate from it. As Andrew Gamble argues, "it wants to be both the leading financial centre in the EU, but retain its global reach - both within Europe yet outside it too, just as it is both inside and outside the British economy".[14] The City's fortunes have been inversely related to the success of the British economy in the 19th and 20th centuries. It has always been remote from the 'real economy'. Indeed, the City has retained its pre-eminent position despite Britain's relative decline as an industrial power. While America was the world's most powerful economy by 1919, New York did not supplant London as the world's leading financial centre.

It was aided too by a state that placed far fewer restrictions on its financial sector than were common elsewhere, and succeeded in surviving huge challenges to its position, including the suspension of the gold standard in 1931 and the decline of sterling as an international currency after 1967. An alliance between the substantial class of rentiers in the UK who depended on financial investments for their income, and the industrial, political and bureaucratic interests associated with the British state and British Empire, ensured that the City view was upheld in major crises during the 20th century. "When major choices had to be made, the issue has generally been resolved in favour of Britain's traditional links with the world economy"[15].

The City was able to seize advantage of successive British Government's policies on deregulation and liberalisation, while capitalising on its traditional strengths. The expertise of the City and the trust placed in it were assets that gave it competitive advantage throughout the 20th century. Until the mid-1980s, the City was always strongly demarcated. The banking sector is a prominent example. The City's retail and deposit banks were very different to building societies specialising in mortgage lending. But in the early 1990s, financial 'supermarkets' emerged as several building societies demutualised. The banks began to offer mortgage loans, with growing competition for saving from money market funds - all posing new regulatory challenges[16].

London is now a huge market for overseas investors, and indeed conducts more business on the financial markets than New York and Tokyo combined. Almost a third of the daily turnover in the world foreign exchange market occurs in London. It is the main global centre for international fund management, the under-writing and trading of international bonds, and 'over-the-counter' derivatives trades. London has always had a strong foreign element, and immigrants originally established some of the City's most traditional institutions - including Rothschild's, Warburg's, and Kleinwort Benson. Indeed, part of Labour's long-standing difficulty with the City has been the tendency to assume it should be fundamentally orientated towards 'British interests'.

It was this context - and the impact of globalisation and liberalisation since the 1960s - that led to a revision of the social democratic conception of the state in the world economy. For 70 years, Labour had alternated between two distinct positions on the economy. On the one hand, seeking to realise Labour's socialist objectives within the constraints imposed by the international capitalist economy. On the other, using the power of the nation-state to insulate the national economy from these constraints, building 'socialism in one country'[17].

In reality, Labour's policies tended to reflect both perspectives with protectionist strategies gaining ascendancy during periods of world recession, such as the 1973 crisis. When Labour embraced the Alternative Economic Strategy (AES) in 1975, it reflected a mood of profound crisis and bitter disappointment for the party, as both the 1964-70 and 1974-79 Governments were forced to depart from a social democratic trajectory towards deflationary fiscal and monetary policies. The AES recommended public ownership, planning, price controls, industrial democracy, and import restrictions to reflate the British economy and reverse industrial decline. It marked a radical break with Labour's revisionist past, though the leadership was always hostile to the AES programme[18].

Labour's refusal to fully come to terms with the internationalisation of the British economy until the late 1980s inevitably caused great damage to its credibility. Instead, it sought at various junctures either to control the City, to turn the City inward to focus on the domestic economy, or indeed to by-pass City institutions altogether. As a consequence, Labour lacked a coherent and serious City policy. There had been periodic efforts to establish advisory panels such as the 'City Group' in 1931, an unofficial group of City experts who were sympathetic to Labour and advised the Shadow Chancellor, Hugh Dalton[19]. But in general, the party's problems were compounded by the lack of direct experience among Labour politicians of how financial institutions and markets actually function, during a period in which the City was changing rapidly.

Indeed, such disinterest reflected Labour's underlying hostility towards the type of capitalism represented by the City. As Kerry McCarthy has persuasively argued, there was a deep strain within the British ethical socialist tradition, "that regarded 'usury' as morally reprehensible and reacted with distaste to gambling and profit". "It bridled at unscrupulous City traders 'gambling' with the nation's wealth. Profits should be earned, not made in the 'casino economy'".[20]

To the Labour Party - the party of labour - the City was indeed the worst example of unfettered market capitalism. Labour has never been a Marxist Party and, even during its lengthy obsession with public ownership, has always in practice accepted the market economy. "It has often been reluctant, however, to articulate its acceptance of market capitalism as the party of organised labour *against* organised capital"[21], making any rapprochement with the City - a profound strategic shift - difficult to achieve in the post-war era.

Labour's Modernisation: the Post-1992 Phase

Labour's reappraisal of the City was therefore problematic and at times, deeply contested within the party. These difficulties were exacerbated because at the beginning of the 1990s, leading figures *within* British business were developing a full-blown alternative to Anglo-Saxon shareholder capitalism, posing a major challenge to Labour's newfound acquiescence to City interests.

The 1980s was the heyday of the takeover boom, as acquisitive predators such as Hanson and BTR used their highly valued shares to launch a series of ambitious takeovers. From late 1983, there was a flurry of activity in which both British and foreign banks took over stock exchange firms. Meanwhile, in combination with City firms, ministers used their statutory powers to start deregulating and modernising City practices. In the process, the City became an unparalleled site for international capital operations, with Japanese banks lending more from the City than British banks. By 1989, the broad financial sector was the engine of growth of the British economy, employing 2.6 million people. It represented 19.8% of GDP in 1989 compared to 11.6% in 1979. Between 1985 and 1989, the financial sector grew at an annual average of 8.9%, compared to 4.1% for manufacturing industry, and 4.2% for the non-financial service sector[22]. The City was the core driver of Britain's capital accumulation strategy.

But in a famous 1990 lecture, the management guru Charles Handy insisted that companies were 'communities not properties', and that 'profits are a necessary but not sufficient condition of success'. Businesses were not just assets to trade on the stock market.

In 1988, the CBI had produced a hostile report criticising the focus of financial institutions on short-term profitability, and the lack of a long-term commitment to UK manufacturing industry. Even the Conservative Trade & Industry Secretary Lord Young complained in 1989 that the City was failing to back 'Britain's bright ideas'. The City retaliated by arguing that scepticism towards long-term investment was a rational reflection of weak economic management, but the concept of 'shareholder value' was under sustained attack.

Indeed, as Geoffrey Owen has reflected, Britain's financial system has long been a 'whipping boy' among the 'declinist' school of economic historians[23]. Before 1914, manufacturers had complained that the City's banks or financial institutions did not support them, as Britain's hegemony was under threat from American and German competition. The concentration of financial expertise in the City was geared not towards the needs of domestic manufacturers, but raising funds for overseas investment. In the 1930s, J.M. Keynes had supported the creation of a National Investment Bank to remedy these failings[24]. Class divisions reinforced the separation between industry and finance, as traders in the City were thought to be 'gentlemanly capitalists' who despised factories, and had little in common with the self-made industrialists of great cities such as Manchester and Birmingham.

It is possible that the cartel operated by the clearing banks until 1971 caused some distortion in lending patterns. The banks found it easier to supply a standard financial package to clients they knew well than to incur the risk of backing smaller innovative companies without a proven record of profitability.[25] More recently, it was alleged that the capital markets in the City had put too much pressure on firms to maximise profits in the short-term, placing managers under constant takeover threat if profits were temporarily depressed, while obviating long-term investment strategies. British industry was too reliant on takeovers as a means of correcting managerial failure, since hostile takeovers are costly and disruptive, often directed at the wrong targets. In Germany, hostile takeovers were very rare.

The view that the City was largely responsible for Britain's weak relative economic performance was widely held. The claim made is that the Treasury-City-Bank of England nexus has served Britain poorly, exerting a malign influence over economic and industrial policy, and producing a political elite that is careless of its manufacturing future. For some, the Thatcher years represented the final, complete and blatant triumph of the financial interests of the south over northern manufacturing interests.

Improvements during the 1980s were only superficial, and the fundamental problems of the British economy remained unresolved, these critics argued. The economy only appeared to improve because expectations about British economic performance have been lowered so much. As David Coates puts it:

> The UK had spent the first four decades of the post-war period locked in a process of cumulative economic decline caused by inadequate levels of investment in plant and equipment, and that growth trajectory remained firmly in place at the century's end…positioning the UK as predominantly an off-shore warehouse economy…The UK economy remains disproportionately a service-based economy, internationally competitive in financial services, but otherwise centred around low-pay service provision to a slowly growing domestic market.[26]

Any reformist government in the 1990s would therefore be confronted by demands to elevate City reform at the deepest institutional level as a high priority. That Labour was able to resist such momentum seems extraordinary when seen in this light. But it reflected an intellectual reality with serious consequences for its governing strategy. The critique of City institutions looked less plausible than it first appeared, while confidence in the alternative German and Japanese social market models was steadily collapsing.

In fact, 'New' Labour decided in 1995-96 to break decisively with Will Hutton's model of 'stakeholder economics' elaborated in *The State We're In*. Hutton had argued that the City was opportunistic and greedy, insisting on unduly high-cost capital, short payback periods, and an inherent bias towards takeovers giving short-term rewards to the stock market at the expense of long-term investment. Instead, stake holding needs to be broadened in companies and institutions, creating a bias towards long-term commitment from owners. "The financial system needs to be thoroughly republicanised", Hutton argued[27].

He advocated the German social market model where, it was argued, industrial structure encouraged co-operation, long-term investment, and high productivity. In 1996, Tony Blair briefly adopted the language of stake holding in his infamous Singapore speech[28]. Yet Hutton's argument was already being strongly criticised from *within* the left, and stakeholder economics was forced into retreat.

Interests are not directly represented within the state in a way that the 'dominance of finance' thesis suggests. 'The City' was not a unified force capable of imposing itself on a reluctant state after 1945. For example, the liberalisation of financial institutions during the 1980s was not universally welcomed within the city. By opening up the system to more international competition, only the interests of the most globally competitive were served. This perspective tends to emphasise the relationship of forces between the ruling-class, the working-class, and the state, but neglects relations within the bloc of dominant interests, and the relationship of those interests to the state[29].

Meghnad Desai argues that Hutton had ignored the greatest problem of recent British economic history, namely the dramatic collapse of manufacturing profitability in the 1970s that the Thatcherite model had effectively, if brutally, resolved. Hutton also overstated the importance of the City to British industry that relied on new equity for barely 10% of new investment, and understated how the City was changing to become more international and meritocratic, Desai argued[30]. The largest fund management companies were American, with a large proportion of non-UK employees, radically altering City culture while shattering the myth of 'gentlemanly capitalism'.[31]

Since the abolition of exchange controls in 1979, the UK economy had to come to terms with the infinite mobility of international capital, a point largely ignored by *The State We're In*.[32] Evidence from the UK also showed that poorly performing sectors - shipbuilding, cars, and machine tools, for example - had very few hostile takeovers. In the US, the electronics industry is a high-performer requiring long-term investment, but is driven by a takeover culture[33].

It was immediately obvious by the mid-1990s that neither of the world's two 'stakeholder economies' - Germany and Japan - were performing strongly. The unemployment rate in Germany compared badly to the UK. In *The Blair Revolution* Mandelson and Liddle argued that the German model was incompatible with the global market economy, and that Germany would have to become more like the UK since product markets were weak, while its firms performed poorly on the capital markets as profitability fell dramatically.[34]

The premise of *The Blair Revolution* was that it was dangerous for a centre-left party to seek to weaken the primary of shareholder value. This would destroy the external discipline that the threat of takeover places on companies to keep them efficient and profitable, "protecting the sleepy at the expense of the thrusting and go-ahead", and impair Labour's economic credibility.

By 1997, against the background of a sustained bull market and ceaseless takeover activity in the UK, the fundamental importance of shareholder value was entrenched and unassailable, reinforcing the necessity of Labour's rapprochement with the City and its financial institutions. A 'new industrial compact' emerged in which senior management accepted the importance of regular dialogue and performance appraisal with institutional investors, as shareholders reigned supreme.

The most surprising change has been the greater readiness of German companies to embrace the Anglo-American concept of shareholder value. Foreign investors hold an increasing proportion of the shares of German public companies. Even more remarkable was the hostile take-over bid for Mannesmann by Vodafone, the British mobile telephone company in 2000. Despite initial opposition to the bid from politicians and trade union leaders, the outcome - a victory for Vodafone - was determined by shareholders. Although it has not unleashed a flood of take-over activity in Germany, it demonstrates how extensively the Anglo-American conception of shareholder value reached by the late 1990s[35].

Labour's New Economics

Transforming Labour's policies on the economy became a high priority for the party leadership after the disastrous 1983 defeat: 'managing the economy' has steadily increased in importance in modern electoral politics, as politicians seeking office have to prove themselves as competent economic managers. Labour's poor reputation had several causes as the party of high taxation, inflation, sterling crises and sluggish growth.

The overriding imperative during the 1992-97 period was for Labour to project itself as a competent and reliable manager of the economy following the dramatic exit of sterling from the Exchange Rate Mechanism in September 1992. To make Labour electable, it had to convince voters, commentators and City analysts that they could manage the economy as successfully as the Conservatives, instead of repeatedly plunging the economy into crisis.

The focus of Labour's macro-economic strategy shifted to a monetary framework providing exchange and interest rate stability, reducing the importance of full employment as a formal policy objective. John Smith and Margaret Beckett had impressed the City prior to the 1992 election with their commitment to defend sterling's rate within the ERM, protecting a future Labour Government against any loss of confidence in the financial markets.

Labour's focus was no longer on insulating the domestic economy from international competition. The claim that Britain could restructure the world in its own interests and confront successfully its domestic problems looked untenable. This was lent force by two developments in the 1980s. First, the dramatic erosion of UK manufacturing and the need to reconstruct Britain's industrial base. Second, globalisation meant that the unilateral pursuit of Keynesian demand management would be subverted by the international financial markets, exemplified by the failure of Mitterand's socialist administration to 'go it alone' in France during the early 1980s[36].

As Andrew Gamble notes, "a watershed had been crossed in the 1980s, as the Thatcher Governments restructured the British economy as a free market economy with a smaller public sector and weaker trade unions"[37]. The new framework was put in place involving deregulation, the reduction of taxes, privatisation and the free movement of capital, "representing a decisive change in UK political economy"[38]. As a result, Labour was to focus increasingly on how to make British companies internationally competitive within an open, interdependent world economy, enabling wealth creation to flourish. During the 1992-1997 period, Labour was to subtlety re-cast the debate further.

It moved from being the party of industry and not the City, with a vision of a developmental state involving a significant strengthening of the Department of Trade & Industry (DTI), to a rejection of corporatism in all its forms. Labour no longer sought to moderate the City's short-term bias by strengthening the regulation of takeovers to reflect the 'public interest', and instead thoroughly embraced the principle of shareholder value.

It continued to advocate some moderation of City behaviour, praising 'more committed owners', while arguing for pension fund trustees to exercise greater control over fund managers taking a 'long-term view'. But intervention was largely restricted to upgrading industrial and human capital in the economy, responding to the accelerating pace of industrial innovation. Labour understood that the regulatory framework in which it operates primarily determines the competitiveness of any financial centre. It believed that the City should not be over-regulated in comparison to its competitors, coinciding with increased anxiety about London's future competitiveness within the European Community in an era of intense capital liberalisation.

Rather than importing models from abroad, or reforming City-industry institutional relations in a German-style direction, Labour sought to offer moderate incentives for change within an Anglo-Saxon framework. Instead, a new economic discourse was shaping Labour policy in the 1990s embracing competition, efficiency, productivity, dynamism and profit. 'Stake holding' it was argued imposes rigidities and constraints on companies when the route to dynamism and success, as Europe was beginning to realise, was flexibility. "As time has passed, 'New' Labour has shifted away from Europe and has instead been drawn to North America, Australia, and the Anglo-Saxon model of capitalism. This shift to a more market-orientated and individualistic form of capitalism has been crucial to the emergence of a distinctively *new* Labour, and has made it less likely that Britain will participate more fully in European integration".[39] The contest between Labour and the Conservatives now focussed on which supply-side strategy could best re-energise the British economy.

Conclusion

By the time of its election victory in May 1997, Labour fully accepted that the internationalisation of the world economy made action by any one country futile, and that the City must operate unencumbered within global capital markets. It had thoroughly reinvented its economic strategy since 1979, and this re-thinking had far-reaching implications for Labour's views not just of macro-economic policy or the mixed economy, but the City itself. The party was moving decisively beyond protectionist and Keynesian policies. The UK would continue its integration into the world economic system, involving free movement within product, capital and labour markets.

This is the most convincing explanation of why the shift in its policy on the City occurred, and why it was consolidated during the 1992-97 phase of Labour's modernisation. Its constant initiatives to woo the City were not primarily concerned with accommodating the demands of capital, but encouraging the City to sound more positive about Labour's programme, precisely because such authoritative analysis had a profound impact on electoral opinion and its governing authority. Voters' views of the Labour Party's economic competence were based partly on an assessment of past performance, and whether or not Labour was perceived as a party that would credibly respond to business interests.

This argument rejects the claim that in its City policies, Labour had simply accepted the 'Downsian' model of electoral competition focussing on the median voter and market research to shape it's political and policy strategy. Neither was it simply driven to appease capital because of 'structural dependence'. There are areas where there is some evidence that Labour altered its policy to impress the private sector and the City such as the training levy. But in others it maintained its commitments - such as the windfall tax on the privatised utilities where it deliberating communicated the policy in advance as a 'one-off' allowing share prices to adjust - and the National Minimum Wage. To claim that Labour set out to follow public opinion rather than lead it - as reflected in its City policies - is a wholly inadequate explanation.

It was encouraging the City to endorse Labour's programme that mattered, as market confidence impacted on the electorate's broader assessment of the party's economic credibility and competence. The 'prawn cocktail offensive' aimed to neutralise negative City comment - but also reflected a wider shift in the climate of ideas - as alternative models of social market capitalism appeared exhausted. There was no credible intellectual framework for economic management with the potential to inform 'New' Labour's domestic statecraft that did not involve an accommodation with financial capital. As Helen Thompson suggests, "it is highly unlikely that any British Government will be motivated by ideology in economic policy-making beyond the very short-term…economic management is a crucial determinant of electoral performance". [40]

The economic landscape had also changed profoundly in the intervening 18 years since Labour was last in power. The Thatcher Governments' strategy was far from successful, as many critics have noted. Productivity and investment remained stubbornly low, there was relatively little improvement in the skills base, and investment in science, infrastructure and the public services had been under-funded. But as Andrew Gamble argues, "it made sufficient structural changes to allow a new political economy to emerge by the 1990s"[41]. 'New' Labour's strategy was also a reflection of profound re-thinking within the Labour leadership about perceived economic, social and political changes: globalisation, the information age, flexibility and insecurity. This led Labour inevitably to revise its historical relationship with financial capital and the City.

So, understanding *why* Labour's relationship with the City was transformed in the last two decades - and consolidated in the 1992-97 period - requires a deeper explanation than the imperative of electoral pragmatism. The party had to produce an economic strategy that was sufficiently viable to win the 1997 election. Blair and his colleagues entered office seeking to recreate a governing competence for the Labour Party that drew a line under the political catastrophes of the 1974-79 Governments, and their efforts to modernise the British economy.

It is perfectly legitimate to contend that Labour's reconciliation with the City has gone too far, imposing unacceptable limits and constraints on a social democratic modernisation project for the British economy. Substantial criticisms of the party's programme by 1997 could still be made.

The central premises of 'New' Labour's 'Third Way' - globalisation as irresistible and inescapable, the necessity of individual adaptation to new technology, the imperative of geographical and occupational mobility, the reality of mobile capital and new global competition - have been strongly contested by some critics[42]. Globalisation is a highly contentious concept. Anyone assessing contemporary economic policy has to make a judgement about its extent and its impact on the freedom for manoeuvre in domestic economic decision-making.

Nonetheless, the 'catch-all' rationale for explaining 'New' Labour policies - naked electoral ambition and strategic 'triangulation' - is inadequate, and should receive closer attention and critique within the social and political sciences.

The quality of ideas does matter in the long term, enabling Labour to rethink its economic strategy, and in turn to reconstitute its relationship with the City through a long process of change and renewal in the 1980s and 1990s.

In conclusion, J.M Keynes was surely right to argue that ideas fundamentally determine political action:

> The ideas of economists and political philosophers, both when they are right and when they are wrong, are more powerful than is commonly understood. Indeed, the world is ruled by little else. Practical men, who believe themselves to be quite exempt from any intellectual influence, are usually the slaves of some defunct economist…soon, or late, it is ideas, not vested interests, which are dangerous for good or evil.[43]

Notes

[1] As defined by Kerry McCarthy in McCarthy, K. 2004, 'The relationship between the Labour and the City 1971-1997' in *Paper to the Economic History Society Annual Conference, Royal Holloway College, 2-4 April 2004.*
[2] Hay, Colin, 1994, "Labour's Thatcherite Revisionism: Playing the Politics of Catch-Up" in *Political Studies* 42, pp. 700-7
[3] Hill, R. 2001, The Labour Party and Economic Strategy 1979-97, Palgrave Macmillan Press, London.
[4] William Keegan of The Observer newspaper coined the phrase 'prawn cocktail offensive' in 1988.

[5] Bulpitt, J. 1986, 'The Discipline of the New Democracy: Mrs Thatcher's Domestic Statecraft', in *Political Studies*, Vol. 34, No.1, pp. 17-35.
[6] Keynes, J.M. 1936, *The General Theory of Employment, Interest and Money*, Macmillan Press, London.
[7] See H. Thompson, 'Economic Policy under Thatcher and Major', in Ludlam, S. and Smith, M.J., *Contemporary British Conservatism*, Palgrave Macmillan, 1995.
[8] Hill, R. 2001, op. cit.
[9] Gamble, A. 2003, *Between Europe and America: the future of British politics*, Macmillan Press, London.
[10] Ibid.
[11] Ingham, G. 1984, *Capitalism Divided? The City and Industry in Britain*, Macmillan Press, London.
[12] See Gamble, A. 1982, *Britain in Decline*, Macmillan Press, London.
[13] See Owen, G. 1999, *From Empire to Europe: The Decline and Revival of British Industry Since the Second World War*, Harper Collins, London.
[14] Gamble, A. 2003, *Between Europe and America: the future of British politics*, Macmillan, London.
[15] Ibid.
[16] See Owen, G. 1999, op. cit. The financial and banking system also has a decisive influence on which countries succeed in particular industries. The availability of venture capital is a crucial underpinning of industrial and commercial success.
[17] The phrase 'socialism in one country' was attributed to the Labour Minister Nye Bevan, veteran of the 1945 Attlee Government and a radical socialist.
[18] For an excellent account of the AES programme, see Coates, D. 1984, *The Context of British Politics*, Hutchinson, London.
[19] Other key groups in the development of Labour's economic strategy in the 1930s include the XYZ Club and the New Fabian Research Bureau. Two of the main contributors, Hugh Dalton and Hugh Gaitskell, went on to become Chancellors of the Exchequer in the post-war Labour Government.
[20] Mc Carthy, K. 2004, op. cit.
[21] Ibid.
[22] Data quoted in Thompson, H. 1996, 'Economic Policy under Thatcher and Major' in Ludlam, S and Smith, M.J. (ed.'s) *Contemporary British Conservatism*, Macmillan Press, London.
[23] See Owen, G. 1999, *From Empire to Europe: The Decline and Revival of British Industry Since the Second World War*, Harper Collins, London.
[24] See Keynes, J. *The General Theory of Employment, Interest and Money*, Macmillan Press, London. The inter-war, period presented a difficult challenge for Britain arising from the depression in world trade, and the financial difficulties experienced by the big exporting industries such as

cotton textiles and steel. The banks have been criticized for not doing more to help these industries by promoting mergers and rationalization.
[25] Owen, G. 1999, op. cit.
[26] See Coates, D. 2000, *Models of Capitalism*, Polity, Cambridge.
[27] See Hutton, W. 1995, *The State We're In*, Jonathan Cape, London.
[28] Tony Blair in a speech to business leaders, Singapore, February 16th 1996.
[29] See Jessop, R. 1982, *The Capitalist State: Marxist Theories and Methods*, Blackwell, Oxford.
[30] As symbolized by the liberal newspaper The Financial Times, the only major broadsheet to endorse Labour in the 1992 election - an early victory for the 'prawn cocktail offensive'.
[31] Desai, M. quoted in Hill, R. 2001, *The Labour Party and Economic Strategy1979-97*, Palgrave Macmillan, London.
[32] Hutton, W. 1995, op. cit.
[33] See Owen, G. 1999, op. cit.
[34] Mandelson, P. & Liddle, R. 1996, *The Blair Revolution: Can New Labour Deliver?*, Faber and Faber, London.
[35] See Owen, G. 1999, op. cit.
[36] It retrospect it has been argued that the collapse of the Mitterrand experiment was the nail in the coffin of 'go it alone' 'reflation in one country' economic strategies. The socialist-communist Government came to power in May 1981 with an agreed economic programme based on reflation and public ownership that was similar to the AES.
[37] See Gamble, A. 2003, *Between Europe and America: The Future of British Politics*, Macmillan Press, London.
[38] Ibid.
[39] See Driver, S. and Martell, L. 1998, *New Labour: Politics after Thatcherism*, Polity Press, Cambridge.
[40] Thompson, H. 1996, op. cit.
[41] See Gamble, A. 2003, op. cit.
[42] See Coates, D. 2000, op. cit.
[43] Keynes, J. M. 1936, *The General Theory of Employment, Interest and Money*, Macmillan Press, London.

Further Reading

Brittain, S. 1969, *Steering the British Economy: the rise of the Treasury*, Secker and Warburg, London.
Bulpitt, J. 1986, 'The Discipline of the New Democracy: Mrs Thatcher's Domestic Statecraft', in *Political Studies*, Vol. 34, No.1, pp. 17-35.
Cairncross, A. 1992, *The British Economy since 1945*, Basil Blackwell, Oxford.
Coates, D. 1984, *The Context of British Politics*, Hutchinson, London.
Collignon, S., et. al. 1994, *Europe's Monetary Future*, Pinter, London.

Driver, S. & Martell, L., 1998, *New Labour: Politics after Thatcherism*, Polity Press, Cambridge.

Dunn, J. 1990, ed., *The Economic Limits to Modern Politics*, Cambridge University Press, Cambridge.

Ferri, P. ed. 1998, *Prospects for the European Monetary System*, Macmillan, London.

Gamble, A. 1982, *Britain in Decline*, Macmillan Press, London.

Gamble, A. 2003, *Between Europe and America: the future of British politics*, Macmillan Press, London.

Hall, P., ed., 1987, *The Political Power of Economic Ideas*, Princeton University Press, Princeton.

Hay, C. 1994 'Labour's Thatcherite Revisionism: Playing the politics of catch-up', in *Political Studies*, 42, pp. 700-7.

Hill, R. 2001, *The Labour Party and Economic Strategy 1979-97*, Palgrave Macmillan, London.

Hutton, W. 1995, *The State We're In*, Jonathan Cape, London.

Ingham, G. 1984, *Capitalism Divided? The City and Industry in Britain*, Macmillan Press, London.

Jessop, R. 1982, *The Capitalist State: Marxist Theories and Methods*, Blackwell, Oxford.

Keegan, W. 1984, *Mrs Thatcher's Economic Experiment*, Penguin, Harmondsworth.

Keynes, J.M. 1936, *The General Theory of Employment, Interest and Money*, Macmillan Press, London.

McCarthy, K. 2004, 'The relationship between the Labour Party and the City 1971-1997', *Paper to the Economic History Society Annual Conference, Royal Holloway College, 2-4 April 2004.*

Owen, G. 1999, *From Empire to Europe: The Decline and Revival of British Industry Since the Second World War*, Harper Collins, London.

Thompson, H. 1996, 'Economic Policy under Thatcher and Major', in *Contemporary British Conservatism*, Steve Ludlam and Martin J. Smith, Macmillan Press, London.

Wickham-Jones, M. 1986, *Economic Strategy and the Labour Party: Politics and Policy-Making 1970-83*, Macmillan Press, London.

Thompson, N. 1996, *Political Economy and the Labour Party: The Economics of Democratic Socialism, 1884-1995*, UCL Press, London.

Roberts, R. & Kynaston, D. 2001, *City-State: A Contemporary History of the City of London and How Money Triumphed*, Profile Books, London.

Chapter Seven

Conservatives and the City

Howard Flight

The City of London is of increased importance to all three political parties. The financial services industry employs over one million people; it accounts for more than one third of UK Corporation Tax revenues and has overseas earnings of approximately £20 billion per annum, funding a not insignificant part of our manufactured imports.

Britain is again a global leader in financial services in a comparable way to the 50 years before the First World War. The ownership of City businesses is largely international and, indeed, senior staff are also increasingly international. Keeping the business in London depends essentially on London being competitive and user friendly in the key areas of taxation and regulation. Otherwise businesses and people can and will move elsewhere easily. The challenge and the risks are that London and the UK are now less competitive in both these key areas. This is the all-important background to my own experience and involvement in seeking to restore good relations between the City and the Conservative Party.

When I was a child in the 1950s my father worked in the City; I well remember going to children's Christmas Parties at his office in Lothbury. Then, from top to bottom, most people working in the City, and in particular clerks, were stalwart Conservatives. I remember imbibing the basic City view that Conservative governments were positive for the stockmarket and the exchange rate, whereas a Labour government was likely to run into devaluation and associated economic problems. Interestingly, the latter was a major negative for Labour right through the 1960s, as I remember discussing with the late Edward Heath in Cambridge in 1968 and agreeing why Harold Wilson's enforced currency devaluation would be bad for Labour at the ensuing 1970 General Election which Wilson, surprisingly, lost.

The City was overwhelmingly supportive of Margaret Thatcher's supply side revolution – even though the early 1980s were financially painful; but at the 1997 General Election I estimate that as many as 40 per cent of those working in the City voted New Labour. I well remember speaking to a large City audience in 1998 at which I assumed, mistakenly, that their politics would be mostly Conservative and critical of New Labour – to my cost!

What happened in the interim? First of all, in people terms, the City and the Conservative Party became increasingly divorced from each other. The number of Conservative MPs with a substantial City career background dwindled to a handful. As I encountered in the 1990s, it became a positive disadvantage in seeking to be selected as a Conservative parliamentary candidate to have a City background. Several of the measures taken by the Major government, as part of their attempt to reduce the fiscal deficit, caused considerable offence in the City particularly as there was little or no consultation. The City perceived Major's promises to lighten the excessive 40 per cent Capital Gains Tax burden and to relieve inheritance tax were empty.

Above all, it was in the City that the Conservative Party lost its key reputation as the better manager of the economy as a result of the ERM membership debacle and Black/White Wednesday. In business terms, to the City the then Conservative government came across as unprofessional and less than competent, even though the economy recovered strongly, post our exit from the ERM and on the back of both a cheap exchange rate and low interest rates and, more fundamentally, the supply side reforms of the Thatcher governments. In the 1990s the Conservative Party never got adequate credit in the City for the great market reforms of the 1980s which have also underpinned the City's dramatic success and prosperity over the last 15 years. Indeed, it is arguable that "Big Bang", ending City cartels and monopolies in the 1980s, has actually resulted in far greater earnings to City businesses and remuneration to City executives!

There was a time in the 1990s when some argued that the increasing euroscepticism of a majority of Conservative MPs damaged the Party's reputation with the City. In my view this was not true. One or two leading City figures were strong europhiles and strong supporters of joining the Euro prior to its launch. This was nothing new. Walter Baghot, the great constitutionalist and leading banker of his day, had been a great supporter of Britain joining the Silver Franc which was the common European currency of the 1870s and 1880s, before it fell apart in the early 1890s. For a few, there was a rather naïve fear that unless the UK joined the Euro, the City would lose out on banking and foreign exchange business. I do not believe this view was shared by a majority of City employees and indeed it was my observation that they were generally eurosceptic throughout. The main point in this territory is, however, that once the Euro had been established, without the UK joining, all the Euro foreign exchange and related business moved to London from the smaller financial centres of Europe. London actually benefited from the creation of the Euro without having to join the Euro – just as it had benefited from the establishment of the Euro Dollar and Bond markets in London, without adopting the US Dollar as our currency. Once this was seen to be the case, the City generally lost interest and has been increasingly hostile to the UK economy getting further dragged in to the over-regulated, over-taxed, unreformed and socialist economic regimes of Continental Europe! I suspect, however, that the Conservative Party lost some credibility with the City as a result of the doctrinaire europhile views of some of its leading figures in the 1990s, which have turned out to be mistaken.

I believe the onset of financial regulation, viewed increasingly by the City as too expensive and too intrusive, has only limited relevance, at least so far, to Party politics. It was a Conservative government which brought in financial regulation and a Labour government which changed it, with the FSMA and the establishment of the FSA as a single regulator – at the time with broad City support. From the time when, as Shadow Economic Secretary to the Treasury, I led for the Conservatives in the Committee Stage of the FSMA in 1999, I have spent a great deal of time both discussing regulatory issues with City institutions and in seeking to diagnose what regulatory reforms were needed. Broadly, I found that I was the first and virtually the only Conservative politician since the onset of financial regulation in 1986 who had entered into a dialogue with the City on this important territory. What this illustrated, more than anything else, was the separation, if not divorce, between the City and Conservative Party politicians which had occurred in people terms over the previous 20 years.

When I arrived as an MP at Westminster in 1997 I found significant hostility towards the City among Conservative ranks - some of this, at least, based on a view that people were earning too much in the City! In the City, the Conservative Party had certainly lost its reputation as being the political Party representing the City and its interests. Here Gordon Brown, although at heart an old-fashioned, Scottish, socialist, who has returned to Labour's bad old tax and spend ways, had the shrewdness to press two political buttons which made New Labour substantially popular with the City. The first was giving independence to the Bank of England to manage monetary policy and the second was reducing the rate of Capital Gains Tax on longer-held business assets to 10 per cent. The City had wanted previous Conservative governments to act similarly in both of these areas.

Running up to the 2001 election, apart from firmly-committed Conservative Party loyalists, I found it difficult to drum up much general support for the Conservative Party in the City of London. Indeed, a number of eminent City entrepreneurs displayed public support for New Labour and many others voted New Labour in 2001 as well as 1997.

Although I did not take on the formal role of Conservative Party Envoy to the City of London until Autumn, 2004, unofficially I started on this task as early as 2001, when Shadow Economic Secretary to the Treasury. Going into the 2001 General Election campaign, I had a large number of meetings with City groups and City businesses which were essentially about stirring up the loyalists. In 2002, as Shadow Chief Secretary to the Treasury, and motivated by friends in the City saying to me that it was time the Conservative Party had a presence in the City, I agreed to set up the Conservative City Circle. This involved, essentially, substantial networking by me, Neil Pidgeon and a group of other dedicated Friends amongst our contacts in the City. We built up a database of over 5,000 supporters. We set up six key sub-committees covering each of the main areas of City activity and held a large reception for approximately 1,000 supporters every six months. In absolute number terms, arguably, we only scratched the surface. In addition, while City Circle is about political involvement and not fundraising, it has also served to feed a large number of individuals who have provided substantial financial support in several different ways via the Conservative Party Treasurer's Department. Above all, City Circle established a known and recognised return of a Conservative political presence in the City, and a conduit for political input from the City to the Conservative Shadow Cabinet.

I also believe that its success reflected a growing change of attitude by the City, back towards the Conservative Party. The City, much more than the population at large, perceived the long-term damage to our economic prosperity which will result from Brown's excessive and wasteful increase in public spending. The Labour government has, moreover, become increasingly hostile to the City of

London in its tax policies. As time passes the political pluses of Bank of England independence and the lower business Capital Gains Tax rate are increasingly taken for granted; in the meantime there is growing criticism of Labour's attack on share option schemes, its nightmare anti-avoidance policies, excessive regulation and too much centralised, economic micro-management. Indeed, the more politically active members of the City are again looking to the Conservative Party to offer radical supply side market economy reforms reducing taxation and downsizing the public sector to boost our growth rates and improve our economic flexibility. Personally, I now detect a much broader and greater interest amongst leading City entrepreneurs to be involved politically with the Conservative Party than has been the case for a decade; but they await a radical and robust Conservative approach.

Looking forward, I view the return of closer relations between the Conservative Party and the City of London - and the wider business community - as politically important. Above all, the Conservative Party has to get back its reputation of being the better manager of the economy, which was the main reason why it was in power for the majority of the 20th Century. The Conservative Party needs, desperately, the active support, advice and public backing of the City and the business community. The Party needs to avoid the arrogance born the 1990s, which turned substantial numbers of key individuals in the City and the wider business community against us. The Party needs to heed the advice of those actually responsible for running businesses. The new leader of the Conservative Party will need to be City and business friendly and to have the positive support of the City.

Particularly following the Railtrack revelations, Labour has lost its honeymoon of 1997-2001 with the City and is perceived as increasingly bad news both economically and fiscally; but the Conservatives still have a lot of friends to make and to win back.

Chapter Eight

The Private Finance Initiative: Issues and Prospects

Sanjiv Sachdev

The Private Finance Initiative (PFI)/Public Private Partnerships (PPPs) are key mechanisms in the government's broader agenda of renewing (better funded) public services – in the words of a former minister they are a "cornerstone of the government's reform programme"[1] Competition from the City led private sector is seen as a source of innovation, spurring the efficiency of the public sector. A consequence has been a sharp increase in the role of outsourcing and the private sector in public service delivery. It is estimated that the scope of public sector outsourcing will grow from £32 billion in 2004 to between £40 billion and £60 billion by 2006-7.[2] As of 2005, PFI contracts worth nearly £43 billions have been signed. Areas of the public realm once almost exclusively undertaken by the public sector – such as defence and criminal justice - have seen the private sector play an increasingly prominent role. In other sectors, such as health and local government, the role of the private sector grown significantly – thus some 56 per cent of all adult and children's personal social services are provided by the private and voluntary sectors, against 40 per cent in 1997 – a market worth more than £9 billion a year; companies have taken over the running of schools in nine local authorities; in health it is estimated that the NHS will soon spend £4.5 billion on privately provided clinical services.[3] The potential scope of private sector involvement is dramatic as is illustrated from a world view; the work of the United States Department of Defense is carried out by 734,000 private sector staff per annum, compared with 700,000 permanent government employees[4], and a quarter of prisoners in Australia are now in private prisons.

The Origins and Scope of the Private Finance Initiative.

The Private Finance Initiative remains controversial. It has stoked the fierce opposition of many trade unions to PFI/PPPs,[5] and taken centre stage at Labour Party conferences and has been subject to widespread criticism.[6]

PFI itself is a prominent form of Public Private Partnerships, the latter being an umbrella term embracing joint ventures, the Private Finance Initiative (PFI) and contracting out. All seek to achieve closer partnerships between the private and public sectors. PFI was devised in 1992 by the then Conservative Chancellor Norman Lamont as a way of funding public services while minimising the initial expense and therefore the need to raise taxes. Under the most common form of PFI, the private sector designs, builds, finances and operates (DBFO) facilities based on 'output' specifications decided by public sector managers and their departments. A condition which was "a sensible transfer of risk to the private sector" according to former Chancellor of the Exchequer Norman Lamont.[7] With the PFI the public sector does not own an asset, such as a hospital or school, but pays the PFI contractor a stream of payments for the use of the facilities over the contract period. Once the contract has expired, ownership of the asset either remains with the private contractor, or is returned to the public sector, depending on the terms of the original contract. Contracts of 25 to 30 years duration are commonplace – a steady rate of return that was attractive to many contractors. PFI was seen as complementing privatisation in extending private sector involvement in public services. In the words of one exponent Sir Alastair Morton: "This [PFI] is the Heineken of privatisation – taking the private sector to the parts of the government machine not reached by previous privatisations and contracting out".[8]

Like Compulsory Competitive Tendering before it, but on a larger scale and with a broader scope, PFI/PPPs represent a potentially dramatic shift in the focus of the public sector, away from being a direct provider and towards being a regulator and procurer of services (in the jargon of 'New Public Management' from 'rowing' to 'steering'). Their scale is significant: by December 2004 677 PFI deals had been signed with a capital value of nearly £42.7 billion.[9] PFI is also the dominant model of procurement for new hospitals and prisons. Table 1 sets out the contracts agreed by December 2004:

PFI deals signed by Department as at December 2004

Department	Number of signed projects	Capital value (£ million)
Cabinet Office	2	347.7
H.M Customs and Excise	2	170.3
Constitutional Affairs	13	306.4
Culture, Media and Sport	7	68.6
Environment, Food and Rural Affairs	13	632.7
Transport	45	21432.1
Education and Skills	121	2922.8
Health	136	4901.2
Trade and Industry	8	180.8
Work and Pensions	11	1341.0
Foreign & Commonwealth	2	91.0
Home Office	37	1095.0
Defence	52	4254.8
Inland Revenue	8	453.8
Office of Deputy Prime Minister	61	972.1
Office of Government Commerce	1	10.0
Northern Ireland	39	528.8
Scotland	84	2249.3
Wales	33	551.3
Total	**677**	**42,699.4**

Source: H.M Treasury (2005)

As the table shows, much of PFI spending is on transport projects– some £15.5 billion was spent on the combined contracts to modernise London Transport.[10]

The Labour Party and the Embrace of PFI/PPPs.

The growth of the public sector has its origins in the limitations of market provision for certain public or monopolistic goods. Conventionally, the government's provision of services arose because long-term market contracts are 'incomplete'; i.e. difficult to specify, expensive to monitor and enforce, and uncertain in their effect. The 'principal', who contracts out the service, has imperfect control of the 'agent', who provides it, and the difficulties increase over time. As Offer argues "Principals lose control over quality and costs, and agents are exposed to exploitation. When co-operation is important, the solution is 'integration', making the agent directly accountable as an employee. Information is more transparent, and costs are controlled directly. Effort is more easily monitored, and compliance enforced. Principal and agent are not discouraged by costly renegotiation".[11] If mishaps occur, it is a matter for managers or engineers rather than lawyers. Moreover, it was contended that when the most efficient scale of operation is a single provider (a natural monopoly) or when users cannot be excluded (a public good). Until the 1980s such integration was common in both public sectors and in large corporations

Since the late seventies, a broader ideological shift turned against this approach. In the United States the 'Leviathan' school of public finance depicted government growth as driven by rent-seeking individuals, politicians, and special-interest groups. The Chicago school of economics took the superiority of market provision as a given.[12] In Britain, Bacon and Eltis famously argued that a bloated public sector was crowding out the market sector.[13] Organisations were urged to divest, to concentrate on their core activities and divest themselves of their other activities; Peters and Waterman urged firms to 'stick to their knitting'.[14] A plethora of terms has emerged to cover the use of the private sector/outside organisation for activities that were formerly undertaken in-house: outsourcing, subcontracting, market testing, contracting out and externalisation[15].

This embrace of the market and the private sector spread to centre-left governments and parties. Many centre left thinkers shared the critique of Osborne and Gaebler that government had become "bloated, wasted, ineffective"[16] failing to adapt to a rapidly changing world and advocated greater private sector involvement in delivering public services as an answer to what was seen an overstretched state and public sector sluggishness. Thus the leading Third Way advocate, Anthony Giddens contends that "[s]ome of the inadequacies of Britain's public services are more to do with inertia, poor management, overmanning and bureaucratic sloth than lack of resources"; and that "firms working in the commercial sector are likely to be better managed than state agencies – not merely because they are commercial, but because they have been exposed to competition."[17] Kelly, then of the Institute of Public Policy Research (IPPR), states that "There now appears to be no widely accepted account of the limits of private sector involvement in public services".[18] A leading advocate of PPPs and Downing Street advisor,

Julian Le Grand, maintains that in the 21st century "Central government or local authorities will still be financing welfare services. But they will no longer be providing the service concerned or, if they do, their role will be increasingly that of a residual provider".[19] The private sector is seen as a more efficient, effective and innovative provider of public services, with competition as the spur to these efficiencies.

This is a fundamental shift in centre left thinking. Traditionally, as Marquand states "In most of western Europe, the great achievement of the second half of the nineteenth century and the first half of the twentieth was the creation of a public domain, ring-fenced from the pressures of the market place, in which citizenship rights rather than market power governed the allocation of social goods."[20] Indeed, the provision of certain services "through market means would demean their citizenship quality".[21] This approach was explicitly rejected by Chancellor of the Exchequer Gordon Brown. Within a context of substantial funding increases to public services, he maintains that "we should normally tackle market failure not by abolishing markets but by strengthening markets and enabling them to work better". Moreover, "the bracing winds of competition… should apply to the public sector as well as the private sector".[22]

For New Labour "[d]emonstrating a full hearted commitment to the future of public services while at the same time striving to recast the relationship between public and private sectors was proclaimed as a leitmotif of the Government's 'new politics.'"[23] The private sector and competition were paramount to reforming (better funded) public services. As prime minister Blair stated: "By instigating a competitive tendering process PPPs can also help to drive up cost efficiencies and encourage innovation in public service delivery",[24] echoing Conservative Michael Howard, who as Home Secretary (1993) extended private sector involvement in the Prison Service, in the grounds "that competition is a spur to higher standards and greater efficiency."[25] Labour has "introduced the private sector into areas where the Conservatives feared to tread"[26] - plans to open the NHS to competition from the private sector and to lease NHS facilities and second staff to the private sector accord with this approach.[27]

Labour's promotion of PFI/PPPs has come under widespread criticism from traditional centre-left opinion.[28] The most vigorous assault is from the Health Policy and Health Services Research Unit.[29] However, even here, critiques of PPPs tend to be less on ideological terms (public ownership, democratic control, equity) and more on pragmatic grounds (value for money, efficiency, complexity) indicative of a wider loss of intellectual confidence.

Extending the Tent: PFI/PPPs and the Rapprochement with Business and the Private Sector.

As a mechanism for public service reform, PPPs hold three particular attractions for New Labour. Firstly, using the private sector to reform public services enhanced the party's credentials as being "business-friendly". New Labour "was obsessed with recruiting business people to their cause, because they believed that one of their party's serious weaknesses was the perception that it did not understand wealth creation".[30] As Kelly argues, promoting PPPs would "prove, once and for all, that the centre-left has dropped its historical ambivalence to the profit motive and to demonstrate that the new government's commitment to social justice need not unsettle the business community".[31] The revision of Clause IV of Labour's constitution, abandoning the aim of extending public ownership, set the basis for this business friendly stance. Correspondingly, the importance of ownership was seen by the IPPR's Commission on Public Private Partnerships as "overblown" and "increasingly a second order issue".[32] Instead, in accordance with the NPM credo, outcomes are emphasised. Business and City anxieties of a return to 'old Labour' were placated as a clear break from the rhetoric and behaviour of past Labour governments became evident (see Patrick Diamond in this volume).

Secondly, the quality of public services is believed to improve through using the private sector. Labour's 2001 manifesto spoke of "drawing on [the private sector's] vitality" and argues that a "'spirit of enterprise' should apply as much to public service as to business".[33] The then Chief Secretary to the Treasury argued that PPPs seek "to close the all too clear gap that exists between the quality of public sector buildings, work and facilities, and the services dependent on them, and those of the private sector".[34] (Thus we are presented with the curious argument that ownership is not important, but that the private sector is central, because of its dynamism and efficiency, to public sector reform).

Thirdly, it is argued that PPPs help the government overcome a perceived fiscal dilemma, enabling more investment to take place than the government is able to provide by conventional capital spending.[35] In the words of Deputy Prime Minister, John Prescott: "[The Labour government] can either find the money from private finance or it can take the money in tax increases".[36] This argument is less convincing as the principal effect of 'private finance' schemes is to raise the time profile of expenditure by the public sector.[37] Indeed, in opposition Labour criticised some PFI schemes on the basis that "apparent savings now could be countered by the formidable commitment on revenue expenditure in years to come".[38]

Labour's commitment to 'partnerships' predates New Labour. A limited reference to "joint public-private sector ventures" for rail and road projects was made in 1991.[39] A turning point, in the wake of its fourth consecutive election defeat in 1992, was the document drawn up by Gordon Brown, Robin Cook and John Prescott. This saw:

> …new partnerships not simply in the provision of rail and infrastructure, but also in inner city and regional developments, in training, in housing, in childcare, and in defence diversification work… we also see a limited application in the provision of private finance for publicly-led projects in health and education.[40]

The scope of the proposed partnerships was much more circumspect than current schemes. It was argued that "[services] such as prisons, the rail service, health service and police, which cannot be run by private concerns whose primary goal is profit."[41] Interestingly, the areas of 'limited application', particularly health and prisons, are the very sectors in which PFI growth has been especially strong; by December 2004 the Health department was the second largest in terms of signed PFI deals with a value of some £4,901 million.[42]

Prior to the 1997 election even those in the vanguard of New Labour criticised the 'perversities' of the market in public services, arguing that 'marketisation' had hastened the disengagement between the public and their users.[43] But a marked shift was evident under the leadership of Tony Blair with New Labour's advocacy of PPPs becoming more enthusiastic. In 1995 he told the Confederation of British Industry that Labour had "pioneered the notion of public/private partnership".[44] The 1997 manifesto (far more detailed on PPPs than its 2001 successor) stated that Labour would, in government, "reinvigorate" PPPs.[45] Labour's 1997 business manifesto set out a detailed twelve point plan for PPPs and called on the private sector to play an "increasing role in procuring public services and investment".[46] The role of the public sector was significantly circumscribed; a key architect of Labour's PFI policy, the former paymaster-general Geoffrey Robinson MP, argues that "Having agreed a detailed specification for a proposal, the whole idea of the PFI was that the private sector should be left to get on with it".[47]

In government, an early piece of legislation passed by Labour was the National Health Service (Private Finance) Act, announced within a fortnight of coming to power and which received Royal Assent in July 1997. This simplified and expanded the PFI process following the first 'Bates review', initiated by the then paymaster-general Geoffrey Robinson MP, which reported in June 1997. These reforms were wholly technocratic, with no indication of them being informed by wider social democratic principles, such as improved labour standards.

Curiously, the language of Labour's 2001 and 2005 manifestos was much more muted than its predecessor. In 2001 it argued that "Where private sector providers can support public endeavour, we should use them".[48] However, such was the sensitivity of the issue in Scotland that the Scottish Labour Party's manifesto omitted this (somewhat oblique) sentence. The Welsh assembly has also been significantly more cautious in its approach to PPPs. The 2005 Manifesto reaffirmed New Labour's commitment to 'driving innovation through diversity of provision'[49] an implicit acceptance of further private sector in-roads in public service delivery.

Contracting out Responsibility?

The shift to a third party for the delivery of services also often shifts much of the responsibility for that service. The potential reputational risk to firms in the event of contract failure can be considerable. As Crouch notes "Henceforth government is responsible only for policy, not for operations".[50] In the name of efficiency, outsourcing can absolve the State of responsibility. If matters go awry blame can be placed on the contractor (Balfour Beatty in the case of the railways, Group 4 in the case of prisoner transport, WS Atkins in education are three notable examples). Arguably a contracting out of accountability

- to unelected bodies - is also taking place. As a character in David Hare's examination of the privatisation of the railways puts it: "The truth is that nowadays governments want to shed responsibility. The whole move is to put yourself in a situation where you are not responsible – nobody can blame you".[51]

Moreover, as noted in the instances of both the railways[52] and gangmaster labour[53] the chains of subcontracting that follow from these initial contracts and the often complex company structures involved, makes pinning down who is responsible for any breaches in legislation difficult.

The shift of the State from provider to commissioner and regulator has coincided with a broader shift of risk from employers to employees. To a degree, it enables an abdication of responsibility for the welfare of public service workers; to which the abandonment of the 'good employer' model can be seen as a part.

Moreover accountability can become muddled and confused, to the detriment of citizens as well as to the governance more generally. This is well illustrated for example in cases where prisoners escape from the custody of private security firms or where the public are unhappy with the quality of service they are getting from their water supplier. In both cases, the elected authorities claim to be no longer answerable (on the grounds that these are 'operational' matters) while the private firm may claim they are still fulfilling the contract.[54]

The Centrality and Neglect of Workforce Issues in PFI/PPPs.

The IPPR Commission found "few other issues in the debate over PPPs that are so controversial" as those concerning the workforce.[55] Large numbers of workers are affected; according to a leading contractor, Capita, some 80,000 workers had transferred to the private sector under PPPs.[56] Trade unions have been particularly concerned at the emergence of a two-tier workforce, where new recruits receive poorer terms and conditions than employees who have been transferred from the public sector.[57] Yet despite the scale of controversy, the numbers of workers involved and the existence of the PFI initiative for over a decade, there is little robust evidence about its impact on public service workers.[58]

Indicative of the paucity of research are publications by International Financial Services London (itself sponsored by KPMG, Pricewaterhousecoopers, Norton Rose and the publicly funded

Partnerships UK). In a 2001 edition it claimed that "empirical evidence suggests high levels of satisfaction among transferred employees on signed deals". When asked to produce this empirical evidence, IFSL was unable to do so. A later edition replaced the term "empirical" with "anecdotal". As Morgan and Allington note of sub-contracting more generally, "what does cause surprise is the extent to which these measures have been embraced with little regard for the consequences".[59] For a government committed to evidence based policy making this neglect is of serious concern.

The 2001 manifesto did make a clear commitment that "[the] Private Finance Initiative (PFI) should not be delivered at the expense of the pay and conditions of the staff employed in these schemes",[60] bringing Party policy into accord with the advice of Osborne and Gaebler for whom preventing the deterioration of pay and benefits was a precondition of reform. But in practice, enforcement of this commitment has proved to be difficult.

From its inception, changing labour practices were central to the success of PFI projects. The Conservative politician, David Willets argued that "Many of the efficiency gains from bringing in private money and management come from escaping traditional NHS labour practices. Many of the firms involved would not wish to negotiate with NHS unions, nor accept conventional job demarcations".[61] Private contractors claim that the efficiencies they secure in managing employees are keys to the success of PPPs. The IPPR Commission maintains that "it is precisely in the area of the organisation of work that the private sector might make a significant contribution to the management of public services".[62] This is unsurprising given the labour intensive nature of many public services; for example, in the prison service staff costs account for about 80 per cent of prison running costs.[63] Moreover, the Treasury claims that PFI "has allowed for considerable innovation in workforce practices".[64] Prime Minister Blair himself has called for public services to "modernise working practices",[65] and for "more flexible staff working practices".[66] However, despite the centrality of workforce management to the alleged greater efficiency of PFI schemes, the implications of such changes for the workers in public services have had little in-depth examination. The House of Commons Health Select Committee (2002) expressed its disappointment "at the lack of evidence backing many of the claims made. Despite numerous requests to the private sector for examples of innovation we received few." An Office of Government

Commerce study examining employment relations matters was set in motion in October 2000 but later abandoned for reasons that remain unclear. The process of enhancing workers rights in PFI contracts has been a difficult one for the trade unions, according to one observer on the developments in local government: "[g]uarantees were followed by inaction and Tony Blair finally gave in only under severe pressure at an acutely fragile period of his premiership, as he faced rebellion over Iraq".[67]

More generally, the initial findings of the Working in Britain in 2000 Survey[68] suggest that the conditions of employees in the private sector are significantly inferior to that of the public sector. The survey found "a much more generous attitude to 'fringe' benefits in the public sector. A much larger proportion than in the private sector are likely to enjoy sick pay as well as maternity pay beyond the state minimum, an occupational pension, the opportunity for career breaks and childcare assistance."[69] The contrast between the two sectors is set out in the table below.

Benefits; the sector contrast in 2000

% of employees	Private	Public
Occupational pension	54	80
Sick pay beyond statutory minimum	59	78
Company car/van	25	10
Subsidised transport	14	19
Discount purchases	38	18
Subsidised meals	25	26
Loans to employees	10	16
Private health care scheme	26	12
Maternity leave beyond statutory minimum	22	43
Childcare assistance	2	10
Career breaks	5	18

Source: *Taylor, 2002*

The difference above is most evident with pensions. While there has been a trend in the private sector to shift investment risk from the company to the individual, public sector pensions have been "comfortably above the amounts that have been going into all but the very best private sector final salary schemes".[70] This pattern is replicated in the patterns of public and private prison service provision, set out below. More generally, for the first time since the

1970s – when the public sector was far larger than today – more public sector than private sector employees have final salary pensions[71] Moreover, leading PPP contractors, Rentokil Initial and Compass also have the highest accrued defined benefit pensions for directors but have shut such schemes for employees.[72]

Some robust evidence on pay and conditions in the Prison Service found pay and conditions in private prisons to be markedly inferior to those in the public sector.[73] The cheaper running costs of the private sector were, according to the House of Commons Public Accounts Committee (1998) "almost wholly to do with different wage rates and different staff levels, and also pension arrangements and different lengths of the working week." As Table 3 illustrates. the average basic pay for a Prison Officer in the public sector was £23,307 compared to £17,148 in the private sector.[74]

Comparison of pay and conditions for Prison Officers and Prison Custody Officers (2003-4)

	Prison Officer (Public)	Prison Custody Officer (Private)
Average starting basic pay[75]	£16,896	£16,076
Average basic pay	£23,307	£17,148
Pay range	£16,896-£25,788[76]	None more than c.£3,000
Av. Weekly contracted hrs	39	40.9
Overtime pay	Time off in lieu, or up to 9 hrs a wk for 13 wks at standard rate	None, flat rate or 1.5x
Pension	Final salary scheme (retirement at 60). Employer contribution equivalent to 14%	Money purchase scheme (retirement at 65). Av. employer contribution 4.5%, av. employee contribution 3%
Annual leave (days)	25-33	20-23

Source: *DLA MCG Consulting (2004)*

For prison officers, the private sector pay packages are significantly inferior to those in the public sector. Average basic pay sharply lower (public sector rates are some 43 per cent higher), when the value of pension and holiday benefits are added this difference rises to 60 per cent. The overall pay scales are much more modest, the contracted working hours longer, the overtime and annual leave arrangements less favourable (public sector staff get, on average, 7.5 days more leave) and, crucially, pension provision is markedly inferior. Importantly, as private sector rates are comparators in the PSPRB analysis for the public sector, they now act as a drag on most public sector rates.

Furthermore, high levels of labour turnover are a serious problem. The average resignation rate in PFI prisons among Prison Custody Officers 25% - ten times the rate (2.6%) among their public sector equivalents.[77] According to Richard Tilt, the former Director-General of the Prison Service in England and Wales before the introduction of competition "it was very difficult to negotiate down pay rates and conditions of service…it becomes a slightly more viable option once you get a degree of competition".[78] Competition is not seen as a force for higher pay. However, after a prolonged battle, union efforts succeeded, in the so-called 'Warwick agreement', in securing commitments from government that the pay and conditions of private providers will not be inferior to those prevailing in the public sector across the public services.[79]

PFI: Fading Fortunes?

One of the key virtues of the PFI was argued to be the ability to build speedily and within the agreed budgets (at the risk of incurring penalties). But more recently the disadvantages of such projects have been increasingly highlighted. Crouch's argument that "long-term contracts are a curiously rigid and inflexible instrument to be adopting during a period which is normally seen as one requiring particularly rapid adaptability and flexibility" has had an echo in the department of health.[80] Furthermore, there is a real question about the extent of the risk actually transferred to contractors, and the ability to monitor it.[81] Moreover, the contract mechanism has been under greater scrutiny:

> The contract specifies a flow of future services, but makes little allowance for changing needs, technologies, and modes of provision. PFI contracts protect only against cost overruns, provide few incentives to improve quality, and lock the community into rigid contracts in a time of rapid change. Price cap regulation provides few incentives to maintain and improve quality, or to create services not envisaged by the contract. The are no rewards for the learning-by-doing that drives innovation and progress, except the reduction of costs, which benefits the contractor alone.[82]

Conclusion: from 'parasites' to partners.

One of the strongest continuities with the preceding Conservative administration, PFI/PPPs have been extended, embedded and enthusiastically promoted, by New Labour. They represent a potentially fundamental shift in the focus of the public sector, away from being a direct provider to becoming a procurer and regulator of services. As part of a broader agenda to renew (better funded) public services, Labour has gradually, but eagerly, turned to the private sector. With the zeal of a new convert it has embraced what Marquand calls the "cult of private sector managerialism", characterising the public sector as tardy and unresponsive, and the private sector as dynamic and innovative.[83] It is has thus reinforced rather than challenged neo-liberal models of public service provision, while seeking to protect the level of that provision. We thus have the curious sight of a centre left government embracing and extending an initiative begun by a fervently pro-market Conservative party as a central component of its public service reforms. Moreover, we see a party founded on the ethic of co-operation promoting competition as the guiding force of reform and an evident shift from a concern to shield citizens from the inequities of markets to a relish, as the then Health Secretary put it, in the "dynamism of the market".[84]

The revisionism that has led to this accommodation with the private sector is profound. Orwell characterised businessmen such as Lord Beaverbrook as 'parasites'[85]; more recently John Lloyd has called for 'partnerships with capital'. [86] Scepticism towards the private sector and the efficacy of markets, evident even in the mid-1990s, has markedly diminished. The hostility of and towards the City and financial markets has seemingly been neutralised. Concerns about the implications of PFI for workers seem more dependent on levels of trade union disquiet than on the careful consideration of the evidence.

Advocacy of the market and the private sector is central to New Labour's public service reforms; the market is associated by it to conceptions of modernity and the private sector is seen as part of coalition-building exercise, embracing business support to extend the 'political tent' of New Labour to areas untouched by 'old' Labour. However, the triumph of NPM extends beyond New Labour into wide reaches of centre-left. Its success may, in part, be due to the lack of a credible alternative. Thomas Kuhn's work on scientific revolutions may have some pertinence here – the mere disconfirmation or challenge never dislodges a dominant paradigm; only a better alternative does.[87] Critiques without antidotes, however compelling, fail to find a wider, sustainable resonance.[88]

While important differences remain between the major political parties (particularly around levels of public spending), these are arguably of degree than direction. The areas of contestation have narrowed and important areas of consensus are evident in public service reform; both Labour and the Conservatives accept a greater role for markets, a significant role for the private sector and a greater emphasis on commissioning with less attention paid to direct providing. There is arguably, in the area of public service reform the emergence of a political monoculture, where all the major parties promote greater 'choice' (albeit with different degrees of emphasis); centre-left or Right express concern about 'restrictive practices'[89] and all foster a 'dynamic and entrepreneurial' public sector. The major parties can be cast as offering different variations of the same public service reform theme, rather than distinct alternatives. In doing so, New Labour risks further diminishing the traditional role of the centre-left as defenders and promoters of the 'public realm' against market intrusion, and furthering the continuing ideological 'hollowing out' of social democracy; it risks the danger, identified by one Cabinet minister,[90] of being painted as a party of technocrats and managers, indistinguishable, a la Orwell's 'Animal Farm', from the very forces it sought to overturn and thus endangering some of the key sources of its recent electoral success.

Notes

[1] Alan Milburn cited in *Commission on Public Private Partnerships,* Institute of Public Policy Research (IPPR), 2001. p.33.

---

[2] Timmins, N. 2005a, "Growth of the Service Provision Business" in *Financial Times*, 18/04/05.
[3] Timmins, N. 2005c, "NHS to Spend £4.5 bn on Private Care" in *Financial Times*, 26/09/05.
[4] House of Commons Foreign Affairs Committee, 2002, *Private Military CompaniesHC992*, TSO, London.
[5] Unison, 2003, *A Fair Wages Clause,* Unison, London.
[6] For example, Crouch, C. 2003, "Commercialisation or Citizenship" in *Fabian Ideas,*606, Fabian Society, London; Leys, C. 2003, *Market Driven Politics*, Verso, London; Offer, A. 2003, *Why Has the Public Sector Grown So Large in Market Societies?*, Oxford University Press, Oxford; Pollock, A. et al, 2001, *Public Services and the Private Sector*, The Catalyst Trust, London.
[7] Lamont, N. 1992, *House of Commons Debates*, Vol. 2134 col. 998, 12/11/92.
[8] Sir Alastair Morton cited in Eglin, R. 1995, "Private Finance, Public Interest" in *Management Today*, May, pp. 60-64.
[9]H.M Treasury, 2005, see www.h.m.treasury.gov.uk/document/public_private_partnerships
[10]Allen, G. 2003, *Private Finance Initiative*, House of Commons Research Paper 03/79, House of Commons Library.
[11] Offer, A. 2003, op. cit., p.8.
[12] Ibid.
[13] Bacon, R. W. and Eltis, W. 1976, *Britain's Economic Problem: Too Few Producers*, Macmillan,London.
[14] Peters, T. and Waterman, B. 1982, *In Search of Excellence*, Warner Books, New York.
[15] 'Offshoring' can be said to be distinctive from the above terms in having an international element, with the activity that was formerly undertaken in country A now being undertaken in country B.
[16] Osborne, D. and Gaebler, T. 1992, *Reinventing Government*, Plume, New York, p.12.
[17] Giddens, A. 2002, *Where Now for New Labour?*, Polity Press, Cambridge, p.56.
[18] Kelly, G. 2000, *The New Partnership Agenda*, Institute of Public Policy Research, London.
[19] Cited in Pike, A. 1996, *In Partnership, Subject to Contract*, Economic and Social Research Council.
[20] Marquand, D. 1997, *Decline of the Public*, Polity Press, London, p.5.
[21] Crouch, C. 2003, op. cit., p.5.
[22] Brown, G. 2003, *A Modern Agenda for Prosperity and Social Reform*, Speech by the Chancellor of the Exchequer to the Social Market Foundation, 03/02/2003, accessible at www.hm-treasury.gov.uk
[23] IPPR, 2001, op. cit., p.17.

[24] Blair, T. 2002, *The Courage of our Convictions,* "Why the Reform of the Public Services is the Route to Social Justice" in *Fabian Ideas*, 603, Fabian Society, London, p.14.
[25] Cited in *Privately Managed Prison: At What Cost?*, January, Prison Reform Trust, London.
[26] Timmins, N. and Cox, B. 2001, "A Public Realm" in *Prospect*, January.
[27] Timmins, N. 2005b, "Hewitt Denies BMA Claims of Privatising Healthcare" in *Financial Times*, 23/09/2005
[28] For example, Hutton, W. 2002, "Risky – No Matter How you Slice It" in *The Observer*, 28/04/2002; Hattersley, R. 2005, "This Ideology is Destroying our Services" in *The Guardian*, 07/03/2005 and Cook, R. 2005, "A Manifesto like this would actually Motivate our Voters" in *The Guardian*, 04/02/2005.
[29] For example, Pollock et al, 2001, op. cit.; Gaffney et al, 1999, "PFI in the NHS – Is there an Economic Case?" in *BMJ*, Vol. 319.
[30] Peston, R. 2005, *Brown's Britain*, Short Books, London, p.102.
[31] Kelly, G. 2000, op. cit.
[32] IPPR, 2001, op. cit., p.33.
[33] Labour Party, 2001, *Ambitions for Britain*, The Labour Party, London.
[34] Smith, A. 2000, "Delivering Better Public Services" in *New Economy*, Vol. 7, Issue 3, September.
[35] Mandelson, P. and Liddle, R. 1996, *The Blair Revolution*, Faber and Faber, London, p.89.
[36] Cited in Brown, C. 2001, "In-charge Prescott Warns off the Unions" in *The Independent on Sunday*, 05/08/2001
[37] Corry et al, 1997, *Public Private Partnerships*, IPPR, London; Robinson, G. 2000, *The Unconventional Minister*, Michael Joseph, London.
[38] Alastair Darling then shadow Chief Secretary cited in Suzman, M. 1997, "Spending Fears Cast Shadows over PFI" in *Financial Times*, 11/01/1997.
[39] Labour Party, 1991, *Opportunity Britain: Labour's Better Way for the 1990's*, April, The Labour Party, London.
[40] Brown, G. Cook, R. and Prescott, J. 1994, *Financing Infrastructure Investment*, The Labour Party, London.
[41] John Prescott MP, 1994 cited in Thompson, P. 2000, "PPPs in Criminal Justice" in *New Economy*, Vol. 7, Issue 3, September.
[42] HM Treasury, 2005, op. cit.
[43] Milburn, A. 1996, "Reforming Public Services" for *Fabian Society*, Spring Lecture, 05/06/1996, p.1.
[44] Blair, T. 1996, *New Britain*, Fourth Estate, London, p.113.
[45] Labour Party, 1997a, *New Labour because Britain Deserves Better*, The Labour Party, London.
[46] Labour Party, 1997b, *Labour's Business Manifesto: Equipping Britain for the Future*, The Labour Party, London.
[47] Robinson, G. 2000, op. cit.
[48] Labour Party, 2001, op. cit.

[49] Labour Party 2005, *Britain Forward Not Back*, The Labour Party, London.
[50] Crouch, C. 2003, op. cit., p.21.
[51] Hare, D. 2003, *The Permanent Way*, Faber and Faber, London.
[52] Freedland, M. 2001, " The Marketisation of Public Services" in Crouch, C., Eder, K., Tambini, D., (ed.s) *Citizenship, Markets and the State*, Clarendon Press, Oxford.
[53] Lawrence, F. 2005, "Precarious Existence of Thousands in Britain's Underclass" in *The Guardian*, 10/01/2005.
[54] Corry et al, 1997, op. cit.
[55] IPPR, 2001, op. cit., o.203.
[56] Cited in Timmins, N. 2002b, "New Board to 'Raise Levels of Debate' over PPP Public Services" in *Financial Times*, 22/11/2002.
[57] Unison, 2000, *Contracting Out and the Two Tier Workforce*, Best Value Intelligence Unit, Unison; Sachdev, S. 2001, *Contracting Culture: From CCT to PPPs*, Unison, London.
[58] Sachdev, S. 2004, *Paying the Cost: Public Private Partnerships and the Public Service Workforce*, Catalyst, London.
[59] Morgan, P. and Allington, N. 2002, "Has the Public Sector Retained it's 'Model Employer' Status?" in *Public Money and Management*, Jan-March, p.37.
[60] Labour Party, 2001, op. cit., p.6.
[61] Willets, D.1993, *The Opportunities for Private Funding in the* NHS, Occasional Paper, p.15.
[62] IPPR, 2001, op. cit., p.201.
[63] National Audit Office (NAO), 2003, *The Operational Performance of PFI Prisons,* 16/06/2003, TSO, p.33.
[64] H M Treasury, 2003, *PFI, Meeting the Investment Challenge*, H M Treasury, London, p.69.
[65] Blair, T. 2002, op. cit., p.18
[66] Ibid.
[67] Turner, D. 2005, "Red Tape Burden a Big Labour Pain" in *Financial Times*, 29/03/2005
[68] See Taylor, R. 2002, *Britain's World of Work – Myths and Realities*, Economic and Social Research Council, Swindon.
[69] Taylor, R. 2002, op. cit.
[70] Timmins, N. 2002a, "Popular Pensions shift Pressure onto Taxpayer" in *Financial Times*, 20/05/2002.
[71] Timmins, N. 2003, "Public Sector Pensions Trail in Shift from Final Salary" in *Financial Times*, 18/02/2003. There are 4.7 million employees with final salary schemes in the public sector and 4.4 million in the private sector. In 1997 there were 5 million public sector employees compared to 21.7 million in the private sector (the latter are cited in Morgan, P. and Allington, N. 2002, op. cit.)

[72] Trade Union Congress (TUC), 2003, *Pension Watch 2003,; Analysis of UK Director and EmployeePensions*, online at www.tuc.org.uk.
[73] Sachdev, S.,2004, op. cit.; Prison Service Pay Review Body (PSPRB), 2005, *Fourth Report on England and Wales*, Cm 6478, TSO, London; DLA MCG Consulting, 2004).
[74] PSPRB 2005
[75] Some private prisons pay staff on a lower rate while under initial training. Figures given are for staff after training.
[76] Normal pay scales ends at £24,868. Staff can then receive long service awards.
[77] DLA MCG Consulting, 2004, *Privately Managed Custodial Services*, DLA MCG Consulting, Liverpool.
[78] Public Accounts Committee, 1999.
[79] Income Data Services, 2003, *Government Issues New Rules on Public Sector Contracting*, IDS Brief 728, March.
[80] Crouch, C. 2003, op. cit., p.16.
[81] Power, M. 1999, *The Audit Society (Fabian Society Spring Lecture, 05/06/1999)*, Clarendon Press, Oxford.
[82] Offer, A. 2003, op. cit., p.30
[83] Marquand, D. 2004, op. cit., p.124.
[84] Reid, J. 2005, Limits of the Market, Constraints of the State: the Public Good and the NHS, The Social Market Foundation, London, p.38.
[85] Orwell, G. 1945, "In Defence of P.G. Wodehouse" in Orwell, S. and Angus, I. (eds), 1970, *As I Please, the Collected Essays Journalism and Letters of George Orwell,* Vol. 3, 1943-1945, p. 402.
[86] Lloyd, J. 2001, *The Protest Ethic*, Demos, London., p.86.
[87] Kuhn, T. S. 1970, *The Structure of Scientific Revolutions,* Chicago University Press, Chicago.
[88] For example O' Neil, O. 2002, *A Question of Trust*, Cambridge University Press, Cambridge; Marquand, D. 2004, op. cit.; and notably du Gay, P. 2000, *In Praise of Bureaucracy*, Sage, London.
[89] Willets, D. 1993, op. cit.; Collins, P. 2004, "The Reinventing Government Scorecard" in *Reinventing Government Again*, Social Market Foundation, p.21; Reid, J. 2005, op. cit., p.8.
[90] Hewitt, P. 2003, "Power to the People" in *Progress*, July/August, 2003.

Further Reading

Allen G. 2003, *The Private Finance Initiative*, House of Commons Research Paper 03/79, House of Commons Library
Bacon R.W and Eltis W. 1976, *Britain's Economic Problem: Two Few Producers*, Macmillan, London
Blair T. 1996, *New Britain*, Fourth Estate, London

Blair T. 2002, *The courage of our convictions, why reform of the public services is the route to social justice*, Fabian Ideas 603, Fabian Society, London

Brown G., Cook R. and Prescott J. 1994 *Financing Infrastructure Investment*, Labour Party

Collins P. (2004) 'The Reinventing Government Scorecard' in *Reinventing Government Again*, Social Market Foundation, London

Corry D., Le Grand J. and Radcliffe R. 1997, *Public Private Partnerships*, Institute of Public Policy Research, London

Crouch C. 2003, *Commercialisation or Citizenship*, Fabian Ideas 606, Fabian Society, London

ed C. Crouch, K Eder, and D. Tambini (eds), 2001, *Citizenship, Markets and the State*, Clarendon Press, Oxford

du Gay P. 2000, *In Praise of Bureaucracy*, Sage, London

Giddens A. 2002, *Where Now for New Labour?* Polity Press: Cambridge

Hare D. 2003, *The Permanent Way*, Faber & Faber, London

Institute of Public Policy Research (2001) Commission on Public Private Partnerships: Building Better Partnerships, London: Institute of Public Policy Research

International Financial Services, London (2001) Public Private Partnerships: UK Expertise for International Markets, London: IFSL accessible at www.ifsl.org.uk

International Financial Services, London (2002) Public Private Partnerships: UK Expertise for International Markets, London: IFSL accessible at www.ifsl.org.uk

Kelly G. 2000, *The New Partnership Agenda*, Institute of Public Policy Research, London

Kuhn T.S. 1970, *The structure of scientific revolutions*, London: Chicago University Press

Labour Party, 2005, Britain *forward not back*, The Labour Party

Labour Party, 2001, *Ambitions for Britain*, The Labour Party

Labour Party, 1997a, *New Labour because Britain deserves better*, The Labour Party

Labour Party, 1997b, *Labour's business manifesto: Equipping Britain for the future*, The Labour Party

Labour Party, 1991, *Opportunity Britain: Labour's Better Way for the 1990s*, The Labour Party

Leys C. 2003, *Market Driven Politics*, Verso, London

Lloyd J. (2001) *The Protest Ethic*, Demos, London

Mandelson P. and Liddle R. 1996, *The Blair Revolution*, Faber and Faber, London

Marquand D. 2004, *Decline of the public*, Polity Press, Cambridge

National Audit Office, 2003. *The Operational Performance of PFI Prisons*, TSO

O' Neill O. 2002, *A Question of Trust*, Cambridge University Press
Offer A. 2003, *Why has the public sector grown so large in market societies?* Oxford University Press
Osborne D. and Gaebler T. 1992, *Reinventing Government*, Plume, New York
Peston, R. 2005, *Brown's Britain*, Short Books, London
Pike A. 1996, *In Partnership, subject to contract*, Economic and Social Research Council
Pollock A., Shaoul J. Rowland D. and Player S. 2001, *Public services and the private sector*, The Catalyst Trust London at www.catalyst-trust.co.uk
Prison Reform Trust 1996, *Privately Managed Prisons: At What Cost?*, Prison Reform Trust, London
Prison Service Pay Review Body, 2005, Fourth Report on England and Wales, Cm 6478, TSO, London
Reid, J. 2005, *Limits of the Market, Constraints of the State: the public good and the NHS*, The Social Market Foundation, London
Robinson G. 2000, *The Unconventional Minister*, Michael Joseph, London
Sachdev S. 2004, *Paying the Cost: Public Private Partnerships and the public service workforce*, Catalyst, London
Sachdev S. 2002, "A tale of conflict and neglect: Public Private Partnerships and employment relations", in *Renewal* Vol. 10 No. 3 pp58-66
Sachdev S. 2001, *Contracting culture: from CCT to PPPs*, Unison, London
Smith A. 2000, "Delivering better public services", in *New Economy* Vol. 7, Issue 3, September
Taylor R. 2002, *Britain's World of Work – Myths and Realities*, Economic and Social Research Council
Thompson, P. 2000, "PPPs in Criminal Justice",in *New Economy* Vol. 7, Issue 3, September
Treasury H.M. 2005, www.h.m.treasury.gov.uk/document/public_private_partnerships
Treasury H.M. 2003, *PFI: meeting the investment challenge*, H M Treasury, London
Unison, 2000, *Contracting out and the two tier workforce*, Best Value Intelligence Unit, www.unison.org/resources/index.htm
Unison, 2002, *A Fair Wages Clause*, February, Unison, London
Unison, 2003, *A portrait of neglect, Unison's case for investment in the local government workforce*, Unison, London
Willets D. 1993, *The Opportunities for Private Funding in the NHS*, Occasional Paper

Chapter Nine

Developments in Global Foreign Exchange

Mario Jung and Agnes Oestreich

The volume of international trade as well as of other financial transactions which involve the exchange of currencies has increased significantly over recent years. As a consequence, the global market for foreign exchange is nowadays one of the most dynamic and liquid financial markets in the world. To enable a great variety of economic transactions within this market, there is a need for a variety of different actors. It is little wonder that the volume of foreign exchange trading increased markedly since the fall of the iron curtain and the reduction of international capital controls. Within this context, the City of London plays an extraordinary important role as the world's centre for foreign exchange trading. This chapter aims to demonstrate the City's relevance in this international financial market segment and to explain the aspects which underline London's central function for foreign exchange trading and analyse worldwide developments of the foreign exchange market

After a brief introduction, a general analysis, characterisation and description of the foreign exchange market will be presented. Thereafter, the development of the international volume and the most important types of transactions in recent years will be illustrated. The following central part of this paper describes the City's dominant position in the global market for foreign exchange. The analyses of the foreign exchange market are based on the data of the Bank for International Settlements' (BIS) "Triennial Central Bank Survey of Foreign Exchange and Derivatives Market Activity" and its national variant for the United Kingdom, published triennially by the Bank of England. Furthermore, the time horizon of this analysis covers the survey years 1989 to 2004.[1]

The Foreign Exchange Market

An average daily turnover of 1.9 trillion US dollars was realised in the global foreign exchange market in April 2004.[2] This enormous volume can be largely attributed to the continuing growth in the volume of international trade due to the increasing inter-dependence of single national economies. Nevertheless, the global foreign exchange market with its different segments is a base for many variants in the international financial business. Therefore, it is not surprising that it is the largest, and most extensive financial market in the world.[3]

The most important global currencies perform three important functions. First, they serve as a transaction currency in the international trade for goods and services. Second, they are an asset class in the international financial markets and third the most important currencies are used as reserves in the central banks of industrialised countries. Exchange rates are influenced by a variety of determinants, such as interest rates, the development of inflation rates, monetary policy decisions, developments in the stock and bond markets, political events as well as rates of economic growth. But beside these fundamental determinants there are also non-fundamental factors, such as speculation, which affect the exchange rates. In particular, this is often a trend-following behaviour of agents in the foreign exchange market, also known as herding.

There are many reasons for the exchange of different currencies.[4] The most obvious is clearing, which is directly related to the needs of international trade for goods. Further transactions in the foreign exchange market are caused by an arbitrage motive. These transactions are made due to discrepancies among foreign exchange rates which occur on different trading places at the same time. It is evident that disadvantageous and unexpected developments of the exchange rate, which can cause losses for market participants, may occur in the foreign exchange market. This is the reason for hedging whereby market participants try to protect themselves against this foreign exchange risk in the financial markets. Finally, transactions in the foreign exchange market are made due to a speculative motive. This kind of transaction is possible because changes in the exchange rate affect the composition and volume of the wealth of financial actors.

In this chapter we will describe the development of turnover volumes of these, the most important, transactions in the market for foreign exchange. To understand the functioning of these transactions, it is necessary to give a short overview (see Chart 1).

Chart 1: Instruments in the foreign exchange market

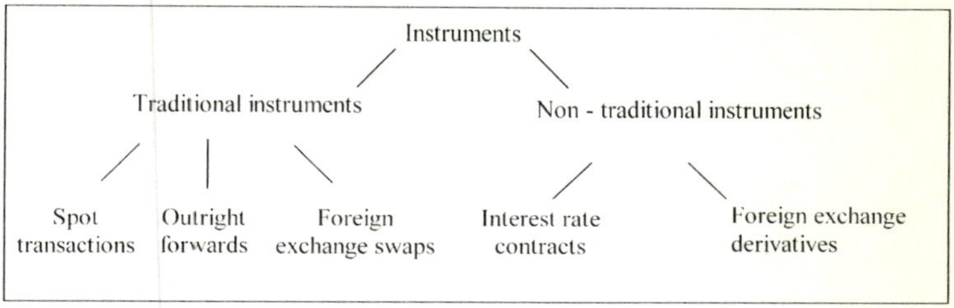

Source: Own creation.

Spot transactions, outright forwards and foreign exchange swaps are the traditional instruments in the foreign exchange market. There are also non-traditional instruments which can be classified in interest rate contracts and foreign exchange derivatives.[5] Within this context, it should be noted that outright forwards and foreign exchange swaps, which belong to the traditional instruments, are also derivatives. Because the focus of our analysis lies only on the so-called traditional instruments, the non-traditional ones are not considered.

The spot exchange market is characterised by an exchange of two currencies between the participants for immediate delivery. The exchange for value or delivery has to be executed within two business days. Consequently, the price of such an exchange is the current exchange rate, the so-called spot rate. In contrast to spot transactions, outright forwards are transactions which are settled at some time in the future (three or more business days later). These transactions are quoted for various delivery dates and for the main currencies. The currencies are exchanged at a price which is agreed on at the current date. The main advantage of outright forwards is the possibility for actors who are engaged in international transactions to protect themselves against foreign exchange risk[6]. Foreign exchange swaps are transactions which involve spot and forward transactions at the same time. This means that two currencies are exchanged for current delivery and the same amount of currencies is simultaneously re-exchanged whereas this re-exchange is settled at a specified date in the future.

The Development of Global Foreign Exchange Market Turnover

The enormity of global foreign exchange should be considered by analysing the growth and type of business over a 15 year period. The volume of this 24-hour international market showed a significant expansion in daily turnover between 1989 and 2004. Whereas the daily foreign exchange market turnover was 590 billions of US dollars in 1989, it grew by more than twice until 2004, when it reached a daily volume of 1880 billions of US dollars (see Chart 2). Since high trading volume causes high liquidity in the foreign exchange market, transaction costs in this market seem to be significantly lower than in other financial markets.

Chart 2: Global foreign exchange market turnover (daily averages in billions of US dollars)

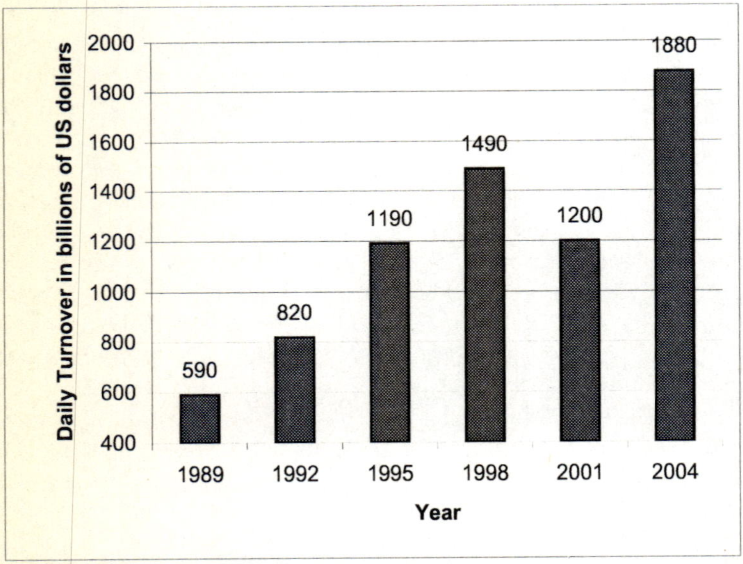

Source: Bank for International Settlements. Data adjusted for local and cross-border double-counting.

During the period, daily turnover grew, year-on-year, at an average a rate of 29.3%, although there was a negative development between the surveys of 1998 and 2001 (-19.5%). This negative growth resulted from different effects. Firstly, the euro was introduced at the beginning of 1999. Consequently, the elimination of cross-trading in the former single currencies of the euro area led to a decreased turnover. Secondly, the volume of inter-dealer businesses in the foreign exchange market fell due to the increasing role of electronic brokerage and due to processes of consolidation in the dealers' business. Although these trends can still be identified, they are less important than in 2001 and are dominated by the following arguments.[7]

Between the survey years 2001 and 2004, daily foreign exchange turnover rose by a remarkable 56.7%. This is a significant growth due to an increased volatility in the international foreign exchange market because of higher investment in appreciating currencies. This also implied higher hedging activities. Interest rate differentials have been a further contribution to the significant growth in turnover. Thus, these caused "normal" and "speculative" investments in high interest rate currencies. Finally, the role of foreign exchange as an exchangeable asset class in the portfolios of foreign investors (beneath equities, bonds and fixed income products) has become significantly more important.[8]

This higher volatility in foreign exchange trading attracted speculators with faster changing market conditions and higher expected gains. But it also entailed higher risks. Therefore, these speculators take in open or uncovered positions which can increase the volatility (and also risk) in the market but which further increase potential gains because they are able to induce a certain persistence in exchange rate trends, at least for the short-run. With this background, two key strategies have been persecuted by market participants in recent years.[9] The first strategy, the so-called 'carry-trading', is based on interest rate differentials. Actors invest in high interest rate currencies in expectation of an appreciation of the target currency against the funding currency. The second strategy, known as 'momentum trading', exploits trends in exchange rates. In this way, actors take long positions in such currencies which follow sustained appreciating trends in the recent past. Generally, both strategies can support or possibly even intensify the current trend of the respective exchange rate. It is estimated that nowadays more than 95% of foreign exchange trading is speculative.[10] It has to be mentioned though that the turnover volumes are denominated in US dollars, so we have to take into consideration the dollar's strong depreciation against other currencies between 2001 and 2004. That is the depreciation of more than 25% against the euro within this period. Hence, the dollar value of the same amount in other currencies was higher in 2004 compared to the one in 2001 which constitutes a simple valuation effect for total foreign exchange turnover.[11]

By taking a look at Chart 3, it can be recognised that there were changes in the composition of global foreign exchange market turnover. The most traditional instrument – the spot transaction – lost its leading role in turnover during the period between 1989 and 2004. Whereas 53.7% of all foreign exchange transactions in 1989 were spot transactions, this share decreased to 33.0% by 2004. It has to be mentioned that this loss is only relative since the spot transactions' volume in 2004 was nearly twice the volume of 1989 (621 billions of US dollars against 317 billions of US dollars). This trend has to be taken into account in the context of the general developments in the international financial markets where innovative and speculative instruments were constructed and implemented. Hence, derivatives also grew significantly in volume and importance, especially outright forwards and foreign exchange swaps.

We have already mentioned that the volume of spot transactions nearly doubled between 1989 and 2004. By comparison the volume of foreign exchange swaps was about five times higher in 2004 than in 1989 (944 billion US dollars compared to 190 billion US dollars), the volume of outright forwards was nearly seven times higher (208 billion US dollars compared to 27 billion US dollars). As a consequence, in 2004 about 61% of the global foreign exchange market turnover were outright forwards and foreign exchange swaps.

The most important transaction currency (see Table 1) in the global market for foreign exchange remains the US dollar with a stable share of turnover of between 80% and 90%. This dominant position of the US dollar results from its leading role as a transaction currency in the goods markets, as a reserve currency for nearly all central banks in the world and as an investment class for international rent-seeking investors and speculators.

Chart 3: The composition of global foreign exchange market turnover (daily averages in billions of US dollars and relating percentage shares of total volume)[12]

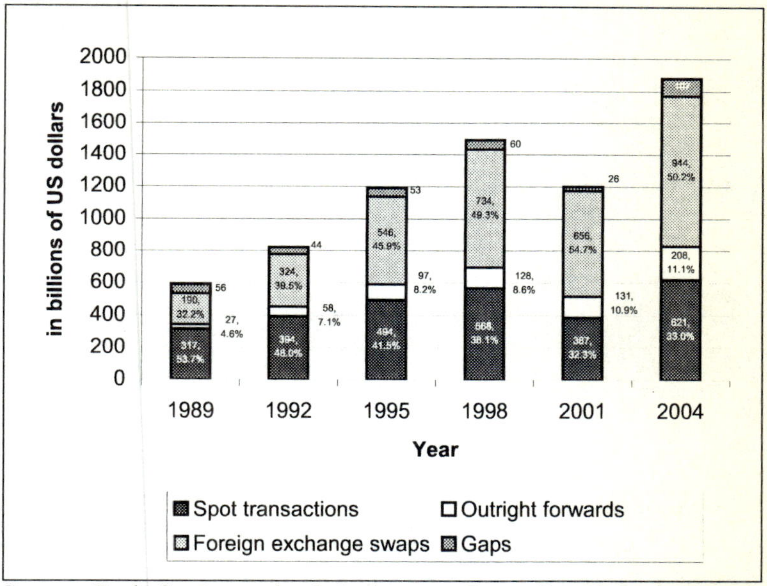

Source: Bank for International Settlements. Data adjusted for local and cross-border double-counting.

Table 1: Currency distribution of foreign exchange market turnover (percentage shares of average daily turnover)

	US dollar	euro	Deutsche Mark	Japanese yen	Pound sterling
1989	90.0	---	27.0	27.0	15.0
1992	82.0	---	39.6	23.4	13.6
1995	83.3	---	36.1	24.1	9.4
1998	87.3	---	30.1	20.2	11.0
2001	90.3	37.6	---	22.7	13.2
2004	88.7	37.2	---	20.3	16.9

Source: Bank for International Settlements. (Two currencies are involved in every single transaction)

For a long time the US dollar was followed by the Deutsche Mark in turnover, but with the implementation of European Monetary Union at the beginning of 1999 the euro as the single European currency became the dominant European currency. The credibility and the independence of the European Central Bank resulted in a high acceptance in the global financial markets. Furthermore, due to the relatively good performance of the euro in the foreign exchange market, the single currency seems set to increase its share of turnover in the future. It may even come to challenge the dollar's dominance.

The US dollar/euro currency pair obtained 28% of global foreign exchange turnover in 2004, followed by US dollar/Japanese yen with 17% and US dollar/British pound with 14%.[13]

London's dominant position in the global foreign exchange market

Trading in foreign exchange is concentrated, with more than 70% of total turnover worldwide in 2004 spread over six countries and specifically over six cities: London, New York, Tokyo, Singapore, Frankfurt and Hong Kong. As can be seen from Table 2, London is the most important place for the global foreign exchange with a share of more than 30% of worldwide daily turnover. This significance can be attributed to the City's interchange function especially between Europe and the USA. Therefore, large transcontinental flows of corporate and currency transactions can arise between the old and the new world. This argument counts also for European transactions with Asia. Hence, financial markets in London are characterised by a high share of financial transactions which are denominated in foreign currencies, especially in US dollar and euro.[14]

London, along with New York and Tokyo, is one of the three most important and biggest financial centres in the world. Whereas Tokyo and New York are global centres especially because of their large domestic markets, the City's primary perspective is an international one. For example, foreign owned banks or other financial institutions held a share of around 72% in London's foreign exchange market in 2004. North American institutions were the most important participants with a share of 45% in trading, followed by EU-Europeans with 14%. Furthermore, in 2003 around 52% of the British banking sector assets were held by foreign banks and in 2004, 277 foreign banks had branches or subsidiaries in the City's financial centre.[15] As a consequence, providing markets and financial services for foreign exchange are the reason for the City's importance in the global financial world.[16]

Even with the UK outside of the single European currency, London has played a key role in the international euro business. Due to the City's interchange function, London provides an important and transparent gateway to the euro for American and Asian investors. Therefore, London holds the key position for the development of the euro markets and financial services in Europe. Hence, for the British, it can be said that, "helping to develop deep and liquid euro markets is arguably the main contribution that we in UK can make to the success of the euro from the 'outside'."[17] Within this context, we want to emphasise the fact, that the volume of traded euros (denominated in US dollars) in the City's foreign exchange market is larger than in all the euro-area countries together.[18]

Table 2: Main trading places of the global foreign exchange market (percentage shares in total daily turnover)

	London (United Kingdom)	New York (USA)	Tokyo (Japan)	Singapore	Frankfurt (Germany)	Hong Kong
1989	25.6	16.0	15.5	7.7	---	6.8
1992	27.0	15.5	11.2	6.9	5.1	5.6
1995	29.5	15.5	10.2	6.7	4.8	5.7
1998	32.5	17.9	6.9	7.1	4.8	4.0
2001	31.2	15.7	9.1	6.2	5.5	4.1
2004	31.3	19.2	8.3	5.2	4.9	4.2

Source: Bank for International Settlements. Data adjusted for local double-counting.

It is not the objective of this chapter to discuss the pros and cons of United Kingdom's potential accession to the euro, but from the City's point of view it can be argued that the euro is more an opportunity than a threat. This results from the great expertise in trading with foreign exchange, the extraordinary banking infrastructure and the great varieties for investments in foreign currencies which London as a global financial centre is able to offer. Though some authors claim that United Kingdom's non-membership in the European Monetary

Union causes "missed opportunities" for the City,[19] it is reasonable to assume that these missed opportunities can be related to the transaction costs of the exchange between euro and British pound, which lead to losses in liquidity compared to the optimal case with a single currency for the United Kingdom and the countries of the current European Monetary Union. But it seems to be quite difficult to quantify these missed opportunities and besides, in total, the City gained from the single currency in its business and turnover: "Although the UK is outside the single currency, the City dominates most euro-related business. It is London, rather than Frankfurt or Paris, which can be characterised as the financial centre of the euro."[20]

Representatives of the Bank of England categorise several structural developments in the euro-markets which have been and are still supported by the City's excellence and innovative structures.[21] As a consequence, these changes offer great potential for City's business, especially in foreign exchange, because these structural developments lead to growth in foreign exchange activity.

Increasingly integrated market trading in the euro across borders

Market trading in the euro becomes more and more integrated across borders, although some market sectors are still not fully integrated. In general liquidity in the euro markets have grown and interest rate spreads narrowed.

Growth in corporate bond issuance

The volume of corporate euro denominated bonds and equity issuance has increased. Since there is no longer currency risk in the euro corporate bond markets, central risk are nowadays credit and liquidity. Furthermore, a tendency in the euro area towards an equity culture which uses the City's supply in expertise and varieties in investment strategies can be seen.

Diversification of investment

Nowadays, global investors diversify their equity and bond portfolios across national or continental borders, which means an investment tendency away from national markets.

Euro financial markets are working quite well

A "natural" result of European Monetary Union is the growth in trading volume in the different financial markets which are already more or less integrated. Due to European harmonisation of wholesale payment systems (TARGET) cross-border activity increased with the implementation of the euro. But problems still arise from the existence of different systems for the trading, clearing and settlement of securities across the European countries. Therefore, it is an important goal in the future to achieve a functioning and efficient integration of these systems.

Having described these structural developments in the euro markets, it is necessary to emphasise the City's fundamental and pioneering role in these processes: it provides a lead through innovation and it is able to set established standards for excellence. Furthermore, London offers financial services and products which are not provided in continental Europe. Beneath these aspects, the City has a unique financial and informational infrastructure which gives London a significant head start in doing foreign exchange business in comparison to other financial centres. One US dollar is one US dollar, no matter where the US dollar is traded. Hence, a single unit of a special currency is a perfectly homogeneous product in the international markets which means that the greatest volumes of a currency are not necessarily traded in the home country but in the trading place with the lowest costs. Because of the City's structure, London is able to offer foreign exchange at the lowest transaction costs worldwide. As a consequence, even with the single European currency, London can hold its worldwide leading position in foreign exchange and as the dominating financial centre in Europe.

The development of the foreign exchange market turnover in London

In 2004, the City's daily turnover of foreign exchange had a volume of 753 billions of US dollars. This amount in 2004 was more than four times higher than the volume in 1989 (184 billions of US dollars).

Chart 4: London's foreign exchange market turnover (daily averages in billions of US dollars)

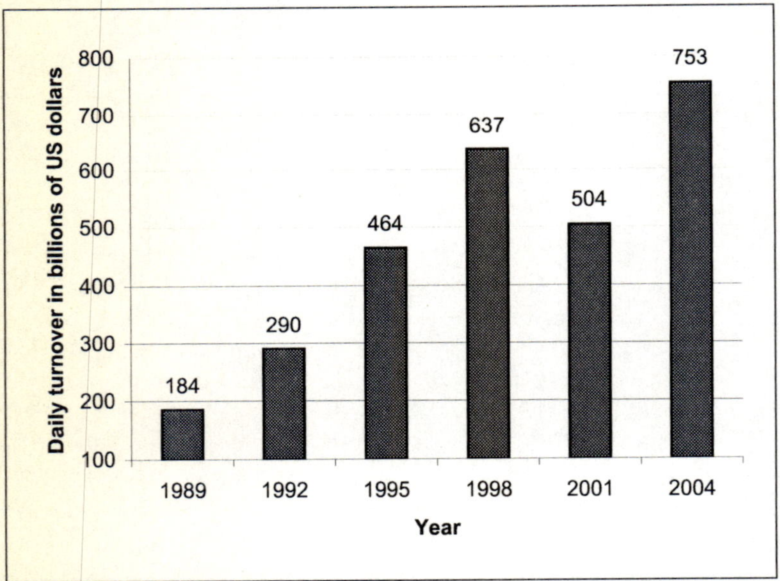

Source: Bank of England. Data adjusted for local double-counting.

The average growth rate between these years was 36.6% (although the trading volume decreased by more than 20% between 1998 and 2001 for). This negative trend was caused by several factors which obtain partly also for the global reduction in foreign exchange turnover, especially the introduction of the euro with the deleted trade between the euro-countries. First of all the consolidation process in the banking sector and the increased role of electronic brokerage led to a decline in inter-dealer business in the City's foreign exchange market. Since several big market players merged, concentration in London's foreign exchange market intensified meaning lower trading volume. What is remarkable is that the market share of the top ten principals in UK's foreign exchange market increased from 50% in 1998 to 58% in 2001; the top twenty from 69% to 80%.[22] Between 2001 and the BIS-survey in 2004 market turnover increased by nearly 50% which can also be explained by the general trends in the global market for foreign exchange. This growth in foreign exchange turnover seems to reflect a longer-term trend rather than a short-term effect. Consequently, 84% of the surveyed banks in the United Kingdom evaluated London's turnover level in foreign exchange as 'normal' in 2004.[23]

Chart 5: The composition of London's foreign exchange market turnover (daily averages, in billions of US dollars)

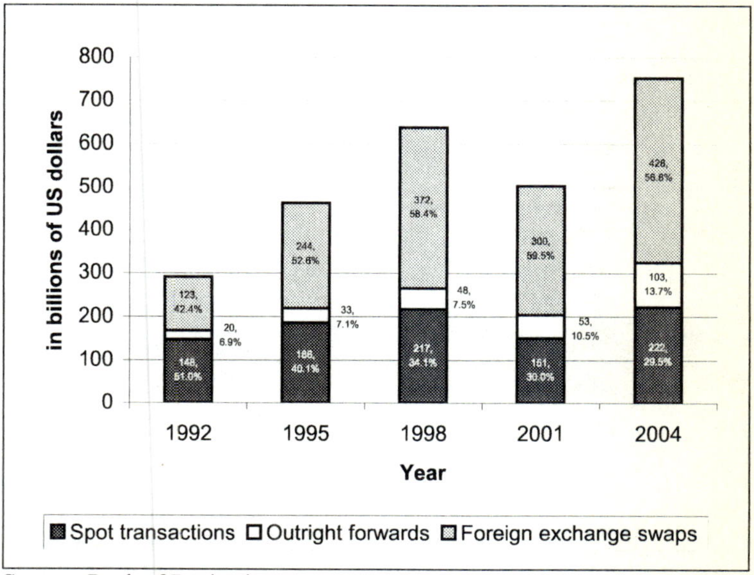

Source: Bank of England.

Developments within the single components were similar to the global ones: spot transactions lost their dominance in their share of total turnover between 1992 and 2004 (from 51.0% to 29.5%) and the volumes of outright forwards and foreign exchange swaps as the most common derivatives grew with high rates. As a consequence, together they account for more than 70% of turnover in 2004 (outright forwards: 13.7%, foreign exchange swaps: 56.8%). Comparable to the worldwide currency distribution of daily foreign exchange market turnover (see Table 1) the US dollar is also the City's favourite foreign exchange currency by trading volume (see Table 3).

Table 3: Currency distribution of London's foreign exchange market turnover (percentage shares of average daily turnover)

	US dollar	euro	Deutsche Mark	Pound sterling	Japanese yen
1992	81	---	41	24	15
1995	84	---	36	16	20
1998	88	---	32	18	14
2001	92	41	---	24	17
2004	90	42	---	28	15

Source: Bank of England. (Two currencies are involved in every single transaction.)

Since the implementation of the single European currency in 1999, the euro took over the role as the second most important currency in London from the Mark. The trading volume of the Japanese Yen is not as big as the global one. Important from the City's point of view is the growing importance of the Pound sterling characterised by an increasing share in London's exchange market from 16% in 1995 to 28% in 2004. This growth became especially obvious after the implementation of the euro.

Conclusion

The global market for foreign exchange has been one of the most dynamic segments in the global financial markets of the last fifteen years: turnover grew by remarkable rates, and considerable innovative investment instruments were tailored to the needs of international actors in the foreign exchange market. This general development was especially supported by the City of London, the main financial centre in the foreign exchange market, with world shares by far greater than New York, Singapore or Frankfurt and Paris. Although the United Kingdom chose to remain outside the euro, London itself gained from the new currency by playing a leading role in the euro markets. As we have seen, the ongoing structural developments in these euro markets are also driven by the City's great expertise in international financial business, its extraordinary informational and human capital infrastructure for the financial sector. Due to the City's role as a mediator between the American, Asian and European continent, London's success is in particular dependent on its international business, especially in the foreign exchange market. Beside London's dominance in the traditional foreign exchange market it should also be noted that in the over-the-counter derivatives markets London plays the leading role with a global share of more than 40% in 2004.[24] Hence, the City was also a dominating actor in the construction of financial innovations which are used in the international trading with foreign exchange.

Since the implementation of the single European currency, London has not suffered from losses in its foreign exchange business which underlines the City's dominant position and relevance in the foreign exchange market. But it is questionable if the undisputed gains from the launch of the euro would not have been higher with the United Kingdom's participation in European Monetary Union

The City's role as one of the top three leading financial centres in the world seems set to remain unchanged, especially its dominance in its foreign exchange activity. This is due to the credibility and acceptance of international banks and exchange dealers. And finally it is significant that London offers a great and unique informational infrastructure, highly skilled human capital and global financial institutions which consider London to be the natural centre of their foreign exchange activity.

Notes

[1] For two graphs relating to London, data material from 1989 was unavailable.

[2] See Bank for International Settlements, 2005, *Triennial Central Bank Survey – Foreign Exchange and Derivatives Market Activity in 2004*, Basel, p. 1.

[3] See International Financial Services, London, 2004a, *Foreign Exchange – City Business Series*, downloadable from www.ifsl.org.uk/uploads/CBS_Foreign_Exchange_2004.pdf, p. 1.

[4] For further information see Yarbrough, B.V.; Yarbrough, R.M. 1997, *The World Economy: Trade and Finance*, 4th ed., Fort Worth, pp. 497-501.
[5] Interest rate options, forward rate agreements and interest rate swaps belong to the interest rate contracts. Currency options and currency swaps can be counted to the foreign exchange derivatives.
[6] See Gandolfo, G. 2001, *International Finance and Open-Economy Macroeconomics*, Berlin, p. 16.
[7] See International Financial Services, London, 2004a, *Foreign Exchange – City Business Series*, downloadable from www.ifsl.org.uk/uploads/ CBS_Foreign_Exchange_2004.pdf, p. 1.
[8] See Galati, G.; Melvin, M. 2004, "Why has FX Trading Surged? Explaining the 2004 Triennial Survey" in *BIS Quarterly Review*, December 2004, p. 68. For a more detailed analysis of the trends between 2001 and 2004 see pp. 69-74 and Bank for International Settlements 2005, *Triennial Central Bank Survey – Foreign Exchange and Derivatives Market Activity in 2004*, Basel, pp. 2, 5-6.
[9] See Galati, G.; Melvin, M. 2004, op. cit., p.69.
[10] See International Financial Services, London (ed.) (2004a), *Foreign Exchange – City Business Series*, downloadable from www.ifsl.org.uk/uploads/ CBS_Foreign_Exchange_2004.pdf, p. 5.
[11] See Bank of England, 2004b, "The foreign exchange and over-the-counter derivatives markets in the United Kingdom" in *Bank of England Quarterly Bulletin*, Winter 2004, p.470. Alternatively, we could have taken the turnover volumes at constant exchange rates. But that would have had the significant disadvantage for the further analysis that the single variants of transactions cannot be calculated at constant exchange rates because of missing data material.
[12] Information concerning the included gaps can be read in Bank for International Settlements, 2005, *Triennial Central Bank Survey – Foreign exchange and derivatives market activity in 2004*, Basel, p. 42. These gaps are mainly deduced from two origins: "Gaps in reporting stem from two sources: incomplete reporting […] in the countries providing data, and less than full coverage of the range of countries in which the surveyed activity takes place."
[13] See Bank for International Settlements, 2004, *Triennial Central Bank Survey of Foreign Exchange and Derivatives Market Activity in April 2004 – Preliminary Global Results*, Basel, p. 12.
[14] See Clark, G.L. 2002, "London in the European Financial Services Industry: Locational Advantage and Product Complementarities" in *Journal of Economic Geography*, Vol. 2, Oxford University Press, p.438 and HM Treasury, 2003, *The Location of Financial Activity and the Euro*, London, p. 10, 2.5.
[15] See International Financial Services, London, 2004a, *Foreign Exchange – City Business Series*, downloadable from www.ifsl.org.uk/uploads/ CBS_Foreign_Exchange_2004.pdf, p. 2.

[16] Clementi, D. 2001, "The City and the Euro: Innovation and Excellence" in *BIS Review* 11/2001, p.1.
[17] Clementi, D. 2001, op. cit., p.2.
[18] See International Financial Services, London, 2004a, *Foreign Exchange – City Business Series*, downloadable from www.ifsl.org.uk/uploads/CBS_Foreign_Exchange_2004.pdf, pp. 1-2.
[19] See for example Davis, E.P. 2002, "The City, Financial-Centre Development and EMU", Presentation given at the NIESR/CEPII conference *British Business and the Euro* in London, 6 February 2002.
[20] Luo, C.-M. 2002, *A Choice between Two Paradigms: What the Euro Implies for the City of London as a World Financial Centre*, UACES European Studies On-line Essays, downloadable from www.uaces.org/E53Luo.pdf, p. 13.
[21] See for the following, Townend, J. 2002, *The euro, the UK and the City of London*, downloadable from www.bankofengland.co.uk/publications/Speeches/2002/Speech157.pdf, pp. 10-11 and Clementi, D. 2001, op. cit., pp.2-3.
[22] See Bank of England, 2001, "The Foreign Exchange and Over-the-Counter Derivatives Markets in the United Kingdom" in *Bank of England Quarterly Bulletin*, Winter 2001, pp.418-419.
[23] See Bank of England 2004b, "The Foreign Exchange and Over-the-Counter Derivatives Markets in the United Kingdom" in *Bank of England Quarterly Bulletin*, Winter 2004, p.472.
[24] See for this and the following Bank of England 2004b, op. cit., pp. 475-477 and Bank for International Settlements, 2005, *Triennial Central Bank Survey – Foreign Exchange and Derivatives Market Activity in 2004*, Basel, p.19. Over-the-counter derivatives are the following: on the one hand, currency derivatives like outright forwards and foreign exchange swaps (integrated in the preceding analysis of this paper), currency swaps and options, on the other hand, interest rate derivatives like forward rate agreements, swaps and options.

Chapter Ten

Governing the City of London in a Global Era: the Promise and Problems of Transgovernmental Regulatory Networks

Richard Woodward

In recent decades regulation of the City of London's financial markets has altered dramatically. The most conspicuous change, and the one which has attracted the most academic comment, has been the growing role of the state in governing the City's financial markets. Since the late 1970s the prevailing system of self-regulation by City grandees has been gradually superseded by a regulatory system underpinned by the state's coercive powers. This process culminated in 1997 with the announcement of a new regulatory behemoth, the Financial Services Authority (FSA), which subsumed the patchwork of existing regulators and later usurped the Bank of England's responsibility for the prudential supervision of the banking system following the passage of the 1998 Bank of England Act.[1] However, the principal focus of this chapter is on the accompanying, albeit less remarked, trend towards the internationalisation and transnationalisation of City regulation (the regional or European dimension of this process is covered by Graham Bishop in this volume). Today, the rules governing the City's financial markets are set within a framework determined by international financial institutions and transgovernmental regulatory networks. This chapter seeks to assess whether this 'quiet revolution'[2] in global financial regulation is contributing to the successful management of the City of London's financial markets.

For reasons which will be explained in greater detail below international regulatory networks have been widely touted by academics and practitioners as an integral part of solution to the conundrums of governing globalised financial markets.[3]

This chapter takes issue with this stance and argues that as they are presently constituted international regulatory networks are part of the problem rather than the solution. This misplaced optimism is the result of a fallacy which infects much of the conventional wisdom on the management of global financial markets, namely that the principal dilemmas are thought to arise from markets 'going global' whilst the jurisdiction of the regulatory authorities responsible for governing them remains bound by the territoriality of nation states. In defining the problem this way policymakers and regulators are able to comfort themselves with the idea that all that is required to ensure the effective regulation of global financial markets is to erect regulatory institutions at the same global 'level' at which markets are operating. Unquestionably the integration of financial markets across national boundaries does create additional difficulties for regulatory authorities including how to reconcile different regulatory structures and accessing information about the overseas activities of domestic financial institutions.

The key point here is that it creates additional difficulties. As Bryant's comprehensive review of global finance points out, financial markets pose unique regulatory challenges even when they are confined within national boundaries. The integration of financial markets across national boundaries merely complicates the problems confronting regulatory authorities.[4] The real problems confronting regulators arise not from globalisation but from the nature of financial markets. Currently, the prevailing attitude of regulators around the globe and the international regulatory networks they have formed is that the market mechanism is the most efficient way of allocating scarce financial resources. Therefore the appropriate role for regulators is interpreted as merely providing the conditions under which market signals can operate most effectively. The problem is that this evangelical faith in the working of the market mechanism is flatly contradicted by a history of financial markets punctuated by "manias, panics and crashes" [5] consequent upon the kinds of behaviour dismissed as implausible or irrational by proselytes of the laissez faire creed who maintain that market activity is underpinned by rational, utility maximising behaviour. If, as George Soros has suggested, "financial markets are inherently unstable, imposing market discipline means imposing instability"[6] the growing importance of pro-market networks of regulators may be endangering financial stability in the City of London.

Transgovernmental Networks and Global Financial Regulation

From the late 1950s onwards the reintegration of financial markets was spurred by the expansion of multinational production, the return of currency convertibility to Western Europe, and the development of Euromarkets combined to speed the reintegration of financial markets. This rise in cross-border capital flows placed a heightened the strains on the Bretton Woods system of international monetary management culminating in its collapse in 1971. The rising incidence of crisis and the financial upheavals wrought by the oil price hikes contributed to a perception that existing forms of international cooperation predicated on conventional international institutions could not, on their own, cope with the consequences of financial globalisation. It was against this background that the promise of transgovernmental relationships began to receive greater attention.

Unlike international organisations, where the principle actors are unitary nation states, transgovernmental relations and networks consist of "direct interactions between agencies (governmental subunits) of different governments where those agencies act relatively autonomously from central governmental control".[7] In the financial domain the principle agencies involved in these liaisons have been national regulatory bodies and central bankers. Networks vary in their intensity and level of institutionalisation. At one extreme, and the primary focus of this chapter, are fully fledged "transgovernmental regulatory organisations"[8] which have a full institutional apparatus including a formal constitution and supporting secretariat. At the other extreme transgovernmental networks can consist of nothing more than bi-lateral or multilateral Memoranda of Understanding (MOU) whereby national agencies agree to exchange information or develop agreements on best practice on an ad hoc basis.

Transgovernmental networks perform a number of functions but arguably their two most important tasks are to act as conduits for the exchange of information, ideas, and intelligence and to promote international best practice. At the most basic level the former role can involve little more than agreement by national regulators to exchange information upon request about a financial intermediary authorised to operate in one jurisdiction but which also conducts financial activities in another. Kapstein maintains that in order to grapple with the exigencies of financial globalisation industrialised countries have evolved the concept of "international cooperation based on home country control".[9] This position holds that it is the responsibility of home regulators to authorise and oversee the activities of domestic institutions operating abroad. The failure of Barings Bank, which was able to evade regulatory oversight by the simple expedient of locating its subsidiary in Singapore,[10] amply demonstrated that accurate and timely information is a crucial prerequisite for supervising the overseas activities of financial institutions.

The exchange of information and ideas also morphs into the network's functions as promoters of best practice. Consisting of leading regulatory professionals transgovernmental networks are vital repositories of expertise. This expertise finds its outlet in developing codes and standards of best practice which signatory regulators are expected to apply in their own jurisdictions. In other words, domestic regulatory practices must be consistent with internationally permitted benchmarks. Though they are not widely renowned amongst the general public the standards enshrined codes like the Basle Committee on Banking Supervision's (BCBS) Core Principles for Effective Banking Supervision and the International Organisation of Securities Commissions (IOSCO) Objectives and Principles of Securities Regulation are widely respected yardsticks applied by those who work in the arcane world of international finance. Importantly, however, these codes of practice have no force in international law and networks do not have any formal enforcement mechanisms of their own. Until recently compliance depended on a strong sense of moral suasion and peer and self assessment. Now compliance with the codes of practice promulgated by networks is routinely gauged under the rubric of the Reports on the Observance of Standards and Codes (ROSCs)[11] carried out as part of the IMF's Financial Sector Assessment Program (FSAP). ROSCs and FSAPs are powerful disciplinary devices because breaches of international standards will be highlighted and are likely to have a detrimental impact on the reputation of the financial centre concerned and the terms and conditions on which institutions located there can gain access to global capital markets.

International Regulatory Networks in the City of London

The City of London is distinguished from other major financial centres such as New York and Tokyo because of the extent to which it offers services to international capital.[12] Of the 691 banks authorised to operate in the UK 501 (72.5%) are incorporated outside the UK and are responsible for managing 56% of the £4,969bn assets held in the UK banking system.[13] As of September 2004 the UK banking sector originated the world's largest share of cross border lending (20%) and cross-border borrowing (22%), an amount larger than any two financial centres combined.[14] The pattern is replicated in the foreign exchange and securities markets. With a daily turnover of $753bn the UK's foreign exchange markets account for 31.3% of the world's foreign exchange transactions, compared with 19.2% in the United States and 8.9% in Japan.[15] In the international bond markets City institutions issued 20% of the world's international bonds valued at $321bn in 2004.[16] The City is also the largest market for foreign equities. According to the World Federation of Exchanges London was the leading location for cross-border trading in equities, accounting for 44% of global turnover in 2004. Moreover, the total of 340 foreign companies listed on the London Stock Exchange in July 2005 is second only in number to the 448 listed on the New York Stock Exchange.[17]

The international dimension of the City's business means that it has always been vulnerable to external shocks. Throughout the 1980s the free market zeal of the Thatcher administration led to the progressive opening of the City's markets to foreign competition. This liberalisation programme unquestionably helped to secure London's pre-eminence as the hub for international financial activity. However, the further influx of foreign owned firms and capital left the City uniquely exposed to the vicissitudes of global finance and "compelled British financial regulators to collaborate more intensively with their counterparts in other jurisdictions".[18]

British financial regulators have been in the vanguard of those nurturing transgovernmental relationships. In 1974 Gordon Richardson and George Blunden, respectively the then Governor and head of banking supervision at the Bank of England, met to discuss means of fostering international co-operation amongst national regulators. Their dialogue pointed to the possibility of forming a committee of central bank supervisors whose chief purpose would be to act as a forum for the exchange of information. Later that same year Richardson proposed this idea to the Group of 10 central bankers gathering at Basle. The meeting concurred and what eventually became known as the Basle Committee on Banking Supervision was born. Subsequently UK authorities were one of the first signatories to IOSCO, the transgovernmental network responsible for the international regulation of securities, while the 1990s saw the extension of transgovernmental practice to the field of insurance with the inception of the International Association of Insurance Supervisors (IAIS).

By the late 1980s the relationship between UK regulators and overseas brethren had deteriorated markedly.[19] However, the scandals engulfing the Bank for Credit and Commerce International (BCCI), Barings Bank and the Sumitomo Corporation were humbling events for the City's regulatory community and reawakened interest in international cooperation. The significant thing about these episodes was that, obvious though the shortcomings in domestic regulatory procedures undoubtedly were, they each had a clear international dimension which better collaboration between national regulatory authorities might have forestalled. The creation of the FSA gave fresh impetus to initiatives aimed at repairing the fabric of transgovernmental relations. For the first time the Financial Services and Markets Act 2000, the legislation which proscribes the overarching framework for the FSA, enshrines in statute the principle of international co-operation. The Act insists that, providing certain conditions are met, the FSA must use its power to assist overseas regulatory authorities.[20]

The Financial Services and Markets Act also lays down four statutory objectives for the FSA: to maintain confidence in the UK financial system, to protect consumers, to reduce financial crime and to promote public understanding of the financial system. With the possible exception of the final objective each of these undertakings has a significant international component. However, the FSA's regulatory philosophy proceeds from the premise that "there is no possible way, in this current environment, of hoping to police all investment activity on a host state basis".[21] Therefore in order to meet its statutory objectives the FSA pledged as part of its "new approach to regulation" to be "influential on the world stage, helping to raise standards, maintaining the position of the UK as a global financial centre and protecting consumers of UK regulated firms".[22] The FSA has eagerly embraced the international components of its work. First, the FSA has expanded its international endeavours with alacrity. In the four years from its inception the FSA more than doubled its membership of international committees to 144 and as of 2001 had in force 168 bilateral and multilateral MoUs with other regulatory agencies.[23] In addition to these formalised arrangements the FSA has instigated a range of informal initiatives. To take one example every six months the FSA meets with the Federal Reserve Bank of New York and the Swiss Banking Commission to discuss the supervision of Credit Suisse and UBS.[24] Second, international regulatory responsibilities have prompted the FSA to remodel its internal architecture. Unlike some regulators the FSA does not possess a designated international affairs division. However, in 2001 of the International Policy Committee was inaugurated at the FSA to act as the focal point of the organisation's external regulatory relations. However, the FSA decided that with the growing importance of international matters to FSA deliberations it would be more sensible for decisions about international strategy to be taken in a common framework and the committee was disbanded as part of the FSA's internal reorganisation in 2004.

In other words the growing importance of the international regulatory dimension necessitated further architectural change. Finally, British financial regulators have been lauded for their strong record of incorporating and enforcing international codes and standards. In 2003, the International Monetary Fund's (IMF's) Financial System Stability Assessment noted that "U.K. systems of regulation and supervision are in general fully or largely compliant show (sic) a high degree of observance with international financial sector standards and codes".[25] Indeed the report identified no substantive flaws in the international aspects of City regulation and confined itself to making minor technical recommendations, especially in the field of insurance, to reflect the sophistication of the City's markets.

Thus, the last two decades have witnessed a steadily escalating commitment to the principles of international co-operation to the extent that today "the international policy arena already accounts for most initiatives affecting the regulation of UK financial services".[26] The question is whether and to what degree this commitment is helping to secure stability for the City of London's financial markets.

Transgovernmental Networks and Governance in the City of London

To briefly recapitulate, the 1970s saw rising unease about the disjuncture between regulatory bodies whose power stopped at the borders of sovereign states and financial markets which were increasingly integrated across these boundaries. Under these conditions there was declining confidence in the capacity of domestic regulatory institutions to effectively supervise their own financial markets and fears that the emancipation of markets from political authority might lead to outcomes antithetical to political and social stability. The solution advocated by the regulatory community was a qualitative and quantitative expansion of international collaboration to meet in order to try and secure at international level the benefits secured by domestic regulators at the national level. Although much of the remainder of this chapter will be critical of the ideology underpinning leading transgovernmental networks it would be churlish not to acknowledge their achievements. It is generally agreed that transgovernmental networks have had a number of beneficial effects in the City and elsewhere including enhancing the quality of financial surveillance, bolstering trust through promoting mutual understanding and assistance, building regulatory capacity in emerging markets, and augmenting the capacity of regulators to maximise compliance with domestic regulatory measures.[27] Given the extraordinary complexity of London's global interlinkages it seems certain that networks must have made a contribution to the financial and regulatory soundness of the City. Nonetheless, a closer inspection of the policies promoted through transgovernmental networks ought to give cause for concern.

First, transgovernmental networks have by and large acted to facilitate rather than negate the integration of financial markets.[28] Therefore even if one accepts that the main dilemma confronting regulators is the continued integration of financial markets then networks appear a self-defeating response to the problem. Second, it is the contention of this chapter that the principle problems arise not from the globalisation of financial markets but from the pathologies inherent in all financial markets. Domestic regulators, and the transgovernmental networks they have spawned, have bought into a deeply flawed analysis of how financial markets operate and, it is argued, have contributed to the development of codes and practices that threaten financial stability in the City of London.

This second area of concern pertains to type of regulation and the notion of the public good. As Underhill argues "regulatory agencies ostensibly shape the market environment to accomplish a public purpose which the unfettered interplay of private interests would obfuscate".[29] Indeed the four statutory objectives outlined in the Financial Services and Markets Act succinctly encapsulates the FSA's public purpose and are typical of the aims and objectives of financial regulators the world over. However, in the last three decades academic and regulatory discourses on financial markets have come to be dominated to an overwhelming degree by the notion, propagated by neo-classical economists,[30] of the efficient markets hypothesis (EMH). The foundation of the EMH rests upon the premise that all market participants are rational, utility maximising agents equipped with perfect information on which to assess risk and take investment decisions. The prices of financial instruments are determined by the risk assessments made by individual participants. The theory maintains that prices will follow a 'random walk' in response to new information which may alter the perceived risk of a given financial instrument.[31] The market is thus viewed as a stable, self equilibrating mechanism.

According to this perspective instability in financial markets arises principally from two sources. The first culprit is distortion introduced to the market mechanism by some exogenous factor, principally government interference. The second are market failures resulting from incomplete or inaccurate information. This messianic confidence in market forces stands the traditional logic of financial regulation on its head and has generated certain types of policy prescription from regulatory bodies. Whereas previously regulators sought to inoculate social, political and economic institutions against the potentially deleterious effects of financial markets they now perceive their proper role to be to impose market discipline by removing impediments to the free functioning and effective operation of the market mechanism. In other words, rather than seeking to regulate the market mechanism, the market mechanism is being deployed as a tool of regulation, a means of compelling discipline amongst market participants. In the UK particularly "the trend is preference for more market freedom and less state intervention, with the state providing the residual framework required for efficient market operations".[32] Rather than obfuscating the pubic purpose there is an anodyne assumption that the free interplay of market forces can be the effective guarantor of the public interest. Exposing institutions to the discipline of the market will mean fewer financial crises, less financial crime, and more prudent investment decisions obviating the need for huge investor protection schemes.

Each of the major transgovernmental networks has, as an overarching objective, the promotion of financial stability and infer that the best way of achieving this is to ensure that markets work efficiently.[33] The chief means through which this has been pursued is devising a panoply of disclosure standards for firms, exchanges, and states. By enhancing the information available to market participants it is thought that this will lead to better investment decisions and more efficient markets. Seven of the Twelve Key Standards for Sound Financial Systems identified by the Financial Stability Forum (FSF) are sponsored or co-sponsored by transgovernmental networks.[34] A cursory glance at any of them reveals a prominent emphasis on measures that seek to 'purify' markets and ensure that they operate efficiently. This approach to markets also leads to the primary responsibility for day to day supervision being devolved to the senior management of financial institutions. The belief is that markets will evolve powerful incentives for firms to put in place rigorous internal procedures which will ensure prudent investment decisions.

Acolytes of the free market creed confidently assert that "there is no other proposition in economics which has more solid empirical evidence supporting it than the Efficient Markets Hypothesis".[35] Once all economic and social institutions have been exposed to this cleansing and invigorating gale of market forces regulators can recede into the background and allow market forces to efficiently allocate financial resources and ensure stability. However, if these assumptions, which at times are articulated as articles of faith rather than empirically supported theories, cannot be substantiated or can be contradicted then much of the basis of modern transgovernmental regulation is problematic. Evidence contradicting the EMH is repudiated as anomalous or as having its root cause in the aforementioned influence of exogenous factors. Nevertheless, there have always been doubts about the extent to which the EMH amounts to a complete or accurate account of how markets operate.

Even if one accepts the genius of financial markets, there is, as the doyen of financiers Warren Buffet has observed, a massive difference between the belief that markets are always efficient and the belief that they mostly efficient. Indeed Buffet's record could be held up as the antithesis of the EMH. Given that all market participants have the same information it is not possible even for 'experts' to be persistently 'ahead of the curve' and extract higher returns from financial trading, yet he, and other skilled practitioners have consistently outperformed the market. However, once one acknowledges that there might be problems, even if only some of the time, that are inherent to the market mechanism then the supervisory arrangements inaugurated by transgovernmental networks predicated on a belief in the efficiency of markets look less enticing.

The market mechanism can have a number of pernicious effects some of which, paradoxically, are the consequence of the very advantages market forces are supposed to confer. Proponents of the market point to their capacity to innovate and to generate new products to manage the resultant risks. However, many argue that many recent innovations, such as the development and widespread use of derivative instruments, pose a colossal threat to the very survival of the global financial system.[36] In a world of rapid innovation it seems the height of conceit to believe that the risks associated with these products can be fully understood, accurately priced or be contained by an ever more elaborate system of technocratic rules. Moreover, in-keeping with their general pro-market stance regulatory bodies are now preoccupied with promoting the competitiveness and fomenting innovation in the financial centres for which they are responsible. During the transition to the FSA ministers, regulators and senior officials repeatedly emphasised the need for a set of regulatory values that "ensure the right kind of regulatory environment for the capital markets. Regulation must allow for the free play of competition and innovation".[37] There are fears that matters of safety and soundness are being sacrificed for the sake of promoting competition and innovation, indeed that these ends are fundamentally incompatible because the outcomes of innovation and competition may be contributing to unsound or unsafe financial systems.

The idea that markets will evolve incentives for effective risk management and punish excesses ignores the insidious effects of pay and bonus schemes on behaviour in financial markets. Although traders receive a generous salary much of their remuneration comes in the form of bonuses, the size of which is calculated on a relative basis. The effect of this is twofold. Firstly, rather than generating incentives for prudent investment the desire to maximise bonuses creates incentives for excessive risk taking. Second, rather than participants making independent risk assessments based on the available information traders tend to imitate strategies and investments that have proved successful for others, something akin to Keynes' 'beauty contest'.[38] This results in trend following or herding behaviour which can cause markets to considerably overshoot their equilibrium. Perfecting the information available to market participants is of little utility if the information to which they ascribe the greatest importance is that being generated by their peers. Moreover, human beings are not the information processing automatons postulated by the EMH but respond to a whole range of stimuli and whose decisions are inseparable from the social and moral context they inhabit.

The pressure to perform can also result in dishonest or outright malfeasant behaviour. The recent history of the City is littered with infamous names such as Nick Leeson and Yasuo Hamanaka. When financial scandals engulf the City the tendency amongst the press and the City patriarchs is to find scapegoats and to portray them as rotten apples amongst an otherwise honest and sound financial sector. For instance, in the aftermath of the collapse of Barings Bank in 1995 there was a concerted effort to single out Nick Leeson whilst conveniently shielding the culture that had nurtured and protected him and the inherent dangers of the financial instruments concerned.[39] However, reading the memoirs of practitioners in the City and around the world it quickly becomes clear that the attitude and activities of traders is considerably at variance with those postulated by the EMH. These accounts are peppered not only with tales of debauchery but also deceit, mismanagement, and incompetence that call into question the assumptions upon which the promotion of free markets is predicated.[40]

Careful consideration of the official speeches of UK regulators reveals that even they are not totally convinced of the virtues of free markets. Consider these extracts from speeches by Howard Davies, the former Chairman of the FSA, in 2000:

> I do not think that all of this reform, all this market surveillance, all this regulatory good practice, will produce a world free of financial crises. Financial markets are inherently unstable. They are there to manage and intermediate risk. They will go up and down, sometimes dramatically (my emphasis).[41]

> We recognised that that is based in the belief that as long as you can shine light on the industry the market will discipline it.....we recognised that that might not happen. That is why we kept direct regulation on the table, in case market discipline, reinforced with legislative disclosure doesn't deliver the kind of safer conduct that we require (my emphasis).[42]

Or this from Andrew Large, then the Chair of the FSAs's predecessor institution, the Securities and Investments Board, and now the Deputy Governor of the Bank of England with responsibility for financial stability:

> So the question is, can we develop some sort of proxy for a global regulator - a system of interdependent national supervisors perhaps, which can confront the challenges posed by this mis-match, and respond to the real risks of failures and disruption that the global markets and firms generate?[43]

While conceding the impossibility of a zero-crisis environment the interesting about these observations is that they perceive markets to have inherent dysfunctional pathologies the results of which could seriously impair the public good. Yet, having acknowledged the limitations of markets they persist in subscribing to a regulatory ideology, both domestically and in the international domain, that allows markets more and more latitude.

In the past transgovernmental networks have been criticised for a lack of enforcement powers. For instance, many of the countries afflicted by the financial crises in Asia were nominally signed up to the IOSCO and BCBS codes of practice but these principles were frequently ignored by the regulator and the regulated. Moreover, there are a number of systemically significant economies which lie outside transgovernmental arrangements and which pose a potential source of future crises. To some extent these criticisms are misplaced. Ultimately the responsibility for ensuring the implementation of, and compliance with, international standards rests with national regulatory institutions. In addition, membership of transgovernmental networks, though still not universal, increasingly does incorporate most major financial centres and the problems of enforcement have been less prevalent since the advent of ROSCs. Nevertheless, there is one other major difficulty which relates to the structure of existing transgovernmental networks. Many countries, including the UK, have previously had a hotchpotch of regulatory bodies each responsible for supervising a discrete segment of financial activity. However, these arrangements have become anachronistic in an environment where deregulation and financial conglomeration have blurred the distinctions between previously discrete financial markets.[44] States have responded to this by increasingly concentrating regulatory authority with some countries, notably Japan, Germany, South Korea and several Scandinavian countries, following the UK's example by creating single, unified regulatory institution.[45]

Given that domestic regulators are increasingly aware of the shortcomings of sectorally based regulation, it is something of an irony that most transgovernmental ventures to which they subscribe are functionally distinct. In 1975 Miriam Camps presciently observed that "the way most international secretariats are organised does nothing to compensate for the divisions and the rigidities that are inherent in all government structures but rather, tends to intensify them by setting up parallel institutions".[46] Surmounting this problem has involved the development of 'networks of networks'.[47] In some cases this has involved informal networking or the creation of working groups and committees to address issues of overlapping concern. In recent years these relationships have become more institutionalised, most conspicuously through the establishment in 1996 of the Joint Forum, under the auspices of the BCBS, IOSCO and the IAIS, and in 1999 the FSF, billed as a meeting place and co-ordinating instrument for national regulators, international financial institutions and "sector specific international-groupings of regulators and supervisors".[48]

Conclusion

No matter how stringent its regulatory structures the City of London will always be vulnerable to financial upheaval because of the extent of its international linkages. The dangers that the City might be contaminated by the many viruses stalking the global financial system have been exacerbated since the late 1970s by the ongoing liberalisation of the City's markets and the concomitant influx of foreign institutions. Coping with this new environment has necessitated the evolution of ever more powerful state based regulators and the parallel development of transgovernmental networks, which are now very prominent sources of governance for the City of London' financial sector.

It has been argued that by qualitatively and quantitatively enhancing international cooperation, especially through the exchange of information and buttressing trust between different national regulatory institutions, transgovernmental networks have made a contribution to more effective supervision of the City of London's financial markets. However, there is cause for concern. The kinds of regulatory policies presently being promoted by national regulators through such networks, in particular those predicated on their seemingly unshakable conviction that free markets work as neo-classical economists tell us might be imperilling rather than contributing to financial stability in the City. Rather than seeking to reregulate markets at an international level in the public interest transgovernmental networks have moved to extend and entrench private and market interests that can be antithetical to the public good. It is the contention of this chapter is that an excessive reliance on the supposedly self-regulating nature of market interactions is likely to perpetuate the financial crises and scandals that have plagued the City in recent decades. The paradox is that as state and transgovernmental regulation of the City has become ever more systematic and intrusive so "the reality of its regulatory control over a financial centre more wide open than ever to a larger and more unruly world [is] highly doubtful".[49]

Notes

[1] For more detailed analysis of this process see Moran, M. 1991, *The Politics of the Financial Services Revolution: The USA, UK and Japan*, MacMillan, London, ch. 3; Moran, M. 1994, "The State and the Financial Services Revolution: A Comparative Analysis", in *West European Politics*, Vol.17, No.3, pp. 158-77; Augar, P. 2000, *The Death of Gentlemanly Capitalism: The Rise and Fall of London's Investment Banks*, Penguin, London; Woodward, R. 2005, "Globalization and the City of London's financial markets: The emergence of multi-level governance in principal financial centres" in Baker, A., Hudson, D. & Woodward, R. (eds), *Governing Financial Globalization: International political economy and multi-level governance*, Routledge, London, pp. 172-6.

[2] Davies, H. 2000, "C D Deshmukh Memorial Lecture at Mumbai India", available online at

---

http://www.fsa.gov.uk/Pages/Library/Communication/Speeches/2000/sp39.shtml. (Accessed 27 August 2005).

[3] See for example Kapstein, E.B. 1994, *Governing the Global Economy: International Finance and the State*, Harvard University Press, London; Slaughter, A-M. 1997, "The Real new World Order", in *Foreign Affairs*, Vol. 76, No. 5, pp. 183-97.

[4] Bryant, R.C. 2003, *Turbulent Waters: Cross Border Finance and International Governance,* Brookings Institute, Washington , ch. 2.

[5] Kindleberger, C.P. 1996, *Manias, Panics and Crashes: A History of Financial Crises*, John Wiley, New York. See also Chancellor, E. 1999, *Devil Take the Hindmost: A History of Financial Speculation*, MacMillan, London; Haacke, C. 2004, *Frenzy: Bubbles, Busts and How to Come Out Ahead*, MacMillan, New York.

[6] Soros, G. 1998, *The Crisis of Global Capitalism: Open Society Endangered*, Little Brown, London, p. xxviii.

[7] Keohane, R.O. & Nye, J.S. 1974, "Introduction: The Complex Interdependence of Canadian-American Interdependence", in *International Organization*, Vol. 28, No. 4, pp. 596. See also Nye, J.S. & Keohane, R.O. 1971, "Transnational Relations and World Politics: An Introduction", in *International Organization*, Vol. 25, No. 3, pp. 329-49; Slaughter, A-M. 2004, *A New World Order*, Princeton University Press, Princeton.

[8] Slaughter, A-M. 2000, "Government networks: the heart of the liberal democratic order", in Fox, G.H. & Roth, B.R. (eds.), *Democratic Governance and International Law*, Cambridge University Press, Cambridge, pp. 215-7.

[9] Kapstein, E.B. 1994, op cit pp. 8-9.

[10] The causes of the failure of Barings Bank were manifold including lax management, weak internal controls, and regulatory failings at the Bank of England. However, most accounts also assign a role to the weak channels of communication between regulators in London and Singapore which enabled Leeson to continue his manipulations for longer. See for example Bank of England. 1995, *Report of the Board of Banking Supervision inquiry into the circumstances of the collapse of Barings*, HMSO, London.

[11] The main codes and principles covered by ROSCs can be found at http://www.imf.org/external/standards/scnew.htm (Accessed 30 August 2005).

[12] Roberts, R. & Kynaston, D. 2001, *City State: How Markets Came to Rule Our World*, Profile Books, London; Roberts, R. 2004, *The City: A Guide to London's Global Financial Centre*, Profile Books, London; Baker, A. 1999, "*Nebleuse* and the 'internationalisation of the state' in the UK? The case of HM Treasury and the Bank of England", in *Review of International Political Economy*, Vol. 6, No. 1, pp. 79-100.

[13] International Financial Services London. 2005, *International Financial Markets in the UK*, available online at

http://www.ifsl.org.uk/uploads/RP_IFM_2005_05.pdf (Accessed 30 August 2005).
[14] Ibid, p. 6.
[15] Bank for International Settlements. 2005, *Triennial Central Bank Survey: Foreign exchange and derivatives market activity in 2004*, BIS, Basle, p. 12.
[16] International Financial Services London. 2005, op cit p 9.
[17] World Federation of Exchanges. 2005, *World Federation of Exchanges Focus*, No. 150 August, available online at http://www.world-exchanges.org/publications/Focus0805.pdf (Accessed 30 August 2005).
[18] Woodward, R. 2005, op cit p. 177.
[19] Large, A. 1997, "'Planning Blight' in the City", in *The Financial Times* 20 May, p. 23.
[20] The precise conditions for assisting an overseas regulator are set out in greater detail in Part IV, Section 47 of the Financial Services and Markets Act. See HMSO. 2000, *Financial Services and Markets Act*, available online at http://www.opsi.gov.uk/acts/acts2000/20000008.htm (Accessed 30 August 2005).
[21] Davies, H. 2000, "Global Markets, Global Regulation", available online at http://www.fsa.gov.uk/Pages/Library/Communication/Speeches/2000/sp45.shtml (Accessed 30 August 2005).
[22] Financial Services Authority. 2000, *A new regulator for the new millennium*, available online at http://www.fsa.gov.uk/pubs/policy/P29.pdf (Accessed 30 August 2005).
[23] Woodward, R. 2001, "'Slaughtering' the British State? Transgovernmental networks and the governance of financial markets in the City of London", Paper presented to the Global Studies Association Conference, Networks and Transformations, Manchester Metropolitan University, 2-4 July.
[24] McCarthy, C. 2004, "How should international financial service companies be regulated?", available online at http://www.fsa.gov.uk/Pages/Library/Communication/Speeches/2004/SP196.shtml (Accessed 31 August 2005).
[25] International Monetary Fund. 2003, *United Kingdom: Financial System Stability Assessment including Reports on the Observance of Standards and Codes on the following topics: Banking Supervision, Insurance Supervision, Securities Regulation, Payments Systems, Monetary and Financial Policy Transparency, Securities Settlement Systems, and Anti-Money Laundering and Counter Terrorist Financing*, International Monetary Fund, Washington D.C., p. 58.
[26] Financial Services Authority, *International Regulatory Outlook 2005*, available online at http://www.fsa.gov.uk/pubs/plan/iro_2005/iro_2005.pdf (Accessed 31 August 2005).
[27] Slaughter, A-M. 2004, op cit pp. 24-6, 171-85.

[28] Underhill, G.R.D. 1995, "Keeping governments out of politics: transnational securities markets, regulatory cooperation, and political legitimacy", in *Review of International Studies*, Vol. 21, No. 3, pp. 251-78.
[29] Underhill, G.R.D. 1997, "Private Markets and Public Responsibility in a Global System: Conflict and Co-operation in Transnational Banking and Securities Regulation", in Underhill (ed), *The New World Order in International Finance*, MacMillan, Basingstoke, p. 40.
[30] For an illuminating discussion of the shortcomings of neo-classical expositions of notions of the economy and the economic see Watson, M. 2005, *Foundations of International Political Economy*, Palgrave, Basingstoke.
[31] For brief, critical and accessible introductions to the Efficient Markets Hypothesis see Kay, J. 2003, *The Truth About Markets: Their Genius, Their Limits, Their Follies*, Allen Lane, London, chs. 12, 16-19; Chancellor, E. 1999, op cit pp. 242-4.
[32] Baker, A. 1999, op cit p. 86.
[33] See for example International Association of Insurance Supervisors. 2005, "About IAIS", available online at http://www.iaisweb.org/132_ENU_HTML.asp (Accessed 1 September 2005); International Organisation of Securities Commissions. 2005, "General Information About IOSCO", available online at http://www.iosco.org/about/ (Accessed 1 September 2005); Basel Committee on Banking Supervision. 2005, "The Basel Committee on Banking Supervision", available online at http://www.bis.org/bcbs/aboutbcbs.htm (Accessed 1 September 2005).
[34] See Financial Stability Forum. 2005, *Twelve Key Standards for Sound Financial Systems*, available online at http://www.fsforum.org/compendium/key_standards_for_sound_financial_system.html (Accessed 1 September 2005).
[35] Jensen, M. 1978, "Some Anomalous Evidence Regarding Market Efficiency", in *Journal of Financial Economics* Vol. 6, No. 2, p 95.
[36] See for example Soros, G. 1998, op cit; Thomson, R. 1999, *Apocalypse Roulette: The Lethal World of Derivatives*, MacMillan, London.
[37] Smith, A. 2000, "Speech by Chief Secretary to the Treasury, Andrew Smith MP, at the World Stock Exchanges Conference", available online at http://www.hm-treasury.gov.uk/newsroom_and_speeches/speeches/chiefsecspeeches/speech_cst_70200.cfm (Accessed 1 September 2005).
[38] Keynes, J.M. 1973[1936], *The General Theory of Employment, Interest and Money*, Cambridge University Press, Cambridge, p. 156.
[39] Tickell, A. 1996, "Making a melodrama out of a crisis: reinterpreting the collapse of Barings Bank", in *Environment and Planning D: Society and Space*, Vol.14, No. 1, pp. 5-33.
[40] See for example Thompson, R. 1999, op cit; Partnoy, F. 2003, *Infectious Greed: How Deceit and Risk Corrupted the Financial Markets*, Henry Holt

and Company, New York; Leeson, N. 1996, *Rogue Trader*, Warner Books, London; Lewis, M. 1999, *Liar's Poker: Two Cities, True Greed*, Coronet, London.

[41] Davies, H. 2000, "C D Deshmukh Memorial Lecture at Mumbai India", op cit.

[42] Quoted in Financial Times, 2000, "Hedge funds may face direct regulation", 27 March, p. 6.

[43] Large, A. 1997, "A Proxy for a Global Regulator: The Way Ahead for International Supervision", available online at www.fsa.gov.uk/speeches/053097a.htm (Accessed 29 November 1999).

[44] On the case for regulatory unification see Briault, C. 2002, *Revisiting the rationale for a single national financial services regulator*, available online at http://www.fsa.gov.uk/pubs/occpapers/OP16.pdf (Accessed 1 September 2005); Goodhart, C.A.E. 2000, "The Organisational Structure of Banking Supervision", *LSE Financial Markets Group Special Paper* No. 127, available online at http://fmg.lse.ac.uk/pdfs/sp127.pdf (Accessed 1 September 2005).

[45] On the trends towards regulatory unification see Abrams, R.K. & Taylor, M.W. 2000, "Issues in the Unification of Financial Sector Supervision", *IMF Working Paper* No. 213; Narain, A. & Ghosh, S. 2001, "Bank Supervisory Arrangements International Perspectives and Indian Perspective", in *Economic and Political Weekly*, 15 September, pp. 1543-53.

[46] Camps, M. 1975, *"First World" Relationships: The role of the OECD*, Atlantic Institute for International Affairs, Paris, p. 46.

[47] Slaughter, A.M. 2000, "Governing the Global Economy through Government Networks", in Byers, M., (ed.) *The Role of Law in International Politics*, Oxford University Press, Oxford, pp. 177-205.

[48] Financial Stability Forum. 2005, "Financial Stability Forum", available online at http://www.fsforum.org/home/home.html (Accessed 1 September 2005).

[49] Strange, S. 1998, *Mad Money*, Manchester University Press, Manchester , p. 154.

Further Reading

Abrams, R.K. & Taylor, M.W. 2000, "Issues in the Unification of Financial Sector Supervision", *IMF Working Paper*, No. 213.

Augar, P. 2000, *The Death of Gentlemanly Capitalism: The Rise and Fall of London's Investment Banks*, Penguin, London.

Baker, A. 1999, "*Nebleuse* and the 'internationalisation of the state' in the UK? The case of HM Treasury and the Bank of England", in *Review of International Political Economy*, Vol. 6, No. 1, pp. 79-100.

Bank for International Settlements. 2005, *Triennial Central Bank Survey: Foreign exchange and derivatives market activity in 2004*, BIS, Basle.

Bank of England. 1995, *Report of the Board of Banking Supervision inquiry into the circumstances of the collapse of Barings*, HMSO, London.
Briault, C. 2002, *Revisiting the rationale for a single national financial services regulator*, available online at http://www.fsa.gov.uk/pubs/occpapers/OP16.pdf (Accessed 1 September 2005).
Bryant, R.C. 2003, *Turbulent Waters: Cross Border Finance and International Governance*, Brookings Institute, Washington.
Camps, M. 1975, *"First World" Relationships: The role of the OECD*, Atlantic Institute for International Affairs, Paris.
Chancellor, E. 1999, *Devil Take the Hindmost: A History of Financial Speculation*, MacMillan, London.
Davies, H. 2000a, "C D Deshmukh Memorial Lecture at Mumbai India", available online at http://www.fsa.gov.uk/Pages/Library/Communication/Speeches/2000/sp39.shtml. (Accessed 27 August 2005)
Davies, H. 2000b, "Global Markets, Global Regulation", available online at http://www.fsa.gov.uk/Pages/Library/Communication/Speeches/2000/sp45.shtml (Accessed 30 August 2005).
Financial Services Authority. 2000, *A new regulator for the new millennium*, available online at http://www.fsa.gov.uk/pubs/policy/P29.pdf (Accessed 30 August 2005).
Financial Services Authority, *International Regulatory Outlook 2005*, available online at http://www.fsa.gov.uk/pubs/plan/iro_2005/iro_2005.pdf (Accessed 31 August 2005).
Financial Stability Forum. 2005, *Twelve Key Standards for Sound Financial Systems*, available online at http://www.fsforum.org/compendium/key_standards_for_sound_financial_system.html (Accessed 1 September 2005).
Goodhart, C.A.E. 2000, "The Organisational Structure of Banking Supervision", in *LSE Financial Markets Group Special Paper* No. 127, available online at http://fmg.lse.ac.uk/pdfs/sp127.pdf (Accessed 1 September 2005).
Haacke, C. 2004, *Frenzy: Bubbles, Busts and How to Come Out Ahead*, MacMillan, New York.
HMSO. 2000, *Financial Services and Markets Act*, available online at http://www.opsi.gov.uk/acts/acts2000/20000008.htm (Accessed 30 August 2005).
International Financial Services London. 2005, *International Financial Markets in the UK*, available online at http://www.ifsl.org.uk/uploads/RP_IFM_2005_05.pdf (Accessed 30 August 2005).
International Monetary Fund. 2003, *United Kingdom: Financial System Stability Assessment including Reports on the Observance of Standards and*

Codes on the following topics: Banking Supervision, Insurance Supervision, Securities Regulation, Payments Systems, Monetary and Financial Policy Transparency, Securities Settlement Systems, and Anti-Money Laundering and Counter Terrorist Financing, International Monetary Fund, Washington D.C..

Jensen, M. 1978, "Some Anomalous Evidence Regarding Market Efficiency", in *Journal of Financial Economics*, Vol. 6, No. 2, pp. 95-101.

Kapstein, E.B. 1994, *Governing the Global Economy: International Finance and the State*, Harvard University Press, London.

Kay, J. 2003, *The Truth About Markets: Their Genius, Their Limits, Their Follies*, Allen Lane, London.

Keohane, R.O. & Nye, J.S. 1974, "Introduction: The Complex Interdependence of Canadian-American Interdependence", in *International Organization*, Vol. 28, No. 4, pp. 595-607.

Kindleberger, C.P. 1996, *Manias, Panics and Crashes: A History of Financial Crises*, John Wiley, New York.

Large, A. 1997, "'Planning Blight' in the City", in *The Financial Times* 20 May, p. 23.

McCarthy, C. 2004, "How should international financial service companies be regulated?", available online at http://www.fsa.gov.uk/Pages/Library/Communication/Speeches/2004/SP196.shtml (Accessed 31 August 2005).

Leeson, N. 1996, *Rogue Trader*, Warner Books, London.

Lewis, M. 1999, *Liar's Poker: Two Cities, True Greed*, Coronet, London.

Moran, M. 1991, *The Politics of the Financial Services Revolution: The USA, UK and Japan*, MacMillan, London.

Moran, M. 1994, "The State and the Financial Services Revolution: A Comparative Analysis", in *West European Politics*, Vol.17, No.3, pp. 158-77

Narain, A. & Ghosh, S. 2001, "Bank Supervisory Arrangements International Perspectives and Indian Perspective", in *Economic and Political Weekly*, 15 September, pp. 1543-53.

Nye, J.S. & Keohane, R.O. 1971, "Transnational Relations and World Politics: An Introduction", in *International Organization*, Vol. 25, No. 3, pp. 329-49.

Partnoy, F. 2003, *Infectious Greed: How Deceit and Risk Corrupted the Financial Markets*, Henry Holt and Company, New York.

Roberts, R. & Kynaston, D. 2001, *City State: How Markets Came to Rule Our World*, Profile Books, London.

Roberts, R. 2004, *The City: A Guide to London's Global Financial Centre*, Profile Books, London.

Slaughter, A-M. 1997, "The Real new World Order", in *Foreign Affairs*, Vol. 76, No. 5, pp. 183-97.

Slaughter, A.M. 2000a, "Governing the Global Economy through Government Networks", in Byers, M. (ed.), *The Role of Law in International Politics*, Oxford University Press, Oxford, pp. 177-205.

Slaughter, A-M. 2000b, "Government networks: the heart of the liberal democratic order", in Fox, G.H. & Roth, B.R. (eds.), *Democratic Governance and International Law*, Cambridge University Press, Cambridge, pp. 199-235.

Slaughter, A-M. 2004, *A New World Order*, Princeton University Press, Princeton.

Soros, G. 1998, *The Crisis of Global Capitalism: Open Society Endangered*, Little Brown, London.

Strange, S. 1998, *Mad Money*, Manchester University Press, Manchester.

Thomson, R. 1999, *Apocalypse Roulette: The Lethal World of Derivatives*, MacMillan, London.

Tickell, A. 1996, "Making a melodrama out of a crisis: reinterpreting the collapse of Barings Bank", in *Environment and Planning D: Society and Space*, Vol.14, No. 1, pp. 5-33.

Underhill, G.R.D. 1995, "Keeping governments out of politics: transnational securities markets, regulatory cooperation, and political legitimacy", in *Review of International Studies*, Vol. 21, No. 3, pp. 251-78.

Underhill, G.R.D. 1997, "Private Markets and Public Responsibility in a Global System: Conflict and Co-operation in Transnational Banking and Securities Regulation", in Underhill (ed), *The New World Order in International Finance*, MacMillan, Basingstoke, pp. 17-49.

Watson, M. 2005, *Foundations of International Political Economy*, Palgrave, Basingstoke.

Woodward, R. 2001, "'Slaughtering' the British State? Transgovernmental networks and the governance of financial markets in the City of London", Paper presented to the Global Studies Association Conference, Networks and Transformations, Manchester Metropolitan University, 2-4 July.

Woodward, R. 2005, "Globalization and the City of London's financial markets: The emergence of multi-level governance in principal financial centres" in Baker, A., Hudson, D. & Woodward, R. (eds.), *Governing Financial Globalization: International political economy and multi-level governance*, Routledge, London, pp. 171-88.

World Federation of Exchanges. 2005, *World Federation of Exchanges Focus*, No. 150 August, available online at http://www.world-exchanges.org/publications/Focus0805.pdf (Accessed 30 August 2005).

Chapter Eleven

The Changing Ethics of the City

Alex Brassey

When I was asked to write a paper on ethics in the City of London, my first reaction was that it would be an incredibly short paper. Despite the City, for most of its time, having been comprised of paternalistic aristocrats, a change has taken place. The change has been more profound since the 1980s than in any previous period. This paper looks at this and some of the key themes that led to a general decline in ethical standards.

In the first section I shall define what I mean when I refer to ethical standards. It is always difficult when referring to the City of London given its fairly disparate constitution. When I refer to the City, however, I am generally referring to the banks, law firms, accountancy practices, insurance businesses and other financial institutions. I am also referring to the head-offices of major companies. Whilst it is the case a small minority of major UK companies have their head offices outside the square mile, I include the major financial decision making boardrooms of these companies within my definition.

The second section traces how the ownership of 'UK plc' changed immeasurably during the 1980s – in particular I shall focus on the privatisation programme of the Thatcher Government. This section highlights the changing focus of the 'company'. Although the privatisation culture generated a higher level of quantitative efficiency – a neo-classical and monetarist objective – this efficiency came at the expense of a key ethical pillar which had previously been enshrined in the mind set of the board room predecessors.

In the third section I will draw some parallels of 'City and board room culture' with a condition that prior to 1950 was known as 'moral insanity' – nowadays known as psychopathy. The essential feature of a psychopath lies in the inability to empathise with anything outside of the 'self'. The changing structure of the City, I shall argue, led to the inevitable dehumanisation of corporate board rooms.

Finally, I will conclude with the paradox that wider ownership, contrary to the thinking of Karl Marx, has not led to greater freedom or economic utopia. The drivers for the paradigmatic shift that took place in the 1980s have to a large extent back-fired. The City is quantitatively more successful than it has even been in its history but from some standpoints is morally bankrupt.

Throughout this work I have made references to British Telecom, which is in many ways a well run company. BT is being used simply as an exemplar for the points this article wishes to raise. It is a large, prominent privatised company of the 1980s which remains in the FTSE 100. I would have been satisfied in using any number of alternatives. Additionally in regards to pay, remuneration and director bonuses, it is my view that any one of dozens of large companies either in the UK or overseas could have been just as effective.

What are 'Ethical Standards' Anyway?

One of the most often used criticisms is also, sadly one of the least understood. The expression that someone is acting 'unethically' is a charge frequently used against behaviour or actions that one finds 'unacceptable'. Academic philosophy, since the time of Plato[1] has been struggling to explain just what 'ethical' means. The short answer is that no-one knows. Nor is anyone likely to devise a universally accepted definition anytime soon.

In order to make progress with this paper it is important to briefly lay out the different schools of though on what is ethical or 'right and wrong'. I will then suggest a working definition and explain how I intend to apply it to the City.

Broadly speaking there are three models. Firstly there is utilitarianism[2]. Utilitarianism considers whether an action either adds or detracts from the 'good'. So, for example, if raising taxes on balance created more 'utility' (happiness, goodness) than it destroyed, then raising taxes would be 'right'. If the converse was true, then reducing taxes would be 'right'. Utilitarianism looks at the consequences of an action and analyses its effects.

Secondly there is the deontological model. This model looks at the rights, duties and obligations of an agent rather than the consequences of action. One's intentions are being analysed for evaluation, rather than what happens as a result of an action. If one's intentions are 'good', then one is acting ethically, regardless of what happens as a result. The most famous imperative stemming from the deontological school was Immanuel Kant's 'categorical imperative'[3]. This suggested that what was 'right' lay in rational agents only behaving in such a way that they would will all other rational agents to behave. Kant is very much in favour of the 'do unto others' principle.

Finally, there is a model known as 'virtue ethics'. On this construal, originally proposed by Aristotle,[4] what is right or virtuous is that which is in accordance with what is good. This sounds a little circular. However, the attractive element of the theory lies in its flexibility to mould itself to situation. In answer to the question 'what is good?' Aristotle would reply, 'the right thing, in the right place, at the right time for the right reasons'. The obvious next question then would be, 'how does one determine that?' Aristotle proposed that some people were moral experts or connoisseurs – phronimoi in Greek.

In the same way we have wine experts or wine connoisseurs who let the rest of us know what should be considered a good vintage, the phronimoi were the ones who let the rest of us know what was good behaviour or ethical behaviour.

Now I have cleared the ground by considering different general models of ethical evaluation, what can be said about ethical standards in the City? Which model should be used in order to evaluate appropriateness? At the start of this paper I suggested that the City could be said to be morally bankrupt and that ethical standards have declined since the 1980s.

What seems to be fairly universal in all models of meta-ethics (deontology, utilitarianism and virtue ethics) is the condemnation of 'selfishness'. Any system, therefore, which encourages the development of an economy which benefits those in control at the expense of those with no control, would be condemned on any model.

Selfishness for utilitarians would mean less 'good' or utility, for Kantians those in control would be in contradiction and for Aristotelians a selfish exploitation could never be considered virtuous (unless it was in pursuit of a higher goal).

The City of London, now more than ever, champions the profit motive as its fundamental raison d'etre. The profit motive, in turn benefits most those who are in a position to exploit that financial success. Without doubt, the greatest beneficiaries of the increase in profitability of 'UK plc' from any statistical perspective have been the new breed of 'managerial aristocrats' who control the financial decision making function of our economy.

My argument suggests that this 'managerial aristocracy', more commonly known by their tabloid reference as 'fat cats', are motivated by excessive materialism fuelled, in some respects, by greed. Left unchecked, as they have been, they will direct the resources of the considerable enterprises they control to serve their ever-growing whims at the expense of the other stake-holders be they staff, shareholders, customers and the wider community. Nowhere can this apocalyptic vision be seen better than the examples of corporate excess in the case of Enron and WorldCom. In the case of these companies, the excesses of the 'managerial aristocracy' ran the company literally into bankruptcy through fraud.

Prior to the 1980s the City of London remained one of those bastions of inherited privilege. The public school and Oxbridge College which one had attended played a significantly more important role in recruitment then ones ability. Additionally, for those more intellectually challenged, providing ones family were considered to be part of the 'ruling classes', there was no problem securing employment in the City.

The City of London was one of the last places to shed itself of 'upper class' domination – with the possible exception of the Civil Service. However, when one looks back on how the 'upper classes' responded ethically to social circumstance in their corporate decision making, it is clear they felt some, albeit limited, paternalistic, duty to provide for the working classes. Employment generally remained stable; a job generally meant a job for life. The relationship between owner and worker remained fixed for long periods.

The development of the labour and trades union movement in the early part of the 20th century hailed the beginning of a social and economic mobility hitherto unseen. The war, followed by the introduction of the welfare state all contributed to major social change. The growth of the state, however, along with the growth in the power of the trades union movement reached something of a peak in the 1970s.

Something changed in the psychology of the middle and working class voters during the later years of the 1970s which ushered in a new kind of economic and social aspiration. The opportunities of 'the capable' to reach the heights reserved for the upper classes had, for the first time, become a common reality. The meritocratic movement – lead by Margaret Thatcher, a middle class girl-made-good – provided the impetus for what was about to happen to the City in the 1980s.

Thatcher introduced a raft of employment and trades union legislation[5] in response to the widespread strikes seen during the winter of discontent. The age of tripartite governance, (government, CBI and TUC) was over. The immediate impact of Milton Friedman inspired Reaganomics – enacted by Thatcher in the UK through the manipulation of supply-side economics - was to have a profound effect on the structure of the economy[6].

The macro-economic objective of eliminating inflation by reducing wage-inspired inflation expectations inevitably led to a rapid rise in unemployment. The sacking of millions of workers in the early part of the 1980s was sold by Thatcher as a necessary consequence of improving the UK's competitiveness. Supply-side economics, stripping down labour and introducing flexible labour markets became a necessary variable in order to improve economic, allocative and distributive efficiency.

This kind of economic thinking can no longer be reasonably denied. The increased flexibility of the labour market and the recessionary pain experienced by the UK and world economy during the 1980s and 1990s can now be seen to have been effective in reducing inflation and inflation expectations.

This price, however, was not paid by those working in the City, or in fact the government. The price paid for this new supply-side, low inflation, low unemployment regime was the UK working class.

The purpose of this paper, however, is not to analyse the macroeconomic effects of Thatcher's supply-side focus. Rather, my intention is to look at how the stated objectives of government changed creating a less ethically minded City.

The neo-classical / monetarist slant which directed much of Thatcher's economic policy during the 1980s led the City to consider the profit motive as the most important driver of economic performance. Roughly speaking, Freidman / Minford et. al. subscribed to the view that all agents within an economy are rational agents. Rational agents, with rational expectations will perform better with 'incentives'. Money is the primary incentive, therefore, if rational agents think they will get more money for working harder and more efficiently, then the system should be set up to promote this philosophically dubious mechanism.

A system solely designed to reward people's labour with money at the expense of all else was bound to create a generation whose focus was the 'bottom line'. Such a system would be devoid of social responsibility, a system which championed greed, the individual and materialism and a system that contained little ethical value.

The next section takes a look at the way in which this basic philosophy 'cashed out' in terms of company 'mission statements'.

Changing the Raison d'etre

Consider the following:

(1) In 1983 British Telecommunications was a public sector enterprise designed to provide the British public with telecommunications services.

(2) In 1984 British Telecommunications PLC was a private sector enterprise designed to provide the British public with telecommunications services.

(1) and (2) look remarkably similar. In fact the only difference between them is the nature of who owns BT. In (1) it was the British public and in (2) it was still the British public, in the main.

The big difference between (1) and (2) and indeed the reason for privatising it in the first place, lay in the principle of the profit motive. The theory suggested that a company which had to make a profit would be leaner and meaner, more innovative and more competitive than a company in the public sector.

In order to see why this was the case, the argument ran that a company which could afford the best people (by paying them more) would be run well. It would become more efficient and would make profits for the shareholders. The theory looks like everyone is a winner. Additionally, by privatising BT and a whole host of other public sector organisations ranging from British Gas to British Steel and British Airways, the PSBR (public sector borrowing requirement) turned into a PSDR (public sector debt repayment).

The key difference therefore between (1) and (2) above is that (2) contains an implied extra clause. This clause appears as (3):

(3) In 1984 British Telecommunications PLC was a private sector enterprise designed to provide the British public with telecommunications. For profit.

The shift from (1) to (3) indicates that the boardroom focus of those involved in running a public sector organisation to the PLC required a change. It would be unfair to suggest that those involved at boardroom level, in addition to the army of City workers could have done anything else given their new remit.

To counter the inevitable cries of excessive profiteering by the new BT plc, the government set up a watchdog: Office of Telecommunications (Oftel – succeeded by the Office of Communications or Ofcom). Oftel was to ensure that, given the monopoly status of BT, the prices charged to the consumer were fair and reasonable. BT, in other words had to make a profit, but not so much as to upset the British voter.

The principles laid out by the 1984 privatisation were carried through on a whole line of other public sector companies throughout the 1980s and 1990s. Privatisation followed by watchdog appeared from our water to gas to electric.

The government needed to ensure that the privatisation programme was successful. After all, if they were going to sell 'the family silver'[7] they had to ensure that someone would definitely buy it. Additionally, for those who bought shares in the newly privatised industries, a guaranteed initial profit was the best incentive for the government to receive encouragement to sell more or less everything else it could get away with. The privatised companies leapt on their first day or trading – indicating that the price of sale was simply too low. Some of the regional water companies increased in value by 40% within minutes of the shares being traded.

The New Owners

So far, we have established that the newly privatised companies became profit motivated. This much is uncontroversial. The main beneficiaries of this profit, however, were slightly hidden from view.

Under the principles of neo-classical economic thinking, the market determines the price of everything. As indicated above, if you wanted the best management, you had to pay the highest price. It was under these principles that the emergence of the 'managerial aristocracy' began to take a foothold.

The basis for rapid increases in executive pay took place in much the same way as footballers' salaries. The government, by releasing large public corporations on to the stock exchange allowed the executive management of these organisations to effectively name their own price and worth. It should come as no surprise that when you grant a group of individuals the ability to name their own salary, the numbers may look staggering. For instance, between 1984 and 2003 average pay of staff at BT rose 162%[8]. Executive pay on the other hand rose by 189% from 1997 to 2003 and in 2003 rose by 66% alone.

Ben Verwaayen joined BT on 14 January 2002 and became chief executive on 1 February 2002, on an annual basic salary of £700,000. Under his service agreement he was entitled to a pro-rata on target bonus for the 2002 financial year of £122,000. This was increased by the Remuneration Committee to £152,000 "to reflect corporate performance". During the 2003 financial year, Verwaayen was entitled to an annual bonus of £849,000 and relocation expenses of £200,000. His three year package also included a housing allowance of £250,000 per annum until January 2005, and £2 million worth of BT share options[9]. Christopher Bland was appointed (part-time) chairman from 1 May 2001 on an annual salary of £500,000 (for a three-day week), which remained unchanged for the 2003 financial year.

The stories of executive pay rising by several hundred percent as the company profits dived became common place. Staff cut backs, dividend suspensions to shareholders, suppliers would be squeezed during tough times within UK plc. The only area which would put in a consistent meteoric rises year-on-year would be executive pay.

How is this possible? The premise that the owners of the company surely have control over what its employees get paid did not seem to be true. The answer lay in the changing nature of who owned the company.

Continuing with our model of BT, ownership changed from the government to the shareholders in 1984. The next question is, who owns the shares? The answer to that is more or less everyone. Ownership became so disparate as to become irrelevant. The number of people who owned BT shares in 1984 was estimated to be in the 10 millions. No single person or group of people could, under this diversity of share holdings hope to ever be able to hold the executive to account. The same is true for more or less all privatised companies and, probably more concerning, true for most publicly quoted companies.

The value of the largest organisations quoted on the London Stock Exchange extends into the £100 billions. The paradox of ownership then presented itself. If everyone 'owns' the company, who controls it? The answer: the 'managerial aristocracy'.

Ownership of these companies is not just direct i.e. individual shareholders owning shares directly. The majority of ownership is held indirectly. Anyone who owns an equities ISA, or PEP, anyone with an endowment policy, anyone with a pension or with-profits-bond – all these people 'own' a share in the likes of Vodafone, BT, British Petroleum, Shell etc. The fact remains that in the UK today most of our listed companies are owned by everyone and run for the benefit of the 'managerial aristocracy'.

I am not suggesting in this paper that the boardroom predecessors of the 'managerial aristocracy' in the City were benevolent, kindly, altruists. In previous decades, ownership and control tended to be far more closely aligned. This meant that economic and financial power lay in ownership rather than management. Homogenous ownership of industry and other concerns in the City of London brought with it a far higher degree of concern for the company than any managerial association could have.

The City of London, through the rise of the 'managerial aristocrat' has seen multi-million pound 'sign-on' fees, golden handshakes, golden hand-cuffs, performance related bonuses etc. The exploding number of mechanisms which this class of individual has made available to pay themselves has seemingly no limit.

Media Attention

The 'managerial aristocrat' has not been immune or unaffected by the publicity which they have attracted. The government was encouraged to set up what they grandly call 'corporate governance' enquiries to look into the remuneration of executives.

Company executives recognised the need to answer questions raised about their pay. The response has been remuneration committees, set up not necessarily to reduce executive pay, rather as a means to justify the pay increases that were being awarded. The language used when justifying large pay rises for senior executives came in a rather ambiguous style. Consider the following:

In the 2003 BT annual report, it was noted that high remuneration reflected 'excellent performance'. Who was to define what was meant by excellent performance? Other senior executives would judge their colleagues and decide on pay. Naturally, the inevitable situation of senior executives voting each other large increases in pay was the outcome. Pay has often become hidden in different bonus schemes. Take the following from the BT 2003 annual report: The annual bonus plan focused on annual objectives. Performance is measured on a scorecard basis, targets are set at the beginning of the financial year and performance is reviewed throughout the year. Targets for the 2003 financial year were based on 'objectives' such as earnings per share, cash flow, and customer satisfaction. Awards in the form of BT shares were also granted to executive directors and senior executives under the deferred bonus plan (DBP). Awards made in 2003 in respect of performance in the 2002 financial year were equivalent in value to 50% of the executive's gross annual bonus, except in the case of the CEO whose award in 2003 was 100% of gross annual bonus.

The 'managerial aristocracy' might well consider that the more complex the scheme, the less the shareholders and even other staff would be able to understand their pay. The 'objectives' to which these bonuses would relate were of course determined by the senior executives themselves. In this way, their large pay increases could be 'justified' by virtue of them meeting performance targets.

External Pressure

The idea of poor 'corporate governance' led to the establishment of the Cadbury Committee. The committee investigated accountability of the Board of Directors to shareholders and to the society. It submitted its report and associated *Code of Best Practices* in December 1992 wherein it spelt out the methods of governance needed to achieve a balance between the essential powers of the Board of Directors and their proper accountability. The resulting report, and associated code of best practices, published was unsurprisingly well received. The Committee's stated purpose was to "help raise the standards of corporate governance and the level of confidence in financial reporting and auditing by setting out clearly what it sees as the respective responsibilities of those involved and what it believes is expected of them"[10].

The basic problems with Cadbury, and the Greenbury Report[11] which followed, lay in two significant areas. Firstly, the recommendations and investigations were conducted by and for the same people who were the ultimate beneficiaries of the system. Secondly, the recommendations were sufficiently couched to allow for smart minded executive directors to 'substantiate' and 'justify' their remuneration. Clearly the notion of excess and 'managerial abuse' could never be solved by people who had previously been managerial abusers.

The problem of corporate excess presents, in some respects, a philosophical conundrum. On the one hand it must be recognised that government or society cannot legislate for everything – there has to be some kind of social consensus in regards to what is 'acceptable'. On the other hand, it seems impossible to expect voluntary restraint when the benefits of not being restrained are as vast as they appear.

In order to highlight the difficulty of this conundrum, consider the idea that the state wished to enforce the rules of etiquette. Certain types of behaviour, for example burping loudly or chewing food with one's mouth open, instead of being frowned upon were to become offences – bringing with them fines or possibly imprisonment for repeated offences. Clearly, the notion that we could or even would want to legislate for good manners seems counter-intuitive.

In the same way we hope as a society that most people adhere to the social norms of what we take to be 'polite behaviour', however wide that definition needs to be, we also hope that those in control of corporations will also adhere to sensible practice. As we cannot legislate for good or polite behaviour in general society, we also cannot legislate for enforcement at board room level.

The problems inherent in the analogy between etiquette in society and ethical behaviour in the board room also hold for breaches in law. I am not saying that board rooms which break the law ought not to be prosecuted and that we should not seek to legislate at all. Rather I am suggesting that in the same way we have criminal law to ensure a degree of social cooperation, we do not force people to be 'nice or polite' to each other. The problem arises as a result of the fact that there is an incentive to be polite to others in ones society and a disincentive to be rude i.e. social exclusion. In the board room, however, there is a huge incentive to be greedy and heartless, i.e. large pay cheques, and a disincentive to be altruistic i.e.

the possibility of rejection and unemployment. This problem is further augmented, as I explain in the following section, on the basis that few in corporate board rooms today feel any impulse to act altruistically in any event.

Psychopaths in the City[12]

In 1991 Robert Hare developed the Psychopathy Checklist – Revised (PCL-R) to assess the personality disorder of psychopathy. The PCL-R includes 20 items, reproduced below. It should be made clear here that there is no official evidence or study to confirm the personality characteristics of CEOs within major organisations. Clearly it would be difficult, if not impossible, to get consent in order to conduct psychopathy testing for senior managers – this would be augmented in the event that the senior manager in question presented psychopathy. However, it might be instructive just to consider the items, and for readers who are or who work closely with senior City executives, compare behaviour.

Glib and superficial charm
Grandiose sense of self-worth
Need for stimulation or proneness to boredom
Pathological lying
Conning and manipulativeness
Lack of remorse or guilt
Shallow Affect
Callousness and lack of empathy
Parasitic lifestyle
Poor behaviour controls
Promiscuous sexual behaviour
Early behaviour problems
Lack of realistic, long terms goals
Impulsivity
Irresponsibility
Failure to accept responsibility for own actions
Many short-term marital relationships
Juvenile delinquency
Revocation of conditional release
Criminal versatility

According to Hare when one assesses for psychopathy each category is scored as 0 = not present, 1 = some evidence, 2 = strong evidence. The scores are then totalled. If the total is more than 25 then a diagnosis of psychopathy is valid. Of the 20 categories above, just how many members of the 'managerial aristocracy' would score an aggregate of 25 plus?

There are some who would suggest that the PCL-R is a good recruiting tool for a senior management position. Certainly the most effective chief executives, in order to generate a more profitable company, will not take into account the human element of 'downsizing' or sacking large numbers of workers. The decision to cut back where necessary in the pursuit of profit, then is not an emotional decision, it is a qualitative decision made on the basis of the numerical evidence.

It should come as no surprise that a large percentage of Chief Executive Officers in the City of London are qualified accountants. These accountants are trained to look at the bottom line. There is little room for making decisions based on what would be traditional ethical grounds.

CEOs are often charming or charismatic – belying aggressive ambition. CEOs often find their way to the top of the organisation having disposed of allies along the way. It stands to reason that a strong Machiavellian personality type is more likely to succeed in a profit motivated environment than an altruist. Promotion generally occurs from results – quantitative results – not as a result of behaving ethically in ones decision making.

One has to consider the attitude of someone who pathologically believes that their value to the organisation justifies their pay. A man who pays himself £2 million as CEO of BT for example has to believe that what he does during the working day between is worth the same as 100 fully qualified telephone engineers on £20,000 p.a. How else can the salary be justified?

The 'managerial aristocracy' is rife. It does not simply exist within a single organisation – the City is thriving with men and women who aspire to this class of existence. Company money is constantly poured away on lavish expenses. Whose money is it that is being spent on business class air fares and five star hotels? It is of course the shareholders' money. It is money that could have been spent on improving the working conditions of staff; it is money that could have been spent on improving product.

The knife-wielding, cost cutting, hard talking CEO looking to save the company money is the same person who will grant themselves a multi-million pound remuneration package and fly first class at a cost of twenty times the fare of an economy seat. The kind of person who thrives in this kind of environment may be found to have no hesitation, to lack remorse or even guilt. This person may be charming, bold, confident, callous and feel little regret. In other words the supreme champion of the City, this new 'master of the Universe' in the words of Sherman McCoy of Bonfire of the Vanities[13], can be described, academically, as a psychopath.

The 1980s Paradox – Ethical Conclusions

The 'can-do' social mobility culture of the 1980s was best encapsulated by the YUPPIE, young up and coming professional and typified the City atmosphere at that time. The focus of the Yuppie was not laudable or altruistic – they had no interest in helping their fellow man or developing technology for the good. Instead they strived to make as much money as quickly as possible. Ethics played no part – a meaningless word that those outside the circle would use to condemn them.

Perhaps the 1980s yuppie is the 21st century board room director. They have switched their Porsche 911s for Bentleys and Lear Jets. The deregulation of the City's financial services industry in 1986 poured fuel on the fire of materialism.

Since the 1980s massive consolidation has taken place, banks swallowed up other banks as mergers and acquisition activity picked up pace elsewhere. As these companies grew, so the 'managerial aristocracy' moved further and further away from the owners or shareholders, thus avoiding having to answer for their profligacy.

The fundamental tenet expressed by Marx in his seminal work 'Das Capital'[14], suggested that the problem for the majority lay in the principle of ownership. Marx insisted that power lay in ownership and urged the proletariat to rise up and take control of the 'means of production'. Marxist ideology, therefore proposes that in order for the workers to find greater social justice and benefit from their labour, the key would be to take ownership (forcibly). The realities of the late 20th Century suggest this political philosophy contains within it a flaw.

The evidence from the City suggests that ownership now has little to do with control. The plutocratic classes rarely 'own' the entities which they control. Marxist theory with its focus on ownership and its postulation of centralised decision makers may have found a working model in the former Soviet Union, North Korea, China and Cuba. The irony, however, is that the leaders of these nations wielded power in similar fashion to the 'managerial aristocrats' in the West.

The macroeconomic aims of neo-classicist idealism, to improve efficiency through supply side economics, have largely been reached. We now live in a low inflation, low unemployment macro economy. The profitability of our major listed companies has never been so good. The problem remains that left unchecked the 'managerial aristocracy' that controls the City of London will continue their relentless march. They will use all legal (and sometimes illegal) means available to them to inflate their wealth.

To conclude, I would suggest there is a significantly greater need for regulation. The power of the shareholder needs to be bolstered. Senior executives should not be permitted to sit on each other remuneration committees. Instead the pay awards of senior executives ought to be determined by the other stakeholders i.e. the shareholders and the staff, possibly through the unions.

In Germany and other parts of Europe it is a legal requirement for worker directors to sit on the main board of each major company. The decision making function in these companies need to demonstrate and cooperate with interest groups other than themselves. There can be little doubt that this pan-European idea of worker directors would require a sacrifice of efficiency. It is likely that workers' conditions as well as pay would increase the cost of production and potentially harm the profitability of major companies. However, the instances of 'fat cattery' would also doubtless reduce and we could potentially look forward to more 'ethical decision marking' at the highest level.

In order to improve ethics in the City we need more legislation and explicit controls that restrain the profit motive. We need to demand, rather than recommend what is required from the City. The problems of externalities such as pollution emissions, shutting rural bank branches due to cost considerations, inflating insurance premiums and other decisions designed to improve the 'bottom line' need to be dealt with by a strong hand.

In order for this to happen, however, requires that we remove power from those least likely to yield it. Today's City hero perhaps displays psychopathic tendencies and their rasion d'etre is money and power above all else. Do they possess a moral compass?

Notes

[1] For more on this see Plato, 1977, *Euthyphro.* Trans. Burnet, J. Clarendon Press.

[2] For more on this see Mill, J.S. 1998, *Utilitarianism, Oxford Philosophical Texts*, Oxford University Press.

[3] For more on this see Kant, I. 1997, *Groundword of the Metaphysics of Morals*, Trans. Gregor, M. Cambridge University Press.

[4] For more on this see Aristotle, 2000, *Nicomachean Ethics*, Trans. Crisp, R. Cambridge Texts in the History of Philosophy, Cambridge University Press.

[5] *Employment Act 1980, Employment Act 1982, Employment Act 1988, Trade Union Act 1984.*

[6] For more on Monetarism see Friedman, M. 1992, *Money Mischief, Episodes in Monetary History*, HBJ.

[7] In 1986, the former Conservative Prime Minister, Harold Macmillan criticised the Thatcher administration in the House of Lords, for their privatisation programme claiming that they were 'Selling off the family silver'.

[8] Calculated using Technical Officer/C3 max pay which was £9,678 p.a. in 1984 and rose to £25,391 in 2003.

[9] *Report on Directors Remunerations*, Sir Anthony Greener, Deputy Chairman (BT Group) and Chairman of Remuneration Committee, May 2002

[10] *Cadbury Report and Code of Best Practices*, December 1992.

[11] The Greenbury Report on directors' remuneration (July 1995) recommended a Code of Best Practice based on the fundamental principles of accountability, transparency, and linkage of rewards to performance. The Combined Code on Corporate Governance, which was published in June 1998, set out principles of good governance and code provisions which drew heavily on the Greenbury recommendations in relation to directors' remuneration

[12] For more on Psychopathy, see Millon, Simonsen, Birket-Smith and Davis (eds), 2003, *Psychopathy, Antisocial, Criminal and Violent Behaviour*, The Guilford Press.

[13] Wolfe, T. 1988, *The Bonfire of the Vanities*, Bantam.

[14] Marx, K, 1992, *Capital: A Critique of Political Economy Vol 1*, Trans. Fowkes, B. Penguin; Marx, K. 1992, *Capital: A Critique of Political Economy Vol 2*, Trans. Fernbach, D. Penguin; Marx, K. 1992, *Capital: A Critique of Political Economy Vol 3*, Trans. Fernbach, D. Penguin.

Chapter Twelve

Financial Exclusion: an Approach to Economic Development for Global Cities

Alice Rogers and Alexandra Forter

The city has long been at the centre of national commerce. As the bounded geographic location for concentrated wealth generating activities, its vibrancy has long been considered a reflection of the economic development of the larger country. Within the past 25 years, the trans-national nature of economies - as the defining feature of the newest incarnation of globalising processes - has expanded the cities links internationally and, more importantly, its role in the economic development of the nation and its citizens[1]. If as Paul Knox asserts cities are "the natural frameworks for the circulation and reproduction of capital" [2], an attempt to analyse citizen's inclusion in financial markets must come to terms with its asymmetries of information and unequal participation.

Irrespective of ones position with regards to the benefits and costs of globalisation, it is clear that it is aligned with the principles of free markets, deregulation, privatisation, and the consolidation of international financial markets.[3] Most work on globalisation and its relationship to cities is based on transactions between the developed and developing world; little effort has been made to elucidate diverging experience within the developed world, and specifically, its world-class cities.

London provides an excellent location for the study of inequalities in the context of financial successes brought about by globalisation. [4]

London, along with New York and Tokyo, is one of the world's three largest financial centres, with a dominant role in several international financial markets, including crossborder bank lending, international bond issuance and trading, foreign-exchange trading, over-the-counter derivatives, fund management and foreign equities trading. It also has the world's largest insurance market....and more foreign banks and investment houses than any other centre.[5]

The City of London also offers a base from which barriers to financial inclusion can be compared with other cities; as financial institutions across cities respond in different ways to the issue, lessons can be learnt and passed on. The largest of which deals with institutional barriers which the City is addressing through proposals for new money laundering regulations and a growing understanding of the impact of financial exclusion on themselves (socially and economically). At the edge of the City, the financial centre of London, is the community of Tower Hamlets and the home of Toynbee Hall, a settlement house that has been serving the neighbourhood since 1884. In a poignant representation of the diverging experience of development and opportunity, citizens of Tower Hamlets have long endured poverty just as trade and commerce have enriched its geographic neighbours. Most recently, Tower Hamlets has consistently been listed as one of the most deprived neighbourhoods in London with the highest rates of unemployment, slowest rate of business growth and lowest level of basic skills[6].

This chapter is based on the work of Toynbee Hall to address the financial exclusion experienced by its clients in Tower Hamlets and the most deprived communities of London. It is therefore firmly rooted in local reality, and the challenges inherent to building a just experience of development. The chapter will aim to outline the concept of financial exclusion, detail the growing momentum for a financial inclusion agenda in the United Kingdom, and present a specific description of access to banking at the national level with reference to international cases.

How can the trend towards increasing inequality in access to economic development be combated, especially for individuals and households? What potential exists for asset building and wealth accumulation for those on the margins of global cities? The financial inclusion agenda - with its goal of making financial products and services available to all - seeks to integrate those on the lowest incomes into the financial mainstream so that they too may benefit from networks of global resource flows. In many ways, the financial inclusion agenda reflects a wider democratic effort to increase access to information, opportunities, and social integration. The shared vision then is for an individual to be an engaged consumer and citizen catalysing greater integration and growth in society as a whole.

Tremendous effort has been made, especially since 2000, to address financial exclusion. Government initiatives such as the Child

Trust Fund, Savings Gateway and Payment Modernisation of benefits and pensions through electronic transfer appear to be pushing the agenda forward. However, there remain significant disparities between the rhetoric of policy and the infrastructure of implementation. Many households find it difficult or impossible to access quality and free money advice as well as find information about or purchase basic financial products. At a time when money management and economic participation is increasingly dependent on integration into the financial services mainstream, it is essential to delineate the service gaps that need to be filled and the strategies to do so.

What do we mean by Financial Exclusion?

In the United Kingdom, everyday money management is governed by financial services technology. Electronic payment of wages is the norm; cash is being replaced by chip & pin or credit cards; and, bank accounts determine access to a myriad of opportunities and privileges.

The importance of having access to a bank account can not be underestimated; only 12 per cent of employed people were paid in cash in 1998 (compared with 58 per cent in 1978), "having a bank account is, therefore, increasingly a condition of employment" (OFT, 1999: 20)....Cheque cashing agencies have been increasing in number and may charge 7 to 9 per cent of the value of the cheque plus a £2 fee for the transaction....the cost of gas paid by direct debit is 12 per cent less than the cost of a pre-payment meter, and seven per cent less than quarterly cash payments.[7]

As such, financial exclusion is a growing concern as individuals without the ability to participate via these technologies are further marginalised.

Financial exclusion is embedded within the concept of social exclusion that seeks to account for the reinforcing and linked nature of social problems that marginalise individuals and communities.[8] The working definition of financial exclusion, used in this chapter, is the general condition whereby individuals cannot or do not access financial products, services, or knowledge appropriate to their needs.[9] Within this broad conceptualisation of financial exclusion, researchers have contributed depth to the definition by considering the conditions for exclusion such as geography and education[10] as well as the mechanisms generating exclusion such as predatory lending[11].

The Personal Finance Research Centre in 2003 outlined potential barriers to inclusion thereby focusing attention to key aspects of a widespread social problem. The report stated that: "exclusion can come about as a result of problems with access, prices, marketing, financial literacy or self-exclusion in response to negative experiences or perceptions."[12] Elucidating upon the specific barriers of access, products (features, prices and marketing), and financial literacy can provide further clarity as to the nature of financial exclusion at the local level.

Access to financial products or services due to geography or physical presence can exclude vulnerable groups. The process of 'desertification' has been coined to describe the exodus of providers from areas[13]. By generating additional costs to accessing products, a barrier has effectively been generated to entry in the mainstream financial services market. Instead, an alternative financial services market has filled the gap generating opportunities for credit and informal schemes that have a detrimental effect to the objective of moving low-income households out of poverty. Without geographic or physical access to necessary financial services and products, individuals are faced with less security, expensive transaction costs and a general inability to translate their financial relationships into positive outcomes.[14] Recent efforts to overcome the access barrier have included access at supermarkets through cashback, as well as through Post Offices and pay points.

Another barrier is availability of products due to pricing, marketing, or features. Initial bank product development specifically for the low-income market has largely recognised the prohibitive nature of high fees for products. Affordability of insurance products, however, can exclude a wider group through pricing structures that charge high premiums for high risk areas. Moreover, marketing these products to the financially excluded has not overcome a sense that bank accounts and insurance, for example, are for the rich.[15]

Inappropriate features within products pose an additional problem for those making the transition out of the cash economy.[16] The inability to use counter service and sole reliance on chip and pin cards requires basic bank account clients to be versed in computer interface technology and self-management of accounts. In addition, the transition to payment through direct debit and associated charges for insufficient funds is an increasing issue for clients budgeting electronically often for the first time. Responses to these product barriers have included insurance with rent schemes and the introduction of passbook options and the buffer zone facility rather than overdraft on some Basic Bank Accounts.

Financial inclusion is not only having access to appropriate products but also about being financially capable to use those products to improve upon ones situation.[17] The need for increased levels of financial literacy has been identified on a local and national level spurring the Financial Services Authority (FSA) to develop its Financial Capability Steering Group.[18] A need for skill development in budgeting, account management, and critical consumerism are fundamental to ensuring that the effort to include individuals financially is a sustainable development. Isolated initiatives are underway within various institutions, including after-school programmes, job training programmes and credit unions, to deliver these education modules or curricula. In combination with financial literacy, information and generic money advice are key elements to improving the capability of the low and moderate income households currently excluded from most financial advice programmes by cost and qualifying requirements. Again, the FSA has developed a tool for assessing financial capability that could serve to support workers providing advice and information.[19]

As a target for policy initiatives, financial exclusion represents multiple points for potential intervention, the each of which requires its own foundation in skill sets, information, and problem orientation. An effort to increase savings among low-income households may be quite different than one aimed at reducing use of alternative credit providers. An intervention at birth, such as the Child Trust Fund, is quite distinct from promoting pension schemes. Finally, an emphasis on financial education prior to engagement with advanced financial products represents a preventative approach in contrast to the reactive approach of debt advice. Importantly, financial exclusion is not simply about not owning certain products, it is about the ultimate end goal of providing individuals with increased opportunities through building assets and capabilities. As an orienting principle, improving the situation of low-income to no-income individuals and households, can serve to prioritise the uptake of such interventions.

Growing Momentum for the Financial Inclusion Agenda

Over the past decade in the UK, approaches to the working poor or benefit recipients has clearly begun to recognise the need to break the cycle of poverty. By moving beyond pure mechanisms of income transfer, the incorporation of asset-based welfare initiatives, like the Working Tax Credit, seeks to generate opportunities of investment and insurance for the poorest in society.[20] While still maturing as a theoretical and practical initiative, this shift towards a focus on assets and associated capabilities for the individual, household, and community has framed the agenda for much of recent government policy and investment.

The Policy Action Team (PAT) charged by the Social Exclusion Unit with tackling the issue of financial exclusion and setting a government agenda for policy was the first to articulate a financial exclusion agenda.[21] PAT 14 recommended in their final report in 1999: expanding access to banks, credit, insurance and money advice along with the development of credit unions.[22] More recently, these recommendations were reiterated when the Spending Review, in Autumn 2004, announced the formation of a Financial Inclusion Task Force. The Task Force is charged with the coordination and recommendation of policy specific to the promotion of financial inclusion to explicitly target for improvement: access to banking, access to affordable credit, and access to free face-to-face money advice.[23] These three policy targets provide a guide for a preliminary look at financial exclusion. While necessarily reducing the complexity of financial exclusion, it is clear that these policy targets are not interrelated first steps on the pathway to inclusion but also relate intimately to issues such as insurance, pensions, and homeownership.

Access to Banking

Efforts to increase access to banking services aim to reduce the 1.9 million UK households estimated to be unbanked by half.[24] Procedural hurdles required of basic bank account applicants have further compounded the barriers of inappropriate products and geographical access already mentioned. Two fundamental aspects to the application process for vulnerable clients have been the identification and address verification process as well as credit checks.

Bank customers are obliged to provide proof of name and address due to the strengthening of money laundering regulations post 9/11 and anti-fraud efforts. Yet many potential customers do not own the more traditional forms of proof banks often ask for (such as a passport of driving licence). The Joint Money Laundering Steering Group (JMLSG) and the FSA have been reviewing the issue of identification to determine a reasonable requirement that aligns with appropriate risk assessment. The JMLSG proposals include the use of one form of photo identification with either a date of birth or address confirmation needed.

Following this particular objective for financial inclusion policy, the government has initiated several projects to open accounts for individuals traditionally financially excluded. The most recent policy of payment modernisation for benefits and state pension as initiated by the Department of Work and Pensions will be treated in great detail in the next section. Unlike this proposal, other initiatives have sought to incorporate asset-building goals once the unbanked have first entered the financial mainstream through accounts.

The Savings Gateway was the first such initiative that succeeded in opening savings accounts for low income individuals without prior holding of financial products. The National Consumer Council, in its own evaluation of this pilot, highlighted the innovation of matched funding which "offer[ed] a clear and simple incentive for these consumers to save."[25]

Beginning in 2002, Services Against Financial Exclusion (SAFE) at Toynbee Hall[26] and four other pilots around the UK began implementation of the Savings Gateway pilot. The Savings Gateway pilot was a pound for pound savings scheme for low income households to generate incentives conducive to building assets. The government engaged SAFE to serve in the recruitment and support capacity for the pilot, while establishing a link with the bank holding the accounts, Halifax. The outcome of this pilot in Tower Hamlets was the opening of 334 savings accounts. Savings Gateway is currently in its second phase of piloting with extension to a wider audience and a change in the savings incentive.

Access to Affordable Credit

Loosening of regulation in the credit industry in the 1980s opened access to borrowing for those previously excluded. Credit was widely taken up and spending habits changed radically[27]. Indeed, 75% of the individuals in the poorest households state a need to borrow money.[28] In 2003 an estimated 67 million credit cards were in circulation in the UK, outnumbering the population[29]. At the beginning of the twenty first century, there was an estimated savings gap of £27billion[30]. That "one in five people are denied access to mainstream credit from banks," has indeed led to the rise of alternative providers to meet this consumer demand.[31] In turn, consumers of these sub prime products can expect high APRs, encouragement to use "rollover loans," and the threat of asset seizure.[32] While sometimes preferred by consumers, the affordability of these products in comparison to mainstream lenders is high generating externalities for the household such as bad debt.[33]

Third sector providers of credit are a growing area in the United Kingdom with both credit unions and Community Development Finance Institutions leading the way. Initiatives such as Fair Finance, a Community Development Finance Institution focused on personal lending and money advice, have developed affordable forms of credit. This means that money stays in communities (rather than being paid out in higher APR). This in turn assists with regeneration, employment, and, ultimately, sustainable economic growth.

As the credit union development in the UK continues to build scale and resources, the potential for these institutions to similarly contribute to credit availability will be enhanced. Because these institutions focus on savings as a fundamental basis for account management, they are uniquely positioned to encourage households to consider saving for the extension of credit and to orient investments to local community institutions[34].

One example of successful work in this area is ongoing in Birmingham where more than 22,000 members are engaged with credit unions[35]. In tackling financial exclusion, Birmingham credit unions have developed the Factor Four approach which entails: money and debt advice, bill payment and debt repayment services, energy advice and assistance to claim Warm Front and energy efficient grants, and access to affordable credit from a credit union and a Community Reinvestment Trust.

The East Lancashire MoneyLine is a Community Reinvestment Trust that has worked to similarly pool community assets for the promotion of financial inclusion. The organisation has assisted more than 2,000 financially excluded households in its first two years of operation and has already advanced over 1,800 affordable loans[36].

Access to Free Face-to-Face Money Advice

As Sir David Clementi, Chairman of the Prudential plc stated at the OECD Forum, "a market of ill-informed consumers benefits no one." A key element to overcoming financial exclusion is recognising the need for knowledge and access to information about financial services, appropriate products, and basic skills to support money management. Callum McCarthy of the Financial Services Authority elaborates on this state of affairs with some telling statistics:

> Among the adult population in the UK….more than 20 per cent, if asked whether they would prefer to receive GBP30 or 10 per cent of GBP350, opt for the lower figure…A study by the Institute of Financial Services showed that eight in ten people did not correctly identify the term APR as the interest rate and other costs of a loan; and four in ten people admit to not really understanding financial products such as mortgages and ISAs.[37]

Of all three highlighted policy targets, there has been little intervention focusing on local or regional strategies. The FSA's Financial Capability Steering Group's work intends to generate some key recommendations for changing this limitation. In the meantime, money advisers at institutions like the Citizens Advice Bureaus and other voluntary or community organisations are most often managing crisis situations. Some innovative work has been done in the classrooms by credit unions to set up a savings culture whereby young children contribute weekly to an account in their name and learn more about money management in the process. Additionally, the efforts of the Personal Finance Education Group to develop curricula for classrooms has been an excellent resource for organisations and individual teachers seeking to prioritise these life skills within their greater learning objectives.

Institutions for Financial Inclusion

Interventions targeting financial exclusion have not just originated in policy; institutions from the public, private and voluntary/community sector have been engaged with the agenda from the beginning. Practitioners in the voluntary sector have taken on financial inclusion as a subset of community economic development work that combines services to improve personal finance, business development, and social enterprise. Private institutions and for profit companies, many housed in the City, have used their own skills and market position to contribute as well. A key to the rapid development of projects and their implementation in just a short period of time has been the cross sector collaboration and wide range of institutional participation.

Essential to the achievement of any financial inclusion objectives is the role of financial institutions themselves whether they are banks, building societies, or credit unions. Banks, as organised under the British Bankers Association, have committed themselves voluntarily to providing universal banking services. In addition to product development, banks have dedicated resources to the establishment of financial inclusion 'teams'. The responsibility for meeting financial inclusion objectives lies within these teams. According to the level of commitment pledged by the high level management at financial institutions, both human and financial resources are committed to financial inclusion activities.

In addition to Head Office directed activity, banks have undertaken local initiatives (supported by Head Office) to increase the access to banking among the traditionally financially excluded. These isolated initiatives have the potential to serve as models for best practice that could either be scaled up to the national level or replicated in other local communities.

One such model is the Bank of Scotland's work with Big Issue vendors. The homeless vendors selling the Big Issue in Scotland (BIS) and those living in temporary hostels are amongst the most vulnerable people in society. Vendors were unable to access even basic bank accounts due to their lack of identification and permanent address. The bank worked with BIS and the FSA to overcome both of these issues, and then provide over 200 vendors in Scotland with an EasyCash Account helping them to manage and control their finances better. However research then showed that the vendors were not making use of the EasyCash accounts to save. The bank's response was to consider what sort of account and additional incentives would encourage vendors to save and hence build personal assets. The result was the Grand Central Savings Scheme, effectively a Bank of Scotland agency, but with the key innovation that Big Issue in Scotland operates the branch. The outcome has been that over 190 vendors have accumulated balances ranging from 31 to several hundred pounds while providing full time employment for one former Big Issue in Scotland vendor.

Building Societies are largely lumped together with banks, in this analysis as well; however, their unique tradition of serving those excluded from home finance could mean a distinct position for these institutions with regard to serving those currently financially excluded. The regulatory context will be a factor for the development of a unique role for building societies.

> ...While all building societies have not been placed under the same obligation [as banks] six societies have supplied their own version of the basic bank account, and by the summer of 2003, 1,245,342 accounts had been opened[38].

Financial institutions, whatever legal form they take, provide the key access point for clients seeking to overcome financial exclusion because they are often providers of affordable products. As the third sector providers, credit unions and community development finance institutions, establish themselves within this market a restructuring towards serving these low-income groups could occur.

It is important also to consider the role of the voluntary and community organisations. This sector has been engaged with financial inclusion for some time providing ad hoc programming around financial literacy and access to products as needed by their clients. In recent years, it has become clear to the government that the trust and established position within the community of these organisations provides a unique access point to those harder to reach. Increasingly, then, the voluntary and community sector have been engaged to implement policy and establish a grassroots foundation for service delivery.

Cross-Sector Working

The pre-budget report (December 2004) stated that tackling financial exclusion was the responsibility of financial service providers, working in partnership with the government and the voluntary and community sector. This clear articulation of a need for partnership across sectors as well as the prominence given to the voluntary sector is an important shift away from traditional thinking on the implementation of policy through government infrastructure.

Since 2002, SAFE has predominantly served the Tower Hamlets area of London with recent expansion of its outreach throughout London and the South East. As a voluntary sector provider of financial inclusions services and recipient of several key government contracts, SAFE has served as a unique broker of relationship capital to further promote the engagement of multiple grassroots and community providers with private financial service providers.

SAFE began with the specific remit of providing practical services that would help people learn more about managing their money and the 'tools' available for doing that. Through this early work to help local residents with *access* and *education*, additional strategies for tackling financial exclusion were added. Currently, SAFE has four main streams of work focusing on improving financial capability through information, education, advice and access to appropriate products. These include financial education, a debt support programme, improved access to financial services and financial inclusion capacity building.

Overall, by working in partnership with other organisations and financial providers, awareness is raised across the board of the difficulties and costs associated with financial exclusion. Practical co-working also stimulates new and innovative ways of delivering services to meet people's needs so needed to increase financial inclusion. In addition, it builds upon existing infrastructure to minimise necessary additional investment and encourage identification of existing assets in a community.

Partnerships within the voluntary and community sector are important, but working across sectors is vital to the field of financial exclusion. Local projects, such as SAFE at Toynbee Hall, cannot fully support clients without the support and cooperation of the financial services. By building relationships with local bank branch founded on understanding the bank's procedures and minimizing their transaction costs for each client, SAFE has had great success in opening accounts for benefit recipients. Other successful partnerships between the community sector and private sector have been seen through the Business Action on Homelessness's project, Ready for Work with HSBC and Barclays. Similarly banks have supported

Credit Unions and Community Development Finance Initiatives to promote financial inclusion to establish referral systems for additional sources of appropriate products.

Similarly banks such as the Royal Bank of Scotland Group (RBS) support and fund innovative responses to financial exclusion. SAFE at Toynbee Hall's Financial Inclusion Forum, a national forum for financial inclusion projects to network and share best practice, is run in partnership with RBS. This support enables SAFE to share its best practice and experience on a national scale, enabling a local project to learn from local action and develop national solutions. This forum, like other national umbrella organisations offers the potential for national joined up solutions.

Finally models of cross-sector partnerships exist between financial inclusion projects and Government. The work SAFE does with hard-to-reach groups in need of support to access an appropriate account for their wages, benefit or state pension with the Department for Work and Pensions is a model of best practice. We now turn to discuss this initiative in detail and the specific policy target of access to banking. Partnerships and cross-sector approaches, such as this one and those outlined above, offer more potential to the financial inclusion agenda than a reliance on one sector.

Access to Banking in the UK

In 2003 it was estimated that 1.9 million households were without a bank account[39]. While nearly 8% of the total population, among those households in the bottom three income deciles the percentage of households without bank accounts leaps to 65%[40] . By looking behind these larger statistics, clear patterns emerge as to the demographic characteristics of individuals without access to bank accounts. Research has demonstrated that those without access to accounts share much in common with the socially excluded.

The lowest levels of account-holding were found among unemployed people; people with household incomes below 100 a week; people reliant on benefits as their sole source of income; and people with learning difficulties.[41]

As part of the greater issue of financial exclusion, access to bank accounts is a specific point of exclusion that is often complicated by conflicting regulation of banking services and the priority nature of multiple social problems faced by low-income households. In effect, these regulations have generated higher barriers for clients who need to demonstrate their identity and address verification. The regulations, transparency, and technology in UK banking, while important for the stability of the market, may be further contributing to the financial exclusion of the poorest in society. Regulations since 9/11 have focused on tightening up the identity and money transfer capacity of clients. Through data protection regulation as well as fear of fraud, increasingly smaller amounts of data regarding the performance of banks in terms of service to specific client groups is available. And finally, the adoption of increasingly advanced technology has facilitated access to money for some while requiring an increasingly higher skill level of customers.

Bank Accounts as a Gateway for Financial Inclusion

A bank account is often an introduction into the financial mainstream for low-income households. As such, holding and managing an appropriate account at a bank or building society provides individuals with multiple tangible and intangible benefits (see the diagram below for an outline of these benefits). These benefits can additionally expand the choices available to low-income households and open up a pathway for achievement of even greater financial inclusion.

Bank Accounts: Costs and Benefits, Choices and Risk

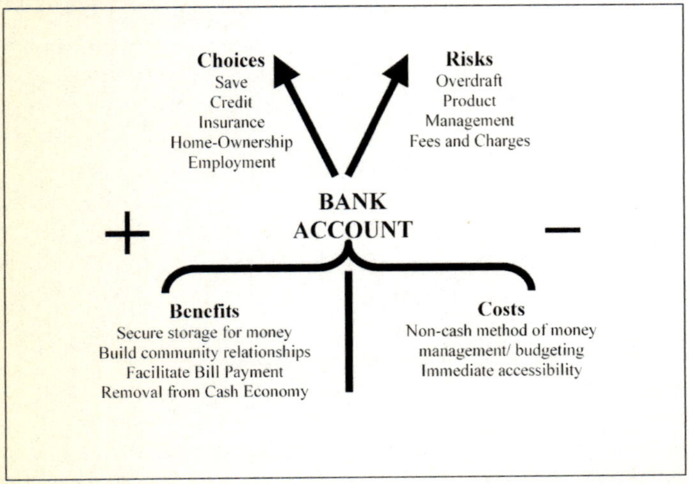

Policy Context

Government policy is often heralded as the main mechanism by which the financial inclusion agenda can succeed. The commitments of the post-1997 Labour Government have indeed demonstrated that significant movement forward can be achieved through this route and initiatives such as the Financial Inclusion Taskforce. These policies have largely been implemented to increase the financially excluded to engage the mainstream financial system rather than vice versa. Questions remain whether additional work to legislate on the role of financial systems is necessary and could propel further forward the agenda. In the meantime, it is important to learn from the current policies as they are implemented and determine the potential for scaling up its results.

One such policy initiative has been the national payment modernisation programme (Direct Payment). In an effort to cut costs, and potentially expand the reach of financial inclusion efforts, the DWP and the Inland Revenue initiated a transition to Direct Payment of all benefits to appropriate accounts. Simultaneous to the development of universal banking services through the Post Office, the Direct Payment initiative also engaged banks and building societies to develop basic bank account products. Additionally, it is estimated that approximately 8 million benefit recipients have transitioned to Direct Payment thereby accessing an account[42].

While still an ongoing initiative, this is the first national effort in the United Kingdom to bank the unbanked. It has required the commitment and participation of private and public sector actors. And most importantly, it has required local level actors to implement the policy. SAFE has taken on this role because of its previous experience with access to banking as well as its networking efforts with grassroots organisations serving low-income individuals.

Market Context

While government pressure was applied to banks and building societies to play a role in the financial inclusion agenda, they have voluntarily developed basic banking products for those on low-income or benefits. The basic bank account product was designed from research into the needs of the financially excluded and complemented by the bank's own research into the market.[43] Since these products were developed in 2003, 5.5 million accounts have been opened[44]. While take up has been high, more detailed information about account use and savings is not currently reported (such as those that go on to close the account due to lack of use or misuse). The basic bank account is a stripped down current account that can provide an introduction to banking and its technologies. However, over time, banks have begun to restrict certain features of the basic bank account such as the buffer zone and counter service, suggesting a tendency to under serve the needs of low-income clients.

Importantly though as a market initiative, banks and building societies are not capitalising on their investment in Basic Bank Account customers by upgrading them to current accounts. Only 26,720 accounts were upgraded in 2003[45]. In combination with case studies on services provided to the unbanked, it is clear that further work needs to be done to develop a business case for banking the unbanked that will at once satisfy bank's profit maximisation goals and mobilise competition for quality service delivery.

Grassroots Context

Grassroots delivery of financial inclusion services has been wide ranging. In many cases, the most developed efforts have been reactive, engaging clients when they have already fallen into debt. However, increasingly, work is being done in the UK to establish a baseline for quality financial capability services, free face-to-face money advice, and general support around accessing appropriate products.

For instance, SAFE's work on access to banking began with the project in 2002 and uses an individualised service delivery model. By taking into account the local context, SAFE capitalises on assets in the community and embeds its access to banking efforts within existing initiatives serving low-income households. SAFE has therefore established strong relationships with social service providers and a reputation for serving the financial needs of low income residents of London.

SAFE has placed the financially excluded individual at the centre of all service delivery to ensure that the process facilitates the transfer of information and individual empowerment to make an informed choice to improve their financial future. While abstractly considered, being excluded both financially and socially, SAFE has found through work with 2,000 plus individuals that there are often key connections that individuals have to their community and friends or families. These support networks often provide the individual information about community based organisations that can serve their needs.

Importantly, financially excluded individuals often present multiple needs and, at times, all of high priority. By working with community based organisations that can address housing, food, job training, and immigration concerns, SAFE has been able to embed its financial services into existing programmes of urgency for the individual. SAFE has used this infrastructure to elevate the role of bank accounts in supporting clients with multiple needs. Thus, for job training programme participants, getting a bank account meets a minimum employability criterion. For housing support programmes, a bank account can serve to facilitate payment of benefits as well as securing a tenancy agreement.

For these individuals, access to banking alone is not a guarantee that financial inclusion has been achieved. Additional work with individuals to deal with debt and/ or learn the skills to manage money is necessary. Moreover, clear guides for how a bank account can catalyse asset building and establish economic security are needed. The progress made in the UK and even more locally in London is based on the development of affordable and appropriate products and provision of quality information, but requires the continued engagement of all sectors to continue to move the financial inclusion agenda forward.

This work alone, however, would not be successful because it does not draw upon the resources within the public and private sector. SAFE has therefore worked to build bridges between national government departments and local councils, and banks and other financial institutions in the neighbouring City. A lack of communication and information between sectors, has mobilised SAFE to promote discussion of the financial inclusion agenda and information sharing about financial inclusion policies with local representatives. In several community initiatives, SAFE has established itself as a resource for information on financial issues.

Financial Exclusion – an International Perspective

The experience of London and the UK is not uncommon to the cities and financial centres of countries around the world. As links between these financial centres are strengthened the experience of financial exclusion for marginalised communities is similarly shared across the globe. A comparison of approaches to financial inclusion from international cities can shed new light on the elements of successful interventions as well as elucidate some common themes across the experiences of financially excluded individuals and communities. The following case studies illustrate briefly some of the achievements within international cities. These cases are categorised roughly by the driving force for the intervention, policy, market, grassroots, or cross-sector. In the specific case of access to banking, international contexts have been varied in terms of the legislative mandate established for banks participation. The strength of the unbanked market alone to propel entry and the delivery mechanisms employed for reaching marginalised individuals with appropriate products and services.

Policy Led

In the United States, the working poor have been offered the Earned Income Tax Credit (EITC) as an innovative policy mechanism to move families out of poverty and reward work. In 2002, nearly 21 million families filing federal income tax returns claimed EITC with an estimated 4.9 million families moving out of poverty as a result.[46] This federal policy is complemented at the state level by EITCs that similarly seek to reduce taxes and supplement wages for the working poor.

In Chicago, Illinois, the EITC initiative has been harnessed to encourage recipients to open accounts. The First Savings Programme - a partnership between the Centre for Economic Progress and ShoreBank - provided free tax preparation for families eligible for the EITC on site at the bank branch with the goal being to open accounts for direct transfer into an account of the EITC. The product offered to participants was a savings account with no minimum balance requirement, a cash card, and no fees. Savers earned interest at the same rate as on other savings products offered by ShoreBank. In just two years, the partnership opened 222 new accounts on the south side of Chicago with initial deposits of $200,000[47].

Market Led

Australia's third largest bank, ANZ, engaged the unbanked on Fiji Islands largely because of the size of this untapped market. ANZ bank estimated that 6.5 million individuals in the Pacific were without bank accounts with 50% of the Fijian population financially excluded. In 2003, staff began research into the needs of those individuals without accounts in Fiji and found that there was both a need and an interest in banking services. ANZ then proceeded to develop banks on wheels that could reach the rural areas of Fiji as well as two products, a savings account and everyday account.

In the implementation of this service, however, ANZ found that many clients sought additional financial literacy advice for themselves and their children. ANZ partnered with UNDP to deliver this service and develop appropriate curriculums. The results are impressive: 25,800 individuals opened accounts saving more than $500,000. The individuals who have benefited from this initiative note the increased security of their money, reduced transaction costs, and increased saving[48].

Grassroots Led

Initiating its work as a non-governmental organization, K-Rep Bank in Kenya came to the conclusion that the constant struggle to maintain capital for programming necessitated a move to banking. Today, the NGO remains alongside the bank and maintains the vision of grassroots and local approaches to working with the poor in Kenya. The bank has 25 outlets across the country and reaches individuals through accounts designed to encourage savings before borrowing[49].

In South Africa, work at the grassroots level has been possible through the establishment of portable banks in rural and outlying urban areas. Standard Bank and First National Bank have been the leaders in this effort setting up these "banks in a box" across the country in an effort to reach the estimated 17.5 million individuals who are unbanked. In addition to providing appropriate products, the banks have focused on transferring information in the hopes of raising the financial capability of the unbanked. An innovative mechanism used by staff is "Train Talk", informal sessions to present information about financial services while people travel by train[50].

Conclusion

Financial exclusion is indeed a pressing issue linked into many of the social concerns currently high on the agenda in the UK and the world; unemployment, education and poverty. As such interventions to increase the engagement of low-income and benefit recipients with the City led financial sector can effect multiple policy targets. Most importantly, though, financial inclusion efforts have the potential to improve the living standards of individuals and households by building up their own capabilities and assets.

It is clear that no single solution exists for reducing the exclusion of individuals from the financial mainstream. Indeed, the most effective approaches seem to understand the local conditions for intervention and build upon existing institutions work in related fields. Certainly by joining up the efforts of multiple institutions, and the resources, the effect on exclusion is multiplied.

Ultimately, the financial institutions of the City are not charitable organisations. The industry does not perceive it as being in their interest to serve low-income clients with low-profit products (such as basic bank accounts) or explaining in detail how these products work. For financially excluded people, a plank is missing on the route to long-term financial health. There is a need to engage multiple sectors in financial inclusion work and to adapt the approach to the private sector to specifically speak to the business case for serving the unbanked.

SAFE's experience with the Saving Gateway has indicated that whilst those with a very limited income will struggle to save (in the pilot these were typically young adults receiving Job Seekers Allowance with housing costs covered through Housing Benefit), participants were enthused at the opportunity to save with a relatively high return for their efforts and commitment. Making certain that interventions to effect financial inclusion are focused on the clients require their participation in developing approaches as well as their own articulation of their needs. Understanding the long-term goals of clients and the reasons for short-term needs is a key to successful programming.

Financial inclusion efforts have a great potential to transform the experiences of low-income individuals and households in cities across the world. By building towards the financial independence of the individual, the opportunity exists for more equitable distribution of wealth and choice for the future.

Notes

[1] Keohane, Robert O. and Josephy Nye. Spring 2000, "Globalization: What's new? What's not? and so what?" in *Foreign Policy*. No. 118. pp. 104-119; Rodrik, Dani. 1997, "Sense and Nonsense in the Globalization Debate." *Foreign Policy*. No. 107. pp. 19-37. See also, Saskia Sassen. 1991, *Global Cities: New York, London, Tokyo*, Princeton University Press: Princeton, NJ.

[2] Knox, Paul. May 1997, "Globalization and Urban Economic Change." *Annals of the American Academy of Political and Social Science*, Vol. 551. pp. 17-27.

[3] *United Nations Comission on Economic Cultural and Social Rights. Statement on Globalization*. May 11, 1998. Found at www.globalpolicy.org/globaliz/define/unstate.htm

[4] In the UK the financial services sector "accounted for 5.3 per cent of national income and the UK's surplus in financial services trade was £17.8 billion, the largest in the world" HM Treasury 2004 p. 1.

[5] "Financial Service." *Country Background*. United Kingdom. EIU Viewswire.

[6] London Borough of Tower Hamlets 'People and Profile', 2002

[7] Moore, Robert. *Access to banking services and credit for UK ethnic minorities, refugees and asylum seekers*. Found at http://www.radstats.org.uk/no075/moore.htm.

[8] Financial Services Authority. July 2000, *In or Out? Financial Exclusion: A literature and research review*, Consumer Research 3.

[9] HM Treasury Report 2004; Regan S. and Paxton W. 2003, *Beyond Bank Accounts*, IPPR; Sinclair S. 2001, *Financial exclusion: An introductory survey,* CRISIS; CRSIS Report 2003

[10] Financial Services Authority. July 2000, *In or Out? Financial Exclusion: A literature and research review*. Consumer Research 3. Pp. 79-84 (geography).

[11] Palmer H. with Conaty P. 2002, *Profiting from Poverty: Why Debt is Big Business in the UK*, New Economics Foundation.

[12] *Personal Finance Research Centre.*

[13] Thrift N. and Leyshon, A, 1997, *Money/Space: Geographies of Monetary Transformation* Routledge; *In or Out? Financial Exclusion: A literature and research review*. Financial Services Authority Consumer Research 3, July 2000.

[14] Sinclair S. Op cit. P.44-46.
[15] Joseph Rowntree Foundation, 1999, *Understanding And Combating Financial Exclusion*. York: Joseph Rowntree Foundation Findings. (March). Ref:369. and Financial Services Authority, 2000, *In Or Out? Financial Exclusion – A Literature And Research Review*. (Consumer research 3). London:Financial Services Authority. P. 18.
[16] National Consumer Council. September 2004, *Mind the Financial Gap: Access to Financial Services*.
[17] NACAB 2003 describes financial capability as ' having the skills, knowledge and confidence to make effective money making decisions'.
[18] McCarthy, Callum. June 27 2005, speech on "Financial Capability Steering Group." *Financial Inclusion Forum*.
[19] Financial Services Authority, , *Building Financial Capability in the UK: the role for financial advice*. Published by the FSA on the advice of the Working Group, July 2004 .
[20] Ippr and Case. *Wealth and Welfare: The role of assets over the life cycle. Preliminary Publication*; Regan, S (ed), 2001, *Assets and Progressive Welfare,* Institute for Public Policy Research, London.
[21] HM Treasury, 16 November 1999, *Initiatives To Tackle Financial Exclusion*. News Release. 190/99.
[22] Policy Action Team, 14. November 1999, *Access To Financial Services: The Report Of Policy Action Team 14*. London: HM Treasury.
[23] HM Treasury, 2004, Promoting *Financial Inclusio,* HM Treasury: London.
[24] *Family Resource Survey*. 2003.
[25] National Consumer Council. September 2004. p. 3.
[26] For more information about SAFE at Toynbee Hall please visit:www.toynbeehall.org.uk
[27] Ambrose, Peter and Liz Cunningham, November 2004, *The Ever Increasing Circle*, Health and Policy Research Centre, University of Brighton: Brighton UK; *Debt on your Doorstep: Who is responsible advice*, AdviceNI, December 2004, www.adviceni.net.
[28] Policis survey in Kempson, Elaine and Collard, Sharon, 2005, *Affordable Credit*, University of Bristol, Bristol. P. 11.
[29] Datamonitor, 'Plastic Nation', November 2004
[30] *Targeting the Savings Gap*, Association and British Insurers and Oliver, Wyman and Company September 2001
[31] Kempsen and Collard, 2005. op cit. p. 25-26.
[32] Ibid. p. 12
[33] Ibid. p. 2;
[34] Conaty, Brown and Mayo, 2004, *Life Saving: Community Development Credit Unions*, New economics Foundation
[35] *The Community Banking Partnership: A joined up solution for financial inclusion*, 2004, New Economics Foundation: London UK

[36] *The Community Banking Partnership: A joined up solution for financial inclusion*, 2004, New Economics Foundation: London UK
[37] McCarthy, Callum. Spring 2005, "Financial Capability" in *Toynbee Journal*. P. 6.
[38] Dayson K. 2005, *Investing in People and Places*, Salford University. p53.
[39] Family Resources Survey, 2003
[40] HM Treasury Report, 2004
[41] Kempson, E. & Whyley, C. 2000, *Extortionate Credit In The UK*, Dept of Trade & Industry.
[42] Author's calculation from DWP statistics
[43] Kempson and Whyley, 1999, *Tackling financial exclusion: An area based approach*; Collard, Kempson and Whyley, 2001, *Payment of Pensions and Benefits: A Survey of Social Security Recipients Paid by Order Book or Girocheque* published for the Foundation by The Policy Press
[44] British Bankers Association www.bba.org.uk
[45] British Bankers Association www.bba.org.uk
[46] Llobera, Joseph and Zahradnik, Bob, May 2004, *A Hand Up: How State Earned Income Tax Credits Help Working Families Escape Poverty in 2004*, Center on Budget and Policy Priorities.
[47] *Money in the Bank: The Extra Credit Savings Programme*, ShoreBank and the Centre for Law & Human Services.
[48] Blacklock, Carolyn, June 2005, *ANZ Bank's Microfinance Experience in the Fiji Islands*, ADB: Finance for the Poor. Vol. 6, No. 2. Pp. 6-8.
[49] Wood, Christina and de Cleene, Sean, *Sustainability Banking in Africa*, CEO Briefing: A document of the UNEP FI African Task Force. UNEP Finance Initiative. Mayoux, Stephane, *In the black: Credit Revolution in Kenya*. BBC. 1 November 2001.
[50] Rathbone, Kevin, 2004, "Banking the Unbanked in South Africa". *Global Regulation*, Deloitte. Issue II. Pp. 4-5. Kitten, Tracy. *Reaching the unbanked: Learning from South Africa's FIs*, www.kioskmarketplace.com

Chapter Thirteen

The City of London, its Bankers and Central and Eastern Europe

Giancarlo Perasso[1]

In 2004, eight new countries of the east joined the European Union and became part of the single market. After the fall of communism, however, Central and Eastern European countries were facing unprecedented challenges in restructuring their economies. These challenges covered the entire spectrum of human activities: from politics to economics, from education to external relations. The transition effort needed external help, both financial and technical assistance.

In this respect, the division of labour rapidly became clear: international organisations were to deal with institution building (help writing laws and regulations regarding the civil society, set up a new judicial system, write the central bank law, market regulations) and macroeconomic support, the private sector was left to play a role in the implementation of structural reform (privatisation, foreign direct investments).

To this end, the marriage between Central and Eastern Europe and the City of London had the potential to be a marriage made in heaven. Has it been the case? In this piece, I will, first, take a look at the role played by the City of London and Central and Eastern Europe and then express some thoughts on the non-financial interaction between the City and Central and Eastern Europe. Finally, I will try to assess whether it was indeed a 'marriage made in heaven'. One word of caution is necessary though. This piece is mostly based on personal experiences, anecdotal evidence and is therefore not a detailed academic assessment. Nevertheless, it will give the reader the flavour of what the opening up of Central and Eastern Europe to the market economy has meant for the City. In this respect, perhaps the most interesting issues have been cultural and I will tackle them in the third part of this chapter.

The Early Days: The Role of the City in Fostering Transition

The fall of communism and the opening up of Central and Eastern Europe was any investment banker's dream. Think of all the areas where City expertise could be employed: privatisation, restructuring and foreign direct investments (FDI); treasury/debt management; and, of course, providing financing for the transition effort. The first section of this paper will examine these items more closely.

Privatisation[2] and FDI[3] played a huge role in the transition process. To begin with, the sheer size of the assets to be privatised was enormous. In some countries, almost 100% of GDP was generated in the state sector. Secondly, the privatisation methods and the political issues related to privatisation were extremely hot issues that had important implications for the activities of investment banks. Without going through all the details of the approaches followed by the various countries, it is fair to say that investment bankers were almost exclusively involved in privatisations where a foreign investor was involved. By contrast, 'small privatisation', such as the transfer of the property from the state to individuals or other similar cases, was dealt with in the more general institutional reform framework.

Some of the privatisation deals were large and provided generous fees for bankers. For instance the Skoda-Volkswagen privatisation in the Czech Republic where Volkswagen paid US$900 mn for 31 per cent of the company in 1991 and then invested heavily in the company to become the sole owner in 2001. Aside from large privatisations, City bankers were involved in most foreign direct investments (FDI) as advisers, arrangers of financing, or other roles. Still, the amount of FDI was relevant for the countries in question but not for City bankers per se: The stock of FDI in Central Europe (excluding the former Soviet Union) was of US$110 bn in 2001, i.e. about 11 years after transition started. If one adds the former Soviet Republics, the grand total reaches approximately US$170 bn. Compare this with US$420 bn of FDI in the UK only over the same period. Central and Eastern Europe was an opportunity for making profits but some of the initial enthusiasm was tempered after a while for two reasons: the market became more and more competitive and fees smaller and smaller and the bulk of privatisation/FDI took place early in the transition and opportunities became fewer.

Debt management and restructuring was another important issue. The former communist countries had a limited involvement in the international financial system as a matter of choice. According to communist economics, the communist bloc (or Comecon, the communist common 'market') had to be self-sufficient and transactions were settled in 'transferable roubles', a notional currency. Overall, the role of finance was limited and money did not fulfil its role as means of exchange, unit of value, and store of value to the same extent as in market economies.

A few countries had a deeper involvement in the international financial system during their communist era. Most notably Hungary became a member of the IMF in 1982 but the first programme was launched only in 1991, when the communist regime was no longer in power. Poland joined the IMF in 1986, when the old regime was already under severe strain, and the first fund programme was launched in 1991. The Soviet Union was never a member but Russia joined the IMF in 1992 and the first programme was launched in that same year.

Still, these countries were not completely absent from the international financial markets as trade credits were extended and government-to-government loans were fairly common. It was the private sector that was not involved to the extent it might have wished.

All this changed after 1989 and the economic recession at the beginning of transition made it, on the one hand, more difficult for some of these countries to repay their external obligations and, on the other, led other countries (most notably, Russia) to borrow heavily in international markets. The City here played a dual role. For the countries in need of rescheduling their debts (as in the case of Bulgaria, Poland and Yugoslavia in the early/mid-nineties), investment bankers acted as advisers in the process as well as being directly engaged in the actual rescheduling procedure. It was an interesting and challenging time. For the countries in need of fresh financing, City bankers were happy to arrange a bond issue or a loan. In this respect, the region, and especially the former Soviet Union, proved to be 'bonus heaven' for many investment bankers. At the same time, these new issues allowed the emerging market asset class to expand significantly, thus providing new investment opportunities for asset managers.

There was, however, a wake-up call: the Russians were not paying. On paper, it was a match made in heaven. On one side there were people who could raise and lend cash; on the other, there were people who needed it to develop their economies. Unfortunately, as in the case of other emerging markets, not everything went smoothly. I still remember Monday morning August 17th 1998 when I gingerly strolled on the trading floor and one of our young analysts suddenly shouted "[expletive] Russia has defaulted on its debt!"

A lot has been written on this topic[4] but a few words are worth mentioning. To begin with, opinions on Russia differed widely at that time. Remember that the IMF was heavily engaged in Russia given the country's dire economic situation (especially with respect to public finances) and that many were playing the 'moral hazard' game, i.e. many were thinking that Russia was too big and 'too nuclear' to fall and, therefore, that the IMF and G7 governments would come up with the money to avoid a default. Consider the following excerpts from a pres conference given by Stanley Fischer, then First Deputy Managing Director of the IMF, on the 13th of July 1998, about a month before the debt default:

> …the Fund has agreed to provide an extra $11.2 billion to Russia this year, of which $5.6 billion will be made available on the passage of the Board's agreement to the program next Monday." …In addition, the Russian Government will tomorrow morning be announcing the details of a plan to convert on a voluntary basis--that is important--GKOs, Treasury Bills, maturing through June 1999, into longer-term, dollar-denominated liabilities at 7 years and 20 years. This scheme is expected to be attractive to the holders of GKOs and is expected to help take some of the pressure off the markets in two ways. One is this rollover problem of GKOs over time, and second, it would reduce the interest bill, and in reducing the interest bill on the ones that are replaced, it is also likely to reduce the interest bill on existing GKOs, because there will be fewer of them[5].

The second measure (the swap of GKOs into longer term, dollar denominated paper) was an idea of investment bankers at Goldman Sachs, a prime example of the involvement of City bankers in debt restructuring.

Unfortunately, investors and many investment bankers took the IMF announcement as evidence that Russia was 'too big and too nuclear' to fall and did not see that the Russian government was in such a desperate situation that the only way out was to suspend the repayment of its domestic debt and ask for a restructuring of its external debt. Of course, many have argued that investment bankers were dumping paper held by the bank onto investors, but my experience was one of great uncertainty permeating the market. As a matter of fact, we were divided amongst those who thought that Russia would be able to muddle through and those who thought that it was just an accident in waiting.

One important development of the Russian crisis was the decoupling of central European countries (the eight countries that joined the EU in 2004) from the former Soviet Union Republics. Until the summer of 1998 all the former communist countries were more or less bundled together. After the crisis, it became apparent that, say, Poland and Hungary had strong institutions, excellent policy makers and stronger economies than Russia or Ukraine. On top of that, negotiations to join the EU were about to start.

The big problem for analysts like me was not so much to sell the idea that central European countries were different from Russia but the idea that joining the EU was a good thing for Hungary, Poland and the other countries. Many of my British colleagues were all strongly anti-EU and anti-Euro, and hence could not see that prospective EU membership was the institutional anchor for these countries to develop a market economy and to achieve economic success. It took some time to win them over and basically it was due to the pressure exerted by continental, mostly German, clients who first saw the similarity between developments in Central Europe and developments in Italy or Spain after the ERM crisis of 1992, i.e., the convergence of bond yields towards those prevailing in the Eurozone. To use City jargon, the 'converge trade' was born and, like any profit opportunities, the City embraced the convergence trade enthusiastically. A new area of business was born and it was probably this development that made the City and Central Europe integrate further.

The Present Interaction between the City and Eastern Europe

To be able to trade, invest in and sell local bonds one has to know the local market very well. This need caused a sharp increase in the demand for young, bright and ambitious Eastern Europeans to come to London and work in the financial sector. Clearly, the changes in the post-communist countries and the possibility of studying abroad allowed City firms to draw on a fairly large pool of young eastern

European graduates who were all too happy to move to London. Initially, it was mostly traders and quant analysts. Currently Eastern European personnel cover all positions and the integration, from the point of view of the labour force, is the same as for other nationalities. Likewise, many eastern institutions have opened branches or offices in the City, thus further advancing the case of the City of London as the most prominent financial centre in Europe.

The economic development and the intellectual sophistication of economic agents and policy-makers in Central and Eastern Europe, together with EU membership for many countries in the region, have made these markets behave like typical G7 markets. Some differences still exist in countries that have not, and probably will not, join the EU (like Russia), but the progress has nevertheless been enormous and, remarkably, in a very short time.

Non-Financial Aspects of the Interaction between the City and Central and Eastern Europe

Perhaps the most interesting aspect of the interaction between the City and Central and Eastern Europe has been the integration of two very different cultures. When the 'wild east' opened up to the outside financial word, it was assumed to be similar to other emerging markets, both by investment bankers and by international institutions. Therefore, scores of investment bankers, analysts and traders who had previously been dealing with Argentina or Indonesia found themselves to be dealing with either un-reformed communist bureaucrats or zealous free-marketers who did not possess a full understanding of the market economy, despite their genuine desire to change the situation. By the same token, investment bankers were used to dealing with officials in, say, Chile where most of them held PhDs in economics from the University of Chicago, and not with officials who had spent their lives studying and applying 'communist economics'.

The dialogue, at times, became farcical. For example, when asked to provide a forecast for the balance of payments, the chief economist of the central bank of a former soviet republic gave me a wonderful spreadsheet which was more a 'source and uses' scheme rather than a proper balance of payments, with all rows and columns ending in perfect balance (as planning in the old communist regime had required). My senior colleague then said: "It all balances out, how wonderful… you do not need our money, then….”; immediately the official snatched the piece of paper out of my colleague’s hand muttering that there must have been some mistake and asked us to come back in the afternoon. As expected, in the afternoon we were given a balance of payments projection with a USD2 bn deficit. Stories like this abound and the ignorance was on both sides.

In some cases, on the contrary, the ignorance of western investors was indeed appalling. I still remember the following exchange in autumn 1998:

> *Client: “Giancarlo, what is your outlook for the Czechoslovak Crown?”*
>
> *Giancarlo: “Which one of the two Crowns?”*
>
> *Client: “What do you mean? Are you making fun of me?”*
>
> *Giancarlo: “Not at all, Czechoslovakia split into the Czech Republic and the Slovak Republic in 1993 and each country has its own Crown. Which one do you want to talk about?”*
>
> *Client: “[expletive], I don’t know, I have to check, I will call you later…”*

Scores of western ‘experts’ also got it spectacularly wrong, viz. the CIA analysis of the communist countries that was a massive overestimation of the actual productive capacity of these countries. In this respect, major rows emerged between bankers and officials when big privatisations where involved. In many cases, the company was a ‘value subtractor’ (i.e. the value of the final product was less than the sum of the value of the inputs and therefore the company needed a major overhaul to be able to generate profits) rather than a ‘value maker’. Local officials were proud of their companies and did not want to sell the country’s ‘jewels’ cheap.

On the other hand, bankers and consultants realised that nobody would have bought those assets at the price requested by officials but they could not afford losing the privatisation mandate and, at the same time, look as if they did not realise how bad the situation was. Add to this the fact that usually the country’s officials pontificated about how skilled the labour force was since everybody in communist societies could read and write “while in South-East Asia nobody can read”, as an official in the former Soviet Union once told me. Reality was a bit different. I remember one case when we went to visit a brewery and the equipment was so old and malfunctioning that each bottle had a different quantity of beer in it and workers were just drinking a bit from each bottle to 'even out' the content in the different bottles. I am sure that they could all read and write and actually had some initiative, but the plant was not an example of best working practices.

This 'pride factor' was particularly acute in the former Soviet Union, and Russia in particular. Officials resented being lumped together with 'third world countries' by investors managing emerging markets funds and some officials actually appeared to be revelling in the investors' pain during the 1998 crisis. For example, the response Viktor Gerashchenko, then chairman of Russia's central bank, gave to an investor asking whether the government or the central bank of Russia were thinking of buying back some of the debt they had defaulted on since that debt was priced at few cents to the dollar: "You know, it could get cheaper…" and then he smiled and his eyes twinkled.

In other cases, the City was seen as a nest of speculators, ready to bring down a country's currency without any respect for the country's history and institutions. City traders (and even analysts in some cases!) were accused of meeting in smoky pubs and deciding which currency to take down next. It was amusing to read articles in newspapers mentioning scores and scores of conspiracy theories like this when the reality was much simpler: if there was a chance of making money by speculating against a currency, no trader would let that chance go. It took some time, but ultimately, this simple reality dawned upon commentators and officials in these countries. It was a learning process for everybody and fortunately conspiracy theories have now almost completely disappeared[6].

Conclusion

The marriage between the City and Central and Eastern Europe has, overall, been a successful one. My view is that the non-financial aspects of the interaction between these two words have been even more crucial than the economic/financial ones in fostering the transition from a planned economy to a market economy. A lot has been done and the progress has been impressive and very fast. Much remains to be done in some countries to strengthen institutions that would guarantee the proper functioning of the market economy, though, and here City bankers can play an important role in establishing a dialogue with the authorities.

Notes

[1] All opinions expressed in the text are my own only.

[2] The literature on privatisation in central and Eastern Europe is almost infinite. See, for example: Giancarlo Perasso, Privatisation schemes and their impact for investors, paper presented at the Royal Institute for International Affairs conference on "Doing Business in an Enlarged Europe", 17 November 2003 and the references quoted there.

[3] The literature on FDI in Central and Eastern Europe is enormous as well. See, for example, Mikael Lönnborg, Mikael Olsson and Michael Rafferty; The Race for inward FDI in the Baltic States and Central and Eastern Europe; http://www.snee.org/filer/papers/196.pdf

[4] See the IMF website (www.imf.org) for a number of technical papers on the Russian Crisis. An excellent non-technical description of what happened can be found in Paul Blustein's "The Chastening" (Public Affairs, 2001) where the (supposed) faults of investment bankers and the IMF are clearly exposed.

[5] See http://www.imf.org/external/np/tr/1998/tr980713.htm for a transcript of the press conference.

[6] Let me add a lighter note. At the beginning, the interaction between City bankers and Eastern Europeans was asymmetric, since the former knew the subject matter better than the latter. Many central and eastern Europeans resented that and tried to get even. As mentioned, we were often seen as 'evil speculators' and nothing else. However, there was one area where Eastern Europeans taught a thing or two to City bankers: drinking. City bankers who thought they could prove their 'machismo' in Moscow or Warsaw by drinking their counterparts under the table were in for some ugly surprises!

Chapter Fourteen

The Future of the City in Europe

Angela Knight

Let me start by saying what the Future of the City in Europe is not dependent upon. It is not dependent upon whether the UK joins the euro, as out of the Euro, the City has continued to extend the breadth and depth of business that it undertakes. For example, London is now the largest European centre for euro exchange business and 70% of European based hedge fund assets are managed from here. The future of the City in Europe is also not dependent upon whether the European constitution is ratified. Whilst this constitution is interestingly seen as too Anglo-Saxon by the French and too centralising by the Brits, ratified or not, it is unlikely to affect the business undertaken by the City.

The City is schizophrenic about Europe. On the one hand, it tends to be pro-European from a philosophical point of view, and talks of the benefits of creating a single market in financial services across the shining future in the EU, while continuing to have difficulties with the European relationships. As is so often the case, theory and reality are a long way apart. One of the problems is of London's making. London sees itself much more as a world financial centre than a regional centre and the numbers give substance to this view. For example, there are over 69 authorised banks in the UK and the London Stock Exchange has more foreign companies listed on it than any other exchange. Statistics such as these underpin the global nature of London. The City has always attracted this business because of its openness and it's welcome to foreign firms providing them with an easy access to markets. It holds a central position between the US and Asian time zones, it has a heavy concentration of financial firms, therefore all types of business can be undertaken, plus having on hand the necessary support systems such as accounting, actuarial, legal and IT. The financial infrastructure is robust; it believes in a proportionate approach to regulation; it is innovative; and of course the *lingua franca* of finance is English. Couple that with the UK culture of "fair play" whereby someone from overseas knows that there are unlikely to be problems but should one arise then it will be dealt with fairly, then these give at least some of the reasons that have made the City the global player it is today.

But despite its global nature (and regardless of the Euro or the EU constitution) it is the EU that will impact most strongly on the City in the short term through a raft of regulatory changes. In the last few years London has found itself up to its neck in the technical detail of the 42 proposals that make up the Financial Services Action Plan (FSAP). In the first instance, this FSAP was heavily supported by the City in theory, as its intention is to bring down the artificial barriers to cross border trading in Europe, particularly for wholesale financial services in the EU. Removing unnecessary barriers to trade is a massively important step, whether it is in the financial world or in any other part of the commercial environment. The reasons are self evident - it is the liberalising of trade that has done so much to improve economies around the world. So just as benefits have accrued in other commercial fields in terms of increased employment, rising GDP and providing the consumer with more choice in goods at a better price, then the same should happen with financial services. But in finance it is not as easy as that!

Looking across Europe, most countries have a stock exchange; there are twenty-five different requirements of reporting a transaction and then every conceivable difference in the clearing and settlement of equities that one can think of. Couple this with the desires of all Governments to get their citizens to save for their future, but no harmony in the methods used and a plethora of different tax breaks in place, then bringing down the barriers for cross-border financial services is a lot harder than bringing down the barriers for the sale of washing machines or computers.

Nevertheless, the FSAP is hugely important for the Future of the City in Europe and its 42 changes are a laudable attempt to address market differences and thereby make it easier for a firm to trade in a number of European countries. If markets are deeper and more liquid then capital gets allocated more rationally which in turn translates into companies investing more appropriately and at a lower cost, hence creating jobs and opportunities. The City has addressed the EU-wide regulatory proposals through its trade associations, through the Corporation of London and through individual approaches, to influence at the Directive creating stage, both in terms of the high level requirements and also the detail as it gets developed. This approach has been extensive and has had some success. However some key flaws remain.

The great open marketplace of London is not necessarily one that other European countries wish to copy, or perhaps more accurately, they do not wish to see it in its totality. Yet too often erroneous assumptions have been made by the City that others want to change their financial centre to make it operate just like London. That is not the case and failure to recognise the legitimate aims of other countries during some of the negotiations has not been particularly helpful to the City's attempts to win some of the important arguments. FSAPs will come and go, but what remains common is that every country will seek to maximise benefits for its own financial services industry. In turn this means at the very least it will seek to minimise the adverse impact of cross border barrier removal and seek to retain local protections for its own citizens. It is a mistake to assume that the removal of barriers is universally thought to be "a good thing". That is a simplistic view which fails to recognise that removal of barriers increases competition and, in a competitive environment, some do not survive!

Unfortunately, for too long the EU emphasis has been on full harmonisation with the idea that only one great central unified core would be able to integrate the European markets. This idea is an anathema to London, and in practice, it cannot and will never work. Full harmonisation makes lawyers rich, but firms despair. It divides regulators and countries. It results in great intelligence and brain power being spent on overcoming regulatory hurdles rather than creating business. It concentrates the best efforts on the change rather than on the future. Whilst differing regulatory requirements, outdated or even discriminatory treatment of foreign market participants, and differing supervisory practices are to be deplored and duplicative regulation that places costly burdens on business need to be got rid of, as far as the EU is concerned, the regulation goal has to be mutual recognition of equivalence. We have to accept and agree each other's systems as being equivalent otherwise we will not proceed any further in creating a European trading block in financial services.

Now having looked at some of the regulatory changes which may help or sadly may well not help Europe grow or foster the future the City and Europe, let me turn to some of the wider economic implications. The long-standing fear in old European countries is that post FSAP, the City will be an even more dominant financial centre, their financial business will trickle away towards London and their own critical mass will be lost - and the numbers partly support their concerns.

Just over a year ago, the EU gained ten new members. There was concern at the time about how these countries would affect the EU and the UK, not least because with the exception of Malta and Cyprus, most of them are the former communist countries of central Europe.

This expansion increased the EU's population by about 18% and it's GDP by 5%. In fact, the Baltic states of Latvia and Lithuania have achieved "Asian Tiger economy" growth rates, whilst Poland has managed 5%. This compares to "old Europe's" 2%, which shows just how much "old Europe" has been in the slow lane. Stock markets in Poland, Hungary and the Czech Republic have sparkled and anyone who has visited either Prague or Budapest recently will have seen just how busy and beautiful these cities are. A serious attraction for many of these countries in joining the EU was not just to erect a stronger barrier against Russian influence but to join with the UK's open, competitive and free trading economy. The financial centre of the City has provided both a magnet for these countries, and a template that they are in their own way following.

We appear to have no problem in getting the message about free markets across in the new member states whose people know about the despair, hopelessness, lack of opportunity, protectionism and isolationism that state ownership produced under communism. Cast off today, they are champing at the bit to see a release of economic freedom across Europe and allow the individual their freedom and initiative to create firms and grow markets.

So whilst having been out of step with "old Europe", the City is in step with "new Europe" and is a pack leader for the new entrants, a pack leader in liberalisation and a pack leader in open economies.

For many countries, the virility symbol of their financial markets is their stock exchange. In the London Stock Exchange, the City has an entity which is hugely international and through the junior market AIM, the Alternative Investment Market, has created one of the most successful (if not the most successful) market in the world for small and medium-sized growth companies. On the one hand it therefore seems quite extraordinary that the LSE should be the subject of a quasi bid both from Deutsche Börse and an even more nebulous offer from Euronext. Yet the recent history of the LSE has been somewhat troubled as in failing to build its own clearing system, and then in failing to be the successful bidder for LIFFE, the London

Futures and Options Exchange, it neither built the deeper commercial base of Deutsche Börse or the broader base of Euronext. With revenues less than either of its two regional rivals, even though its internationality is much greater and the market cap of the companies that have listed on it are huge, the question continues to be asked as to whether or not it will continue as a stand-alone entity. Historically a partnership with the US would have been seen as attractive, as ties with America are seen to be stronger even to this day than those with the EU. Yet an LSE link with the American exchange could well bring the horrors of Sarbanes Oxley requirements placing a further layer of costly rules and regulations on major PLCs who are already implementing the new International Financial Reporting Standards (IFRS), plus meeting the UK's not insignificant regulatory demands. Few would welcome the long arm of the SEC stretching fully into our own markets and indeed it is notable in this context that whilst it is possible for a company to delist from the New York Stock Exchange, it appears to be nearly impossible for them to deregister from the SEC. Therefore, with any US partnerships hampered by SarBox, the options (if they are needed) for the London Stock Exchange lie regionally.

There are always competition issues; however, when major entities seek to continue and when one infrastructure provider amalgamates with another (even though they may be PLCs), the competitive questions need to be addressed in even greater depth. Nevertheless, there is little future in continuing to develop yet more and different trading mechanisms across Europe and merging exchanges not only should mean fewer different trading systems but also greater harmonisation through the entire post-trading chain of clearing and settlement. But takeovers are not the only option. One of the most interesting issues in the future of the exchange debate is that the major users of the exchanges in Europe have not to date used their collective commercial "clout" to promote simplicity and harmonisation instead of the continuation of the current differences. Maybe the answer is a commercial one. Many of the major users of European exchanges have overcome the current barriers of cross border trading and so operate in the various countries and in so doing provide services for others who do not. There is therefore a benefit to their profit from continuing with both cross border constraints and country differences assisted by remuneration policies that reward staff according to the profitability of the local business that they are running. Put together, those same multi-nationals who are on the one hand so keen to bring down cross border barriers could also be one of the reasons why the constraints have remained for so long and commercial imperatives which one would have anticipated would have forced harmonisation in exchange world have not in fact occurred.

It is often said that the wholesale firms have most to gain from the EU. Again this is subject to debate. Much of the regional wholesale business is in fact already undertaken in London with the major subsidiaries of US firms quartered in London, so easier trading across Europe has got to be beneficial for them. Nevertheless, it may not be as beneficial as originally anticipated. Removing constraints brings more competitors and no doubt there will be some firms in hitherto protected European country markets that will seek to retain their business at almost any price – and probably with at very least the covert support of their governments. The jury is therefore out as to who is going to be successful in the pan-European market. In the short term there may well be deeper and more liquid markets but equally profits may also be much less than hoped.

The fund management industry is another potential beneficiary in the short, medium and long term, with the City being the largest centre for fund management in Europe and also one of the largest in the world. However, fund management is also substantial in all EU countries and interestingly, depending on how one calculates the numbers, Edinburgh comes in around third. Fund management is not just an institutional activity and not just UCITS driven; it is also about managing pension funds as well. Competition here is likely to be high and as tax has an inexorable part to play then it may well be that the City's dominance in fund management starts to reduce over the next few years, partly as other centres expand with local constraints lifted; and partly because of the drive of all European governments to get their citizens to save more; and partly because fund management companies will gravitate to their most attractive tax location. So the future for the City fund management industry in Europe is a competitive one.

Lastly, let us look at the position of the private or individual investor. They are, after all, part of the City in the widest sense of the expression as there is still a culture of share ownership in the UK with over 10 million individuals directly holding equities. They are therefore as much a part of the future of the City in Europe as the other sectors. Individuals have often been reluctant to invest outside the UK for a variety of reasons such as language, economic cycle, currency fluctuation, lack of information, costs and lastly because culturally it is much easier if you stay within your own jurisdiction because you understand the law, you know the consequences and have a knowledge of the redress mechanisms. Nevertheless, over recent years UK investors have been increasingly attracted to look overseas for part of their portfolio investments. Inevitably the US has attracted most interest but so have some large companies quartered in Europe. Whilst it may not happen in the short term, if it becomes easier to buy something and the price looks attractive, then the number of customers interested will inevitably increase. It is therefore not unreasonable to anticipate that the interest of UK shareholders in the shares of companies in other European countries will increase over time, though the reverse interest is unlikely to take place whilst stamp duty remains such a substantial financial barrier on purchases of UK company shares. The City has long objected to stamp duty on share purchase but has been rebuffed at its request for reduction or abolition at every stage. The reason for the rebuff is straight forward, and that is because stamp duty on shares raises a very substantial amount of money each year for the Government, and Governments do not habitually abolish a substantial and easy to collect tax. Nevertheless, at some point this inbuilt structural competitive disadvantage in the UK will hamper the City, both in Europe and globally.

Costs are, indeed, a problem. Call centres are a very obvious example of what happens when costs increase more than the customer is willing to pay, but call centres are not the only operation being outsourced. Back offices generally do not have to be in the UK and nor, in fact, do the assets that a firm manages. Looking ahead, the UK's already high cost base is likely to increase with the inevitable result that much of that which does not have to be done here in future will be done elsewhere. And the "elsewhere" will not be in the EU unless the new entrants manage to keep down their costs on a long term basis.

The unfortunate tendency of the EU is of an ever upward pressure on costs driven by social protections. The UK is not immune from these and moreover adds a few of its own. The lights are currently flashing amber – move to red and suddenly business will find better places to base their operations.

But my conclusion is more positive. The City indeed has a strong future in Europe as well as a strong future in competing with other centres around the world. Whilst some of the changes ahead, particularly those which will reduce the barriers to cross border trading, will be beneficial, London will not gain universally and in fact will find some of the proposed changes somewhat constricting to the business it undertakes. Indeed, if the City has to choose between its position in Europe and its position globally, my guess is it will choose its position globally every time.